SIMPLIFIED REAL-WORLD ECONOMICS

A Practical Guide for Managers and Small Business Owners

MICHAEL C. THOMSETT

J.ROSS PUBLISHING

ISBN-13: 978-1-60427-167-6

Printed and bound in the U.S.A. Printed on acid-free paper.

10 9 8 7 6 5 4 3 2 1

For Library of Congress Cataloging-in-Publication Data, please visit the WAV section of the publisher's website at www.jrosspub.com/wav.

Direct all inquiries to J. Ross Publishing, Inc., 300 S. Pine Island Rd., Suite 305, Plantation, FL 33324.

Phone: (954) 727-9333
Fax: (561) 892-0700
Web: www.jrosspub.com

CONTENTS

INTRODUCTION

WHAT DO WE REALLY KNOW ABOUT *ECONOMICS*?

If ignorance paid dividends, most Americans could make a fortune out of what they don't know about economics.

—Luther Hodges (March 14, 1962)
The Wall Street Journal

A business owner deals with economics every day. Questions about cash flow, customer needs and wants, production, wages, taxes—it all comes down to how economics are managed and how economic problems are anticipated and avoided.

In other words, business owners are the ultimate economists of the world. Professional economists offer allegedly sage advice about all things economic. But, have any of them ever run their own business? Have any of them ever had to worry about economic survival, including threats of bankruptcy, business failure, home foreclosure, or meeting payroll? Chances are that few, if any, economists have a footing in the real world of business operations.

As the *real* economists of the world, business owners pay a role in educating others about how the economy really works. It is not efficiently controlled or influenced by the government, which—like economics in

general—is populated by individuals who, in many cases, have never worked in the private sector or confronted the problems that business owners face every single day. A business owner has a great opportunity to educate—employees, fellow business owners, and family members—about how things really work.

For example, how many employees ever consider the problems that management faces in meeting this week's payroll? Or paying for merchandise that is essential to marketing products? Or deciding whether or not to give out raises or bonuses? Chances are that employees have never considered these issues. Why? It is because a large segment of the population is blind to economic reality. This is true in the private sector, government, academia, and even among business owners in some cases. This blindness prevents a realistic understanding of everything concerning the immediate economy (microeconomics) as well as the national and international economy (macroeconomics).

This is the motive for writing this book. Because so many people (perhaps a majority) have never even confronted their own, immediate economic reality, they never have the chance to advance knowledge about how it all works. For most, the economy is like a shiny box that produces electrical current. What is inside the box? How does it work? What happens if it stops working and who will fix it? If the box continues working, these questions simply don't come up; but they should. Knowledge is a powerful tool, and knowledge about the economy is essential to everyone who wants to be in control of their destiny, their financial health, and ultimately, their happiness and security.

This book is divided into three sections. The first section is *introductory* topics, three chapters exploring the basics and universal truths about economics. The second section is *microeconomics*, covering a range of topics of interest to business owners and consumers. The third section is *macroeconomics*, which includes matters pertaining to the entire country and the international community (inflation, employment, taxation, import/export policies). The book is designed to provide information about the economy as well as the underlying principles. The topics in this book are presented without complex and theoretical concepts that are of little interest to the typical business owner. Most business people want to know

the bottom line of economics. How does it affect what I do daily? What outside influences help or hurt my operations? How can I anticipate next month's economic impact? How can I compete effectively and maintain market share? How will I make cash flow next month?

These are the kinds of real-world questions that business owners ask daily—and these concerns are kept in mind on every page of this book. The purpose: to promote practical thoughts and not theoretical concepts. That is what the business owner needs. That's what this book is designed to provide.

ABOUT THE AUTHOR

With a career that's spanned more than 40 years, Michael Thomsett is considered by many as a *financial guru* or financial expert several times over. Always in high demand, Michael is a frequent speaker at financial-based seminars and conventions throughout the world. He is also a prolific best-selling author, instructor, trainer, coach, and blogger.

Michael is arguably the world's best-selling author of options investment educational books, having written more than a dozen on the topic, most notably *Getting Started in Options*, published by John Wiley and Sons, which has sold over 350,000 copies. The rights to this best seller were recently acquired by DeGruyter. A revised edition of the book is now available under the new title of *Options: The Essential Guide for Getting Started in Derivatives Trading*. Michael's first compilation, *Investment and Securities Dictionary*, was named Outstanding Academic Book of the Year by *Choice Magazine* and was also published in paperback as *Webster's New World Investment and Securities Dictionary*. He has taught classes for Moody's Analytics, the New York Institute of Finance, and many others via online platforms. He has also been a guest on numerous financial television programs including NBC, CBS, ABC, CNN, and Fox News.

Early in his career while working as a consultant in the financial services industry, Michael discovered that he had the unique ability to simplify and

convey complex topics, with a focus on practical real-world application, in a way that most business people, managers, entrepreneurs, and individual investors including the novice could easily understand. So he began writing articles regularly for dozens of business, trade, and professional magazines as well as for peer-reviewed academic journals. Between 1985 and 1987 alone he had more than 500 published articles to his credit.

Having developed a love for writing and educating people, with a reputation as a top expert in the fields of investing, accounting, and finance and being well versed in several areas of business and management, Michael made the decision to start writing books. To date, Michael has written more than 90 books on a wide variety of topics in the fields of investing, technical analysis, trading and real estate, bookkeeping and accounting, finance, personal consumer finance, business, and management—including topics such as Six Sigma and project management. In each instance, Michael has chosen areas to write about in which he believed the public would benefit from his unique ability to simplify and convey complex topics in a manner that people can more easily understand with a focus on practical real-world application.

Michael currently lives near Nashville, Tennessee.

This book has free material available for download from the Web Added Value™ resource center at *www.jrosspub.com*

At J. Ross Publishing we are committed to providing today's professional with practical, hands-on tools that enhance the learning experience and give readers an opportunity to apply what they have learned. That is why we offer free ancillary materials available for download on this book and all participating Web Added Value™ publications. These online resources may include interactive versions of the material that appears in the book or supplemental templates, worksheets, models, plans, case studies, proposals, spreadsheets and assessment tools, among other things. Whenever you see the WAV™ symbol in any of our publications, it means bonus materials accompany the book and are available from the Web Added Value Download Resource Center at www.jrosspub.com.

Downloads for *Simplified Real-World Economics* include the figures from the book for classroom or instructional use.

Part I

Introductory Topics

1

BASIC ECONOMICS—WANTS AND NEEDS

Abstract

Economics is all about wants and needs and the fact that those wants and needs can never be satisfied fully. Economics is the study of behavior and the way that behavior functions in an environment of scarcity. If a desirable product is not scarce, it has no economic value. For example, oxygen is abundant and free; attempting to place value on the air that people breathe does not make sense. Scarcity is a requirement for identifying value—and consumer response to the pricing of goods and products is based on that value.

The topic of economics is taught in many universities—but, is it well understood in the business community? Too much of what is called *economics* should be accurately named *political* economics. A bias in the presentation of ideas makes it difficult for people to grasp the fundamental attributes of the topic. Consequently, many economics concepts are based on class envy, desirability of redistribution of wealth, and how governments can and should use their power to tax.

Beyond the biased presentation in some economics courses, complexity is a second issue. Some economics courses, books, and articles are

overly complex, so that most readers are discouraged and lost in the process. Economics is really a simple idea, so it should be taught in a simplified way.

EXACTLY WHAT IS ECONOMICS?

Economics is the study of behavior. The definition varies somewhat depending on the source used. Here are some examples of definitions:

1. Economics is the social science that studies the *choices* that individuals, businesses, governments, and entire societies make as they cope with *scarcity* and the *incentives* that influence and reconcile those choices.[1]
2. Economics is a study of the ways in which people use resources to satisfy their wants. The word *wants* requires little explanation. All of us want the food, clothing, and shelter that we need to stay alive. But most of us . . . want much more. We want cars, television sets, vacation trips—in fact, our capacity to want is almost unlimited.[2]
3. Economics is the study of how society manages its scarce resources. In most societies, resources are allocated not by a single central planner but through the combined actions of millions of households and firms. Economists therefore study how people make decisions: how much they work, what they buy, how much they save, and how they invest their savings.[3]
4. Economics is the study of how scarce, or limited resources are used to satisfy people's unlimited wants and needs. In other words, economics is concerned with how people make decisions in a world of scarcity. Much of the study of economics is focused on satisfying people's wants and needs for material *things*—shoes, cars, medical services, entertainment, and the like. And, although happiness, sorrow, beauty, and integrity are not direct concerns of the discipline of economics, we know that often these values underlie the economic decisions that people make.[4]

Economics can be defined briefly or in greater detail, as these examples reveal. But they all contain the same basic idea: scarcity, wants and needs, and decisions.

Economics
The interaction of scarcity with the wants and needs of consumers, and how decisions are made.

SCARCITY

What makes something scarce? This question must be answered to understand the nature of economics.

Everyone deals with scarcity, regardless of their income level. To someone who is poor, it may seem that wealthier people do not deal with scarcity, but they do. Governments also deal with scarcity when a limited revenue stream cannot possibly pay for all of the infrastructure, social programs, and other initiatives that are brought up and either addressed or deferred.

Example

A new business specializes in providing ready-to-eat meals for home delivery. The concept is that busy people coming home from work are tired and do not want to cook a healthy meal for their children. Many people in this situation turn to fast food as an easy alternative, but health concerns make the ready-to-eat meals industry appealing. The owner established a commercial kitchen in an existing restaurant. Creating a new kitchen is expensive, but a shared kitchen solves problems for both businesses. The existing restaurant does not open until 6 p.m. The ready-to-eat business prepares food between 4 and 6 p.m. The existing restaurant collects rent from the new enterprise and the new enterprise solves the problem of investment in a new kitchen.

In this case, existing kitchen space for rent was scarce. Finding a restaurant in which the schedule was a good fit solved this problem. One business reduced its investment and the other generated rental income. Scarcity was dealt with through coming up with a solution. This example exhibits a core attribute in economics: scarcity leads to choice, and at times, a creative choice overcomes the initial problem.

The same decisions are made even by wealthy consumers.

Example

A business executive has saved her money and invested wisely. Now she is considering starting her own consulting business. But even with a considerable nest egg, she must think about start-up costs and ongoing expenses. These include hiring and paying employees, providing benefits, advertising services, finding suitable office space, and allowing for the reduction in income while a clientele is created. Even though this executive is wealthy by most definitions, she will need to borrow money to finance the new business venture. Not only is money scarce, but finding potential clientele requires competitive effort. The field of likely clients is scarce. One solution is to start out operating from home with a dedicated office space. This cuts down on rent, utilities, and salary expenses. Expansion may lead to creation of an outside office, the addition of staff, and using available capital to attract new clients (rather than paying for overhead).

Even with a considerable nest egg available to invest, the executive recognizes that her savings are a limited (scarce) asset. It must be deployed wisely to maximize the new enterprise's chances for success.

In these two examples of how individuals deal with scarcity, the same challenge is presented. The individual needs to develop solutions based on circumstances, and people at all income levels face scarcity. It is unavoidable. Everyone must choose between available solutions to problems they face, whether it is figuring out how to find a commercial kitchen for a new food business or how to finance a new service business.

Choices such as these are determined by the incentives they provide. For the ready-to-eat meals business, the owner avoided the expense of creating a new commercial kitchen. For the business executive, the incentive was to build a business without committing to overhead that would rapidly absorb capital.

These choices are going to change as the price of goods and services change. For example, if the wholesale cost of food grows by 5%, the food business owner would need to creatively solve the problem of a shrinking margin. Can volume be increased, prices raised, or can alternative food sources reduce the net wholesale cost?

If the executive decided to start her business without hiring any employees, at least initially, that would reduce the start-up expense of the new business. She could also work from home, saving the cost of a lease, utilities, insurance, parking, and other related forms of overhead. The price of starting the business is lowered by starting out slowly and without adding those expenses until they are unavoidable.

WANTS AND NEEDS

Limitation of goods and services—the things consumers need and want—is a constant and realistic feature of the economy. This limitation applies to both sides of the equation. Supply of anything is limited, and supply of resources is also limited.

A principle of economics is that the wants and needs that everyone experiences can never be fully satisfied. All commodities are limited, so there is never enough of anything. In an ideal world, goods and services would be limited, but at a comfortable level. Consumers can satisfy their needs and wants to a degree, but not completely. Those goods and services can be found, but only to a certain degree.

Decisions must be made. An important point to keep in mind is that unlimited supply means that there are no underlying economic constraints. The example of oxygen makes this point. It is free to breathe, so trying to place a monetary value on it would not work.

An exception: a modern fad is the oxygen bar, where consumers are offered flavored oxygen for a price. Someone has figured out how to turn oxygen into a commodity and to create a business out of this. Even so, is this a fad or does it eventually become a new necessity? Opinions will vary and there certainly are a group of consumers who swear by the oxygen bar. These tend to be located at leisure outlets such as nightclubs, spas, resorts, yoga studios, or casinos. It seems that buying oxygen goes along with other forms of *wants* rather than *needs*. Do you *want* mint-flavored oxygen, or do you *need* it?

For the owner of an oxygen bar, costs are low and limited to an initial investment in equipment plus a nominal cost for oxygen:

Oxygen bars provide very high profit margins. It costs an oxygen bar owner about $0.45 per *session* to run the bar, which includes the aroma, nose hose, and oxygen (labor is not figured into this since it is variable). The average session costs the consumer $10.00 for 10 minutes, leaving a $9.55 *profit* for the owner per session or customer![5]

DECISIONS

A discussion of scarcity and choice cannot be undertaken separately. The two are aspects of the same issue—that of *decisions*. Daily life, whether by an individual, business, or government, consists of a series of decisions.

Everyone must make the comparison between cost and benefit. This often-cited cost-benefit analysis is more than a study of raw numbers. It is the most reasonable system for how decisions are made. It may take one of two forms. First is a decision between two different choices, and could be based on price, quality, brand recognition, or level of want for a product. For example, do you select a somewhat more expensive brand of cereal or cola because you trust the company?

Second is a decision to do something or not. For example, can you afford a vacation this year? It might cost more than you can afford, so a few decisions must be made. You can skip the vacation, borrow money, pay for the trip using credit, or select a vacation that costs less than the one you want to take.

Your decision is also going to vary based on circumstances. You have probably heard the advice to not shop for food when you are hungry. A hungry shopper is likely to buy desirable items that are beyond the budget. Eating unhealthy but tasty food brings you heightened pleasure, but once you have eaten half of the potato chips, you might look at the remaining chips and wonder what you were thinking. Your hunger, once satisfied, pointed out how the decision was not a wise one. The decision attribute has two sides: how are decisions made? and equally important, why were those decisions made at the time?

If you begin with the assumption that, as a consumer, you know all of the possible choices that you have (products, prices, value) *and* that you know how much utility each brings, then you will make informed

decisions. Many of the decisions everyone makes are poorly informed or even uninformed.

For example, what is the purpose in paying an exceptionally high price for a handbag or shoes, based solely on the designer label? This is an applicable case because many consumers will gladly pay a high price for the Gucci or Prada purchase when an off-the-rack brand might be equal in quality. Why? Is this irrational or is there an intangible benefit beyond quality? Even with full information about comparative price and quality, many will make an expensive purchase based on branding rather than on quality.

This requires an analysis between cost and benefit. This is not going to be identical for all decisions or for all consumers. Clearly, the purchase of a $500 purse brings some form of benefit that is believed to be greater than a purse of equal craftsmanship costing only $30. The perceived benefit justified the cost of the $500 purse on some level. It might not be real, but it is perceived as real, and that's what matters. The wants and needs of people are assumed to be fully informed. Economists tend to think this is the case. However, in many cases, the choices being made are not truly informed, but are perceived as being informed—an important distinction.

This comes into play in an economic sense in many ways. Do you want to pay $10 for flavored oxygen? Were you one of those 5 million people who in 1975 bought a pet rock? The perceived value was part of a short-lived fad, of course, but even at a cost of about $4 each, the founder of the pet rock brought in $15 million in six months.[6]

These points define the science of economics. Thus, the combination of scarcity, needs and wants, and decisions must be present in all decisions made by consumers, business, and government. Much more may be said on the topic of managing scarcity—and that is the topic of the upcoming chapter.

ENDNOTES

1. Parkin, Michael. (2010). *Economics.* 9th ed. New York, NY: Pearson. p. 2.
2. Van Sickle, John V. and Benjamin A. Rogge. (1954). *Introduction to Economics.* New York, NY: D. Van Nostrand. p. 3.

3. Mankiw, N. Gregory. (2017). *Principles of Economics.* 8th ed. Boston, MA: Cengage. p. 4.
4. Welch, Patrick J. and Gerry F. Welch. (2016). *Economics Theory and Practice.* 11th ed. Hoboken, NJ: John Wiley & Sons. p. 2.
5. www.oxygenbars.com.
6. https://www.bcbusiness.ca/9-dumbest-fads-ever-to-make-money.

2

MANAGING SCARCITY—DECISIONS

Abstract

Scarcity is an essential ingredient in economics. If something is not scarce, it cannot be assigned economic value. The greater a product's scarcity, the higher the price; in addition, a tendency among consumers is to have a greater desire for scarce goods. Balancing scarcity with price and quantity is a constant struggle in the realm of economics. Consumers make choices based on this struggle. Every consumer wants the highest quality of scarce goods at the lowest possible price. Opportunity cost describes how choices are made. This further relies on the concept of marginal analysis, the study of the variables that are involved in choice.

How do consumers make decisions? This is the question that every producer must ask in order to better understand the economics of providing goods and services. The product must be affordable and at the same time, scarce. The price and quantity determine how consumers react, and this is the essence of how decisions are made in the market. It all begins with *scarcity*.

> Scarcity
> The limitation of all goods and services, and of their affordability; the essential element required to set value on anything.

Scarcity is essential before any goods can have value. If something is not scarce, its economic value cannot exist.

If a product is abundant and anyone can access it, its economic value is zero. Some attempts have been made by producers to change this dynamic, but it cannot change permanently. By creating a fad based on artificial scarcity (thus, artificial supply), a producer may create demand in the moment.

ARTIFICIAL DEMAND AND FADS

In 1975, one of the oddest fads in the market was created by advertising man Gary Dahl. His *pet rock* was marketed over a six-month period and 1.5 million were sold at a price of $4 each. These were, literally, rocks, marketed like live pets and complete with cardboard boxes and breathing holes. Dahl, who passed away in 2015, became an instant millionaire. The fad was short-lived but profitable. The origin of this strange fad was described in an article about Dahl:

> Over beers in a Los Gatos bar, Gary Dahl's drinking buddies spewed tales about incontinent dogs, destructive cats, overly fecund gerbils, and vacations foiled because no one could babysit the bird.
>
> Everyone had problems with a pet except for Dahl, who claimed his was hassle-free.
>
> "I own a pet rock," he quipped.
>
> His friends cracked up and turned it into a running joke. Dahl laughed his way to the bank.[1]

This strange example was based on packaging and marketing of an abundant resource, the ordinary rock. The originality of the idea created artificial demand. Although it lasted only six months, that was long enough to be a success. Similar ideas that enjoyed short lives but financial success include Beanie Babies, the Sock Monkey, and Cabbage Patch Kids. However, the idea of artificial demand is nothing new. One of the strangest tales in economic history is that of the 17th century *Tulipmania.*

In the 1630s in Holland, Tulipmania (in Dutch, *tulpenmanie*) was an extreme speculative bubble. These bubbles occur periodically and, even in hindsight, they are normally impossible to comprehend. Why do people speculate with vast fortunes in goods that clearly are overpriced? The

ability to analyze and understand how irrational this is cannot compete with a single human tendency: greed.

Speculators want to get rich quickly, and will risk all they own, even borrowing money to invest more than they can afford. This is seen repeatedly in the stock market even today. Speculators do not learn the economic lessons of the past, but repeat the mistakes made by others. The irrational run-up in prices of single tulip bulbs began in 1636 and by May 1637, prices collapsed—speculators lost everything. Today, the very term itself, Tulipmania often is used as a metaphor to describe speculative fevers and panics. This is defined as situations in which some prices behave in a way that appears not to be fully explainable by economic *fundamentals.*[2]

At the height of this speculative fever, single tulip bulbs sold for as high as 10 times more than the average income of a Dutch craftsman. Typical of such speculative bubbles, prices rose rapidly but then crashed even more rapidly:

> Many individuals grew suddenly rich. A golden bait hung temptingly out before the people, and, one after the other, they rushed to the tulip marts, like flies around a honey-pot. Every one [*sic*] imagined that the passion for tulips would last forever [*sic*], and that the wealthy from every part of the world would send to Holland, and pay whatever prices were asked for them. The riches of Europe would be concentrated on the shores of the Zuyder Zee, and poverty banished from the favoured clime of Holland. Nobles, citizens, farmers, mechanics, seamen, footmen, maidservants, even chimney sweeps and old clotheswomen, dabbled in tulips.[3]

This artificial demand should not be confused with the real thing, based on economic needs and wants. A consumer will purchase bread and milk to feed the family but will not speculate in possible increases in food prices by borrowing money and buying a garage full of one product. Artificial demand is based at times on the greed of a seller, wanting to sell goods for prices that are

Artificial demand
Any form of demand created by generating interest in a product or service when no true economic value exists.

Greater fool theory
speculation, the belief that paying too much for a product or service is rationalized by the belief that someone else (i.e., a *greater fool*) will be willing to pay more.

many times higher than his own purchase price. This relies on the *greater fool theory*, the observation that during times of speculation, prices are not determined by the true or intrinsic value, but rather by beliefs among other speculators that are, in a word, irrational. Under this theory, one speculator pays a foolishly high price in the belief that it can be resold later to a *greater fool*, someone with even greater irrational expectations: ". . . that is, they paid such spectacularly high prices on the assumption that some other nitwit would come along willing to pay even more."[4]

REAL SCARCITY

Artificial scarcity recurs often and despite history's many lessons, it is tried by many, either intentionally or as the result of a current fad. In comparison, real scarcity exists and creates the fundamental points about economics:

There are never enough goods or services to satisfy needs and wants.

A supply of goods and services works best when it is available, but not without limitations. Consumers will value those goods and services on these terms but will not even think about the price of goods or services if the supply is unlimited. Why? Because lack of limitations means there can be no reasonable price.

Prices move based on scarcity and choices made by consumers.

The price asked by a seller will only be paid by a buyer if (a) the product or service is needed or wanted; (b) comparable choices are at best equal or, at worst, of lower value; and (c) a perceived value is accepted so that the price is considered fair and reasonable.

Without scarcity, goods and services cannot have any economic value.

How does economic value exist? How is it created? Without scarcity, the price of goods or services must be zero. In the previous chapter, the example was given of oxygen. It is abundant and is freely breathed. Thus, it cannot be priced and marketed directly.

Every consumer confronts scarcity daily. With a limited income, choices must be made. First, the necessities must be paid for: housing, food, utilities, transportation, and clothing. Next, a family may put money aside in savings for the future. Finally, the remaining *disposable income* can be spent on a variety of goods or services: a new car, a family vacation, a bigger television, a better cell phone. Because disposable income is often scarce, a consumer cannot buy all of these goods and services. Choices must be made.

Disposable income
The income available after paying for necessities and not saved; income available for wants rather than for needs.

In having to decide which discretionary goods or services to buy, everyone deals with scarcity and this is expressed in the choices they make. Scarcity also limits the availability of goods and services. A producer must fund the creation of a factory, equipment and machinery, intellectual property, and labor. All of this is required to produce products offered to the market. But they cannot be produced without limits; even if they could, it would destroy the producer's profits.

For example, if a producer had unlimited funds and could flood the market with an item previously costing $40 each, what would occur? By producing so many of this item that the supply outpaced demand, could they still ask for $40? No, the abundance of supply based on unlimited production capability would destroy the economic value of the product. In this sense, scarcity is a positive force, for both sides. The producer creates enough product to meet demand at a price adequate to yield a profit. The consumer is willing to buy a finite number of products at a given price because that price is reasonable, and the product satisfies a want or a need.

CHOICE BASED ON SCARCITY

Choice and scarcity cannot be separated. Consumers make choices based on the limitations of income, personal preferences, and priorities. This is

unavoidable. Because all goods and services with economic value contain a price, a choice must be made about everything. There is no such thing as abundance without limit.

The same limitations apply to producers, governments, and society in general. Some governmental policies are based on a belief that money is unlimited for the choices made, and by printing more and more currency, those limits can be overcome. However, when money is printed excessively, it dilutes value and leads to bigger problems later. This is another lesson of history. However, even with the ability to print currency, governments—like all consumers—must make economic and political choices.

Governments and consumers must make choices about everything, and these choices are invariably based on defining core values and priorities. A government, for example, may set spending policies based on social justice and welfare; or on economic progress and economic growth. An individual does the same; choices are set based on priorities, and in turn, priorities grow from understanding wants and desires.

Is it so important to have a high-priced status automobile that you will sacrifice saving for retirement? Is one of your core values being able to enjoy an annual one-week vacation costing one month's salary by delaying the purchase of needed new clothes? Do you want to enjoy a weekly trip to an expensive restaurant, deferring the payment of expenses in your small business?

All these choices define not only your core values, but also how those values affect your economic health. As a business executive, for example, you must approve an annual forecast and budget. Will part of this year's spending be drastically reduced to improve net profits after the past year's unexpected increases? Did you pay for skilled technical expertise, which is considered a long-term investment in improved productivity? Will you focus more on spending money to pursue a larger market share or expand your product line? If you cannot afford to do both, will you take on more long-term debt as an alternative? Or will you cut back on expenses with strict internal controls?

Business managers and executives make choices every day. In this respect, producers are also consumers. For example, it might be necessary to pay large salaries to recruit the experts whom you need to expand your

market. It might also be necessary to invest in a concentrated marketing campaign, product development, or research and development. All of these choices demand judgment, and in business, choice is the result of estimating or understanding the underlying value of an expected outcome. In other words, choices and decisions are invariably based on scarcity; but those choices are not made randomly or carelessly. With awareness of limitations in resources (scarcity), the executive selects between higher expenses that are intended to generate more revenue or internal cuts in order to improve net margins (choice).

Like private companies, governments work with scarce resources to make choices based on perceived value. Does a local county or city invest in public schools, parks, roadways and police protection? Or does it cut back on those services to balance its budget? Are tax increases necessary in order to provide what people need and want? And how far should those tax increases go? Local governments, in the role of consumers, must evaluate available revenues and desirable spending programs and make choices just like individuals. National governments face the same range of issues and must apply scarce revenues to pay for choices made.

EVALUATING OPPORTUNITY COST

The choices made by consumers, governments, and society at large are the result of evaluation. Comparisons between costs and benefits lead to these choices while also remembering the core economic rule that there is never enough resources to satisfy all of the wants and needs—no one can have everything they want.

This is termed *opportunity cost*, the informed evaluation of costs and benefits to a decision. The method by which consumers decide what to buy and what not to buy, the price they are willing and able to pay, and the quality of a product are all part of the analysis of opportunity cost. It also includes what a consumer decides to give up. For example, a business owner invests in the

Opportunity cost
The evaluation of costs and benefits undertaken to arrive at a decision, including knowledge of what must be given up as a result.

> Core values
> The well-defined purposes and goals held by a business or person; the expansion of financial considerations to include nonfinancial ideals about future outcomes of present decisions.

> Mission statement
> A formalized and brief description of goals, aims, and values for a company, expressed and shared with all stakeholders.

> Long-term objectives
> The set of actions and outcomes developed with the mission statement in mind, expressing the desires and underlying values of the organization.

expansion of operations into new markets (research and development, hiring of a sales staff, product development and expansion, and promotion). In order to make this investment, the owner defers increasing his or her compensation and giving raises to staff. The opportunity cost of expansion was based on a belief that future revenue and net profit will justify the decision. Whether that turns out to be a sound decision depends on the success of the decision itself versus what could have occurred by not pursuing an expanded market share and using funds to increase salaries and wages.

This opportunity cost applies at all levels of the economy. A family might decide to purchase a new car but give up their annual vacation. Another family decides to move to a larger, newer home but sacrifices adding to their savings and retirement accounts in order to increase the down payment. The opportunity cost of every decision is likely to involve a *value judgment*, the analysis of a decision or action versus an alternative decision or action.

Opportunity costs are not analyzed solely on the financial merits of one course of action or another. They are based on the *core values* held by the business or person. Therefore, businesses are encouraged to devote time in the development of a mission statement, long-term objectives, and a value proposition. All of these phases may be largely academic if they are developed and then simply filed away. However, when difficult decisions must be made, the defining attributes of a business are essential to making an informed decision and maximizing the opportunity cost.

The purpose of these defining attributes is not only to help a company identify what decisions enhance opportunity costs for the business, but also to help the consumer address their opportunity costs. Why should a customer choose your company's product or services versus those of your competitors? The creation of a competitive advantage is the purpose of this defining exercise, which was termed an *economic moat* by Warren Buffett. The wider the moat, the stronger and more sustainable the competitive advantage.

> <u>Value proposition</u>
> A set of defining attributes about why products or services address customer or client needs; the special or exceptional talents of owners and staff; the qualities in the product and service that set it apart from others.

HOW SCARCITY SHAPES CORE VALUES

Every business has core values, whether these are clearly expressed or not. However, even when those core values are described, they must take scarcity into consideration. Otherwise, the core values will not be practical. For example, core values may be expressed in these ways:

- Capture 100% of the market for our product.
- Become a Fortune 500 company within 10 years.
- Retire within five years with $10 million in net assets.

All of these core values are exciting and optimistic. But are they realistic? Probably not. Few if any companies can capture 100% of a market. It would necessitate putting competitors out of business or acquiring them, and then preventing new enterprises from entering the market. This is not realistic; and even if it were, what is the opportunity cost of acquiring 100% of business, even if it were possible? It does not lead automatically to higher profits; in fact, in order to accomplish these unrealistic goals, a company would have to spend money to defeat competitors. Translation: lower profits.

Becoming a Fortune 500 company is an odd goal. This is not something that occurs because the goal has been set; it is the result of making smart decisions regarding how goods and services are marketed and how

market share is acquired and maintained. Being a Fortune 500 company is a result, not a goal.

Retiring in only a few years with $10 million in net assets is a goal that few people would reject on its own merits. But what must take place for this to occur? The goal is incomplete because it does not lay out the steps required for it to occur.

In each of these cases, the assumed core values are either unrealistic or they ignore the role of scarcity. Just as consumers must set core values for how they conduct their financial and nonfinancial lives, businesses also must develop a plan based not only on desire, but on acknowledgment of scarcity. Everyone—including consumers and businesses—confronts scarcity at every turn. The wants and desires of people and businesses can never be satisfied, due to scarcity. In setting up core values, this reality must be included to ensure that reality dominates the course of action that is planned and followed. This process has a name: *economics*.

Core values for individuals can be reduced to single terms: happiness, wealth, love, respect, security, health, etc. For businesses, core values tend to be more generalized when they are reduced to single words: profits, reputation, esteem, [market] dominance, etc. However, beyond the single words, core values take on greater meaning when expressed with scarcity in mind. In other words, going back to the mission statement—long-term objectives and value proposition—the development of core values can and should include not only the desired result, but the ways in which scarcity is navigated to arrive at the desired outcome. Acknowledging scarcity helps to ensure that core values are not only a focused outcome in the future, but realistic as well.

SCARCITY IN A WORLD OF INEFFICIENCY AND INEQUITY

Efficiency
The application of scarce resources in the best possible manner and for the lowest possible cost.

The fact that scarcity must exist in order to acknowledge economic value leads to a related idea: that of *efficiency*. To most people, this refers to accomplishing tasks in the most expedient manner and at the lowest cost. From a business

point of view, it means using scarce resources in the best possible manner and for the lowest possible cost. If production of all goods and services was accomplished efficiently, it would maximize overall benefit and reduce costs, thus also reducing scarcity.

Society (often referred to collectively as the *economy*) would benefit when production processes were fully operated at maximum efficiency and use. The result would be lower prices and increased quantity of products. An efficient consumer would recognize and reward efficiency by buying more of a product that is needed or wanted, and would benefit from that efficiency by paying a lower cost.

Efficiency addresses a related problem with scarcity. Identification of a fair or equitable distribution of scarce goods is a constant problem. Should fairness be a goal for society, in an economic sense? For example, if a pharmaceutical drug is sold for $6 per pill and some families who need the drug cannot afford it, would it be fair and equitable to adjust the price? Perhaps a wealthier consumer could pay $9 and a poor consumer pay only $3 for the same medicine.

This is a complex issue related to efficiency. Maximum efficiency viewed in isolation would recognize a fair price based on a producer's cost of goods sold and their minimum profit margin—that might be the $6 level. However, someone who needs the medicine and cannot afford it would be subsidized in an equitable economic system. These two ideas—efficiency and equity—often conflict with one another.

> Equity fairness in the economy
> A provision of a needed product or service at a lower cost to those who cannot afford a higher price.

The equitable provision of goods and services needed by everyone is complicated because it requires both a consideration of affordability and a value judgment. A compassionate society wants equitable distribution, so that a family who is living in poverty is subsidized in terms of housing, food, and medicine. Because subsidies cost money, this means that producers who provide products below their marginal cost must be able to raise prices for other consumers; or that if governments subsidize some citizens, they will raise taxes to pay for the subsidies. This demands a value judgment, which is a balance between efficiency and equity. The compassionate society makes the value judgment, which becomes involved with

not only economic considerations, but larger political ones as well—such as, immigration, foreign aid, welfare policies, tax rates, employment and wages, and government spending.

Because these policies and decisions are all based on scarcity at the core of the questions involved, the role of scarcity is more than the obvious establishment of price and quantity or even the decision about how to spend money. Scarcity affects everyone in several ways. Efficiency and equity are the most complex attributes of scarcity.

The conflict generated by this higher level of scarcity is described as competition for a limited degree of resources. Consumers compete with one another. If one group has higher access (can afford a drug, for example) and another group has no access or limited access, the situation is perceived by many as unfair. Even though economic success in terms of earnings distinguishes one group from another, *fairness* is a desirable but often irrational desire.

For example, poverty may be caused by many different factors. These may include lack of education and specialization, obsolescence that makes a skill unmarketable, or ill health reducing or eliminating a family's income. It may also be the result of substance abuse, violent crime, and other poor decisions made by consumers. It is a complex matter. Even in cases when the head of a family makes selfish decisions leading to poverty, should small children suffer as a result? Should they go to bed without enough food or live through the winter without heat?

The compassionate society recognizes that the value judgments made to deal with scarcity cannot be applied universally. In some situations, people are victimized by their own decisions and their families suffer. They need to be cared for by society, and that care should be paid for with higher taxes or lower prices of essential goods and services.

A distortion of this value judgment is based on class envy. Some people believe that equity is the goal of an economy. The wealthier and more successful citizen should be required to pay higher taxes in order to give greater benefits to the less fortunate. This is not based on need alone or even on the idea of subsidizing the less fortunate. It is based on an extreme twisting of the concept of equity, using class envy and even punishment for success to equalize everyone, even beyond the concept of compassionate subsidizing of the poor.

When equity enters the economic picture, the entire study of economics becomes complex and political. What may be studied rationally as the study of behavior and value judgments easily becomes a political view; in this view, economics is seen as a tool for exacting justice or revenge, aimed at the successful business or individual for the benefit of the less successful citizen.

INDUCED SCARCITY

The study of scarcity as the underlying force of economics may be studied not only in terms of efficiency and equity, but also in how scarcity is induced. This is a reference to two ideas: demand-induced scarcity and supply-induced scarcity.

The theory behind these induced forms of scarcity is a starting point for determining how price and quantity are set. Despite a widespread belief that producers may simply raise prices whenever they want to increase net profits, this is not the case. Consumers ultimately determine price by how they react to producer actions.

Scarcity may be broken down into three types. *Demand-induced scarcity* occurs when the consumer population grows, thus setting up greater demand for products or services. In these situations, it might prove difficult for producers to meet demand immediately and the will need to improve methods for creating and transporting goods to market.

Supply-induced scarcity occurs whenever producers limit production, most often due to limitations on natural resources, production capability, and other factors beyond their control. Except for artificial supply-induced scarcity, the influences that cause this cannot be controlled. For example, in 2011, a massive earthquake and tsunami hit Japan. This was the most costly disaster in history.[5]

Demand-induced scarcity
A form of scarcity generated when the consumer population grows or when the demand for a product or service is expanded.

Supply-induced scarcity
A form of scarcity resulting from shortages or unavailability of raw materials, labor, or other requirements of production.

The sole-source Japan-based company Merck KGaA produced Xirallic, a pigment used on new automobiles, and because of the disaster, the pigment was unavailable to the auto industry. Xirallic created a distinct shimmering effect in autos and this could not be reproduced exactly. Both Ford and Chrysler were forced to limit production and marketing of two popular colored autos, red and black. The limitation of the paint supply cost both manufacturers millions of dollars in lost revenue.[6]

This example of supply-induced scarcity was not made by choice. Because the supply chain for the pigment was provided from a single factory, no immediate alternatives were available.

Beyond demand-induced and supply-induced scarcity, *structural scarcity* is found when some consumers cannot access goods or services. This may be due to geographic, demographic, or income restrictions. For example, in some third world countries, some populations might not have access to necessities due to political causes, weather, or wars. This is an example of structural scarcity.

> Structural scarcity
> A form of scarcity resulting from consumers being unable to access goods and services, due to geographic, demographic, or income-based restrictions.

The nature of scarcity is further distinguished by *scarce goods* and *nonscarce goods*. Scarce goods are defined as any goods where demand is greater than supply. As a result, prices will also be greater for scarce goods, and this leads to conflict about which consumers are entitled to acquire goods at a specific price. This conflict is unavoidable; it describes "the possible existence of conflict over the possession of a finite thing . . . my ownership and control excludes your control."[7]

> Scarce goods
> Any products or materials for which demand is greater than supply.

Nonscarce goods are abundant and often cannot have economic value. Not only are they abundant; they are also available to a wide consumer population. They may also be termed *free goods*.

Why are these definitions crucial to a business owner or manager? These are economic theories if studied only as concepts. However, they also hold real-world importance. The example of the

single-sourced Xirallic was used by all the major auto manufacturers. When it became unavailable for an indefinite period following the disaster in Japan, auto companies faced a reality: they could not produce autos on the same basis as before. If they used an alternative material, they would need to track every auto produced so that in the future, replacement parts and body shop work would vary based on which form of paint had been used.

Nonscarce goods
Any products or materials that are abundant, usually having no economic value.

Free goods
Are the ultimate description of nonscarce goods—available to everyone and anyone, and without cost.

For even a small, localized business, the same limitations on demand and supply can easily impact operations and lead to losses. For example, if a business relies on employees belonging to a union, a strike could put a company out of business. For example, a 1989 strike by the International Association of Machinists and Aerospace Workers was supported by Eastern Airlines pilots and flight attendants—closing all domestic operations. This forced Eastern into bankruptcy and they closed permanently in January 1991.[8]

When applied to a small operation with limited capital, a labor strike, the unavailability of an essential raw material that is needed in the production process, or the obsolescence of a product could all spell the end based on changing levels of demand and supply, which are all based on degrees of scarcity. For example, when the auto industry began in the early 20th century, blacksmithing—previously an in-demand business for those relying on horse and carriage transportation—was made obsolete. Those blacksmiths who transitioned into auto mechanics were able to survive; the rest went out of business.

CHOICE AND SCARCITY

The choices made by consumers are based, unavoidably, on the status of scarce and nonscarce goods. This *choice theory* assumes that consumers

Choice theory
The belief that consumers are rational in the way they choose when comparing prices, quality, and reputation of scarce goods.

Perfect information
The belief that consumers make choices based on complete knowledge of all aspects going into those choices.

are rational in how they choose. For example, if price is a primary driver of choice, the rational step is to select the lowest-priced comparable goods. If brand loyalty is the primary driver, the consumer is willing to pay more for acquisition of a known brand. Both choices are rational.

The assumption that choice is rational is based on another assumption—that choices are made with complete and total information about all aspects of a product. This idea, *perfect information*, explains how choice theory works, or at least how it should work.

Consumer behavior, whether informed and perfect or impulsive, is the collective result of choices made. The consumer will prefer one product over another, given comparable pricing and quality. The means for developing a preference is of paramount importance to every business. The distinctions of price are obvious and tangible. However, some choices are made based on other criteria. These include brand loyalty, packaging style and color, the list of ingredients, and reputation of a company and its products. For example, many consumers buy Campbell's Soup out of loyalty and brand recognition. Campbell's, in existence since 1869, is one of the oldest established food companies in the world. However, their product is not necessarily the healthiest soup available. The company reduced sodium content in their soups between 2007 and 2010 in response to criticism of its high salt content. However, by 2011, sodium content was again increased. Based on name recognition and reputation, Campbell's soup products continue to dominate shelf space in retail stores.[9]

In this case, consumers make the choice to buy a product even when alternatives are available with healthier content. This is a choice made by consumers. If it is a rational and informed choice, the high sodium content is not an issue for the family purchasing soup. The brand and its reputation matters more.

Choice theory enables companies to evaluate consumer behavior. Why does a consumer prefer one brand over another? Beyond the obvious differences in price, what other factors, tangible and intangible, go into choices? Beyond simple preferences and brand loyalty, choice is altered when demand and supply are changed. Price is changed as demand changes, and this realization helps to clarify how demand and price interact. Consider a case in which two separate levels of demand are compared. Figure 2.1 presents two demand levels and reveals how price is affected when demand changes.

The assumptions about price and quantity are not independent, but act in harmony with each other. The scale of demand impacts the scale of supply, without exception. Demand A and Demand B intersect with supply at different points on the graph. The greater the pressure from the demand side, the more price and quantity are impacted and must change. Choice is not based on a simple or predictable curve of demand

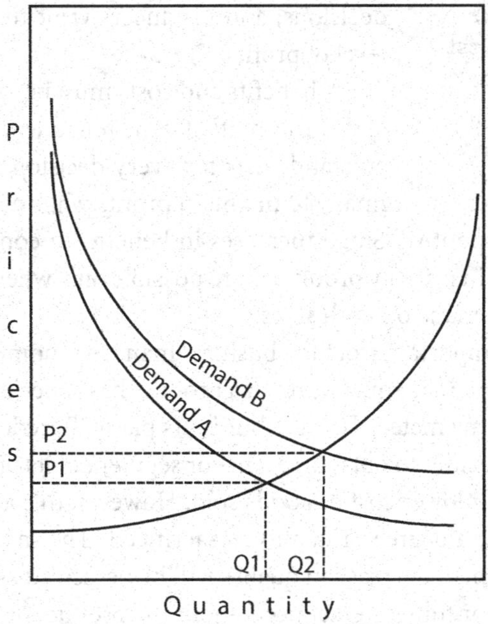

Figure 2.1 How changing demand affects price

and supply. Consumers will prefer the most advantageous qualities in the choices they make, including not only price but many additional factors, packaging and reputation among them. What do consumers think of when they see Campbell's Soup on the shelf next to other brands? Why are the labels dominated by red? What consideration do consumers give to price versus name recognition and label color?

THE ROLE OF MARGINAL ANALYSIS

Marginal analyses
Adjustments in price by producers to achieve the best possible profits, or in behavior among consumers to get the best possible price and quality.

Another crucial test of scarcity and how it affects the interaction between price and quantity is that of *marginal analysis*. This is a quantification of choices made by both producers and consumers. Marginal analysis is the study of how behavior is optimized. For example, consumers want the best possible price and use to result from their decisions; and producers want the best possible level of profits.

All benefits and costs must be studied marginally, meaning that consumers will compare benefits and costs for every decision and producers will increase prices marginally to maintain profits while at the same time remaining competitive. Small increases in benefits to consumers versus small increases in price by producers are possible only when scarcity rules over all choices made on both sides.

Why is this important from the business manager's point of view? Consider this example: a manufacturer of a product has experienced increases in the price of raw materials and labor in its plant. To reduce these costs, management decides to outsource a major segment of its production process, resulting in lower cost of goods sold. However, this also means that to reduce costs, a degree of quality is sacrificed. The manufacturer believes that the small decrease in quality will be perceived as marginal and will not affect consumer perceptions about the product or its price.

Outsourcing does not always accomplish the overall results desired. For example, when moving manufacturing operations overseas, some

have discovered that it is more economically beneficial to keep operations at home: "When quality, the cost of freight, delivery times, and other factors are considered, sometimes it's cost-neutral or cheaper to make products yourself, in U.S. factories, rather than outsource them overseas."[10]

From the consumer's point of view, there might be a willingness to pay higher prices in exchange for other features, such as extended warranties. This gives the buyer peace of mind, although it often is the case that a product is most likely to last longer than the warranty period. The marginal increase in price is based not on complete information, but on perceptions and peace of mind.

In each of these instances, the *economies of scale* are at play. This is the idea that production is improved in marginal costs when higher output does not add greatly to the cost per unit. And consumers are exposed to economies of scale with price incentives: "Buy one, get one free" or "Buy three or more for a 20% discount" are examples.

A danger to any business that manufactures products is the *diseconomies of scale.* This refers to the tendency for marginal costs to rise at a rate exceeding marginal revenues. This occurs when a producer loses profit margin as the consequence of increasing production volume. It is possible that the higher volume of output cannot improve the costs of lower volume. The resulting diseconomies of scale eventually erode profits and force producers to cut back, having failed to generate greater economies of scale.

The producer may apply marginal change not only in price, but also in revenue analysis. Marginal costs are expected to rise when revenue rises and thus makes production more efficient (lowering per-unit cost). However, with competition, it is possible that marginal costs will be forced higher even if marginal revenue does not also improve. Consumers face a similar decision.

Economies of scale
The improvement by producers in marginal costs, which may include a small reduction in quality; the incentives offered to consumers to purchase more of a product for a small discount.

Diseconomies of scale
The loss of profitability because of increased production volume, caused by the inability of lowered costs per unit.

Do they need a two-year supply of a product just to get a small discount in today's price? An informed consumer is likely to question the offer based on whether it even makes sense. Unless the consumer expects prices to rise substantially in the near future, there may be little or no incentive to over-purchase a product today.

ENDNOTES

1. Woo, Elaine. (April 1, 2015). "Gary Ross Dahl, originator of 70s Pet Rock sensation, dies at 78." *Los Angeles Times.*
2. French, Doug. (2006). "The Dutch monetary environment during tulipmania." *The Quarterly Journal of Austrian Economics.* 9(1): pp. 3–14.
3. Mackay, Charles. (1841). *Extraordinary Popular Delusions and the Madness of Crowds.* London, UK: Richard Bentley. Chapter 3.
4. Fox, Justin. (June 11, 2001). "When bubbles burst tulips: Dot-coms. Hey, manias happen. But most don't lead to economic disaster." *Fortune,* http://archive.fortune.com—retrieved November 14, 2018.
5. Branigan, Tania. (March 13, 2011). "Tsunami, earthquake, nuclear crisis—now Japan faces power cuts." *The Guardian.*
6. Boudette, Neal E. and Jeff Bennett. (March 26, 2011). "Pigment shortage hits auto makers." *Wall Street Journal.*
7. Tucker, Jeffrey A. and Stephan Kinsella. (August 25, 2010). "Goods, scarce and nonscarce." *Mises Institute,* https://mises.org/library/goods-scarce-and-nonscarce.
8. Ellin, Abby and Jeanette Torres. (November 19, 2012). "Hostess, Twinkies: 5 Game-Changing Strikes." ABC News, https://abcnews.go.com/Business/strikes-shut-companies/story?id=17743234.
9. Weeks, Carly. (July 14, 2011). "Campbell's adding salt back to its soups." *Toronto Globe and Mail.*
10. Barrett, Rick. (November 10, 2010). "Companies find outsourcing can backfire as quality, customer service suffer." *Journal Sentinel.*

3

COMMON ECONOMIC MYTHS

Abstract

More than most financial topics, the field of economics is beset by numerous persistent myths. This occurs because the political aspects to the economic world provide the motivation to convey a series of beliefs, many of which simply are false. Facts are not as persistent or as satisfying as myths. It has been observed that: "Practical politics consists in ignoring facts."[1] What occurs when myths dominate economic thought and education? The myths are perceived as the reality and, in the minds of many, become reality.

In economics, many beliefs become perceived as truths because they satisfy a political point of view. This is a destructive power in the financial world. A business owner, more than most people, is vulnerable to economic consequences if the wrong decisions and choices are made. However, the myths persist.

ECONOMICS AND TAXES

The first set of myths concern taxes, especially on a federal level. There are three parts to this range of myths.

Higher Taxes Cut Deficits

The first part is a widely held belief that the only way to reduce government deficits is to raise taxes. Approximately half of all politicians promote this idea and to the extent that they win elections, about half of the voters believe this as well. Yet, it is not true.

When taxes are raised, the reality of economics takes over. Businesses hire fewer people because more of their net profits are taxed, and this translates to higher unemployment. With fewer employees than the business wants, productivity also declines. Overall, this leads to a negative economic trend. Ironically, the government collects less in tax revenue when rates are raised because the simple economic *fact* is that *when production is taxed, less production occurs.*

Laffer curve
A belief offered by Art Laffer in the 1980s stating that when federal taxes are raised, revenues fall, and that when tax rates are lowered, revenue grows.

In other words, when the point of maximum revenue has been reached but tax rates continue to rise, net revenues decline. This theory is explained through the *Laffer Curve* (see Figure 3.1), developed by Art Laffer to reveal the relationship

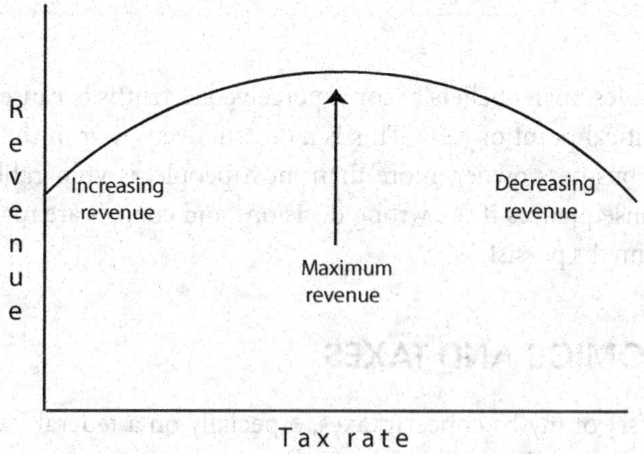

Figure 3.1 Laffer Curve

between tax rates and government revenue. Called *supply-side economics*, this idea—that higher tax rates lead to lower revenues—became the mainstay of tax policies under the administrations of Ronald Reagan and George Bush and, later, of Donald Trump. The theory has been proved time and again as various federal administrations have raised or lowered tax rates. Often called *voodoo economics*, the fact remains that during those administrations, tax rates were lowered. The result: unemployment rapidly declined to multi-generation low levels, and tax revenues rose when applied at lower corporate and individual rates.[2]

Supply-side economics
The belief that lowering taxes and reducing regulation work together to generate greater business activity, leading to greater tax revenues.

Those affected by higher tax rates are small businesses, defined by the Small Business Administration (SBA) as those with fewer than 500 employees. The SBA also reports that 99.7% of all employment takes place in small businesses.[3]

Lower Taxes Only Increase Deficits

A closely related belief is that lower taxes—because they decrease government revenue—add to federal deficits. This is untrue on two levels. First, lower taxes lead to higher revenues because more tax is collected. In 2018, for example, following significant corporate and individual tax cuts, the results revealed the truth about lower taxes:

> *Supply-Side Economics*: Democrats scoffed at Republicans who said the Trump tax cuts would at least partially pay for themselves through higher economic growth. But it looks like the GOP had it right all along, as revenues climb.[4]

The belief that lower taxes only increase deficits appears to make sense, mathematically at least. However, despite any personal political beliefs, facts expose the falsehood of this belief. Deficits can be reduced by a combination of lower taxes (thus, greater private sector activity) and reduction and control of government spending. Deficits are caused not because

taxes are too low, but because the government spends more money than it generates in tax revenue.

This is a profound truth, but it often is overlooked in preference for the myth that tax rates should be raised to prevent deficits. By balancing the federal budget, deficit spending would disappear. In fact, the definition of *deficit spending* is the act of spending more money than revenues received.

The Wealthy Do Not Pay Their Fair Share of Taxes

This persistent myth is easily disproven. The truth is that no matter how you define the wealthy, nearly all federal income taxes are paid by the upper tier of income. Approximately one-half of all people pay no taxes:

> In other words, the bottom 50 percent paid 3 percent. Which small percentile of tax payers also paid 3 percent or more? You might have guessed it. It is the top 0.001%, or about 1,400 taxpayers. That group alone paid 3.25 percent of all income taxes . . . the bottom 50 percent paid nearly 5 percent whereas the top 0.001 percent of filers paid 2.3 percent of income taxes.[5]

Taxes Can Be Used to Redistribute Wealth from the Small Number of Rich People to Others

This may be the most destructive of the tax-related myths in economics. Some politicians and economists view taxation as a means for redistribution—take from the wealthy and give to the poor. As noble an idea as this is, the facts show that it does not work. Trillions of dollars of tax revenue was spent fighting the *War on Poverty* between 1964 and 2017. Spending that amount of money in redistribution of wealth has not worked. According to the Heritage Foundation: "The lack of progress in building self-sufficiency since the beginning of the War on Poverty 50 years ago is due in major part to the welfare system itself."[6]

From 1964 to 2017, the reported national poverty rate in the United States fell from 19% to 12.3%. This was at a total cost of $21.5 trillion. Overall, the War on Poverty was a massive failure, for one very logical reason:

"What turned the War on Poverty into a social and human catastrophe was that the enhanced welfare state created a perverse system of incentives, and people adapted to their new environment."[7]

Despite the statistics about the failure of wealth redistribution, the belief that economics and taxes should be used to accomplish *social justice* persists. Is it realistic to apply economic pressure to move wealth from one group to another? Does it even work? Or, in the alternative, is there an underlying truth?

> *Economics and taxing policy should offer a means for managing financial expectations, paying for essential services, and promoting healthy commerce.*

ECONOMICS AND THE FUTURE

The financial news is full of experts predicting the future. Whether it is the future of the stock market, interest rates, unemployment, or anything else, the myth is that predicting the future is possible. The truth is that no one can accurately predict what will happen tomorrow, next week, or next year. There are simply too many variables.

What does add value is a thoughtful discussion of what *might* happen if specific actions take place first. An expert on interest rates could predict that an increase would have consequences, and those can be articulated. An increase in unemployment, the gross domestic product, or trade policies also will have consequences. What complicates all of this is the compulsion of many, especially in the media, to predict what will happen in the future, and not so much about what could happen if economic policies change.

Economists are wrong just as often as everyone else. However, some like to proclaim their expertise as rationale for making predictions that are impossible to validate. Many have tried to predict the Dow Jones Industrial Average number in a year. How can anyone know how 30 different stocks will move over 12 months? What factors went into the prediction? How do you know you can trust the prediction?

People want certainty. This is true in all aspects of life, even though none of these aspects can be predicted. The financial and economics

experts you see on television, in print, and online have absolutely no idea about what the future will look like. The only authority for predictions about the future is based on charts and graphs or on simple majority opinion. For example:

> According to the National Association for Business Economics' most recent quarterly outlook, the majority of the economists surveyed predict the next recession will occur by the fourth quarter of 2020. Half of respondents said the next big downturn would begin between the fourth quarter of 2019 and the second quarter of 2020. Only about 33% of those surveyed thought the next recession was likely to happen later than 2020.[8]

The problem in relying on the weight of opinion is that majorities are not necessarily right; they more often are wrong. A majority (or even 50-50) is supposed to be a convincing statistic, but it would be ill-advised to subscribe to a belief simply because half of all economists agree with a prediction. In fact, the past reveals that economists usually are not right in their predictions—and to a troubling degree:

> Prakash Loungani from the IMF (International Monetary Fund) analyzed the accuracy of economic forecasters and found something remarkable and worrying. "The record of failure to predict recessions is virtually unblemished," he said.
>
> His analysis revealed that economists had failed to predict 148 of the past 150 recessions. Part of the problem, he said, was that there wasn't much of a reputational gain to be had by predicting a recession others had missed. If you disagreed with the consensus, you would be met with skepticism. The downside of getting it wrong was more personally damaging than the upside of getting it right.[9]

Despite a record of consistently being wrong about the future, experts continue to offer predictions with confidence and certainty. The belief that the future can be predicted is often based on another flawed assumption: that with enough economic *science*, prediction can be made with great accuracy. But economics is not actuarial. An actuary uses statistical

probability to predict how many people of a given age will die each year, *on average.* This is science and is based on observation. When it comes to economics, there are too many variables to justify the level of predictions.

Beyond simply being wrong, economists also tend to disagree with each other. Some will predict a rise of 3% in unemployment over the next year, while others cite 2%, 1%, or zero change. The only common element is the inability to explain why predictions are offered in the first place: "If all the economists were laid end to end, they would not reach a conclusion."[10]

ECONOMICS AND INFLATION

A popular belief, one that makes no sense whatsoever, is that deficit spending is the underlying cause of inflation. Federal deficits have been blamed by politicians, economists, and academic experts for rising inflation. However, there is no correlation between deficit levels and degrees of inflation, at least not directly.

What exactly is *inflation*? It is an increase in prices, leading to a decline in the purchasing power of money. You have probably heard that over 20 years, with 3% inflation, the value of one dollar has been reduced to 55 cents. Inflation can be calculated for any inflation rate using the free calculator at https://www.buyupside.com/calculators/inflationjan08.htm.

Inflation
An increase in prices, leading to a decline in the purchasing power of money.

The cause of inflation is widely misunderstood, with many believing that prices are the actual cause. This was summarized by the observation: "Steel prices cause inflation like wet sidewalks cause rain."[11]

In fact, inflation is caused by adjustments in either demand or supply levels. As these evolve, the result is either *demand-pull inflation* or *cost-push inflation.* This is summarized in Figure 3.2.

Demand-pull inflation
A form of inflation caused by increased demand.

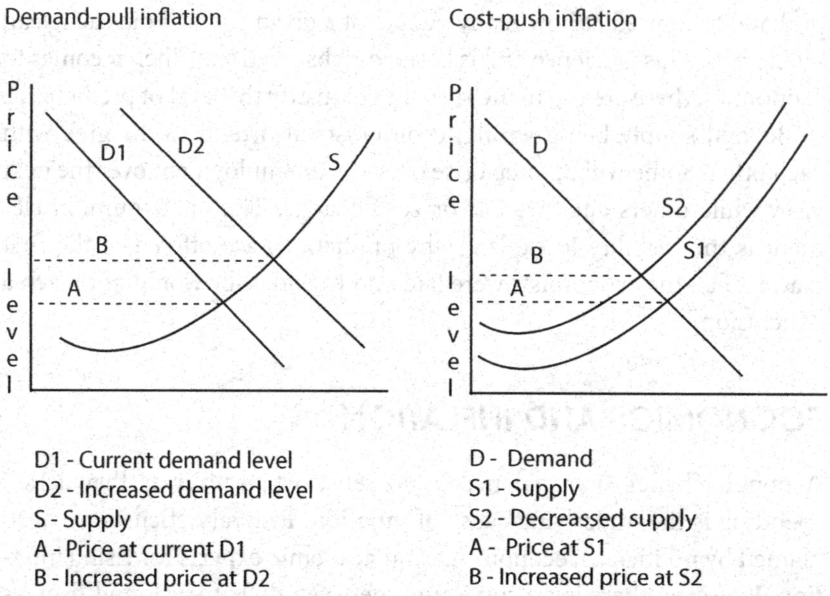

Figure 3.2 Two types of inflation

Cost-push inflation
A form of inflation caused by decreased supply.

In summary, these graphs reveal that prices rise in one of two ways. In *demand-pull inflation*, the level of demand rises more rapidly than production, causing higher prices for the available supply level. In *cost-push inflation*, as a producer's costs increase (for example, for labor or raw materials), the price is increased to maintain the producer's gross margins.

In both cases, *price* is the result of changes in either demand or supply. Price does not cause inflation; it is the *consequence* of evolving demand and supply.

ECONOMICS AND UNEMPLOYMENT

Some economists claim that inflation and unemployment present a type of trade-off, meaning changes in one affect the other. Many economists have argued that if the government takes steps to reduce inflation, it will cause unemployment.

This assumption relies on a belief that the government, rather than the private sector, is the ultimate determinant of all things in the economy. A free market philosophy recognizes the driving force as the market itself and observes that government may try to influence the economy—but should it?

This belief in consequences of government action is part of a philosophy called *Keynesian economics.* Named for British economist John Maynard Keynes, this philosophy was developed in the 1930s to explain the underlying causes of the Great Depression. Keynes argued that a depression was most efficiently ended through increased government expenditures. He also argued that economic intervention by governments could stabilize a weak economy. Also called *demand-side* economics, the Keynesian philosophy is the opposite of supply-side economics, the argument that lower taxes and more reliance on private sector activity is the most suitable way to create a healthy economy.

The Keynesian philosophy sees a direct correlation between government decisions and economic results. This includes the belief that inflation and unemployment have a cause-and-effect relationship. Keynesians claim that controlling deficits and spending leads to permanent prosperity. This means that reducing inflationary policies by government causes unemployment.

Keynesian economics
A set of theories promoted by John Maynard Keynes that government spending can be undertaken to stabilize and improve the economy; also called *demand-side* economics.

An alternative point of view is that governments should adopt a hands-off policy. By allowing the free market to thrive—meaning lower taxes and reduced regulation—unemployment shrinks and the economy thrives. This has been demonstrated time and again through government

policies that provide incentives to businesses to hire more people. This is accomplished by removing regulation and reducing taxes. In both the Reagan and Bush administrations, this philosophy (supply-side economics, or *trickle-down* economics) was shown to work each time it was tried. The myth connecting inflation and unemployment is easily debunked by examining the historical record.

TRUTHS, NOT MYTHS

These myths only scratch the surface of the untruths about the economy and the role of taxes, inflation, and government. Most myths about the economy are arguments about the role of government. In fact, the government has a limited number of roles in the economy:

1. Provide goods and services only when they cannot be provided through private companies.
2. Set up institutions, rules, and regulations to protect the economy.
3. Remove and prevent interference in the economy from outside forces.

To many, including economists in some cases, the belief persists that government's role is to control and influence the economy for the public good. This often is based on a false premise, that "the state knows everything and can do everything." This belief can be divided into three segments. First, government is the best judge of deficiency. Second, government is the best source for adjustments to maintain market efficiency. Third, government does not act out of self-interest, but from a sense of altruism.[12]

This set of beliefs and assumptions is flawed because, in fact, government is both inefficient and poorly informed. This comes not only from the blinding force of political motivation on both sides of the government debate, but also from large-scale inefficiencies. Governments often are led by people who have never worked in the private sector, and who do not understand free markets or economic forces. For example, during the years Obama was president, top officials such as cabinet members

heading up executive branch departments had little or no significant private sector experience. Most advisors had always worked in government and, it could be argued, had little or no understanding of the economy.[13]

In comparison, the Trump administration relies on advisors from the private sector and represents the opposite of the previous administration. This by no means ensures that one side or the other is a magic fix for all economic problems; however, it clearly is preferable for governments, when establishing policies that affect the economy, to consider the opinions of the most experienced private sector advisors—those who know and have experienced the impact of government policies regarding taxation, regulation, and oversight.

Excessive reliance on the many economic myths that refuse to go away (despite all the evidence) translates to the creation of ineffective or destructive policies. To the degree that everyone in the private and public sectors better understand how economic forces work, the economy will be stronger, healthier, and more grounded in the real world.

ENDNOTES

1. Adams, Henry Brooks. (1907). *The Education of Henry Adams.* (1999 ed.). New York, NY: Modern Library. p. 373.
2. https://www.intelligenteconomist.com/laffer-curve/.
3. Small Business Administration (SBA), www.sba.gov/content/small-business-size-standards.
4. https://www.investors.com/politics/editorials/income-tax-revenues-trump-tax-cuts-economic-growth.
5. Tanzi, Alexandre. (October 16, 2018). "Top 3% of U.S. taxpayers paid majority of income tax in 2016." *Bloomberg*, https://www.bloomberg.com/news/articles/2018-10-14/top-3-of-u-s-taxpayers-paid-majority-of-income-taxes-in-2016.
6. Sheffield, Rachel and Robert Rector. (September 15, 2014). "The War on Poverty after 50 years." https://www.heritage.org/poverty-and-inequality/report/the-war-poverty-after-50-years.

7. Woodhill, Louis. (March 19, 2014). "The War on Poverty wasn't a failure—it was a catastrophe." *Forbes*, https://www.forbes.com/sites/louiswoodhill/2014/03/19/the-war-on-poverty-wasnt-a-failure-it-was-a-catastrophe/#52b8eef16f49.
8. De Lea, Brittany. (June 4, 2018). "Next recession not far off, economists predict." *Fox Business*, https://www.foxbusiness.com/markets/next-recession-not-far-off-economists-predict.
9. Shaw, Adam. (September 2, 2017). "Why economic forecasting has always been a flawed science." *The Guardian*, https://www.theguardian.com/money/2017/sep/02/economic-forecasting-flawed-science-data.
10. Attributed to George Bernard Shaw. (May 1933). *The Saturday Review of Literature.*
11. Blough, Roger. (August 1, 1967). *Forbes.*
12. Dollery, Brian and Joe Wallis. (2001). *The Political Economy of Local Government*. Cheltenham, UK: Edward Elgar. p. 48.
13. Kuhn, David Paul. (September 3, 2010). "None of your business. On Obama's Public Sector Cabinet." *Real Clear Politics*, https://www.realclearpolitics.com/articles/2010/09/03/none_of_your_business_on_obamas_public_sector_cabinet_107001.html.

Part II

Microeconomics

4

SUPPLY AND DEMAND—HOW MARKETS WORK

Abstract

Supply and demand, the two essential attributes of any economic system, define what may be provided to meet consumer wants and needs versus the levels of those wants and needs. The two sides do not always match perfectly. When supply is too low to meet demand, prices move upward in an inflationary effect. When a supply is in surplus, meaning there is more available than the current demand, prices move downward. Both producers and consumers constantly strive to move their price points to a point of agreement, called equilibrium, but that cannot be sustained for long. The interaction of supply and demand is constant.

The forces of supply and demand often are cited in business publications and online. However, some assumptions come with these citations and need to be addressed.

First, supply and demand are not controlled by producers. Many people believe that producers and retailers have the power to set the prices of their products at whatever they choose—that the hardware store owner can add 30 cents to the cost of a hammer or the grocery store manager can raise the price of lettuce by five cents.

To a very limited extent, producers and retailers can adjust prices. But in a roundabout way, consumers set the prices, not the producers. Even a

small increase in the price of goods will drive consumers to a lower-cost competitor. When you come to a corner with two gas stations, and one charges two cents less for regular gas, you are likely to pick the cheaper alternative. It's human nature. The same applies when you buy a hammer or lettuce. You are likely to go to the lower-price store every time, all else being equal. The point is this: despite popular belief, prices cannot be raised arbitrarily. It causes loss of business and market share, and customers will go elsewhere if your price is higher, even minimally.

For a business owner, this demonstrates that demand determines price. If you want to maintain market share, you must respect the delicate balance between the price that customers are willing to pay and your need to earn a marginal gross profit.

OVERVIEW, THE NATURE OF GOODS AND SERVICES

You are not only a business owner, but a consumer as well. When you purchase raw materials, you shop for the best deal. Price, discounts, delivery terms, and quality all affect where and when you buy, in what quantities, and under what terms. When you hire people, you also want to pay the lowest reasonable wage for the best-qualified people. If you are required to compete by paying higher wages, you must raise prices—but so must everyone else; thus, the inflation that is attributed to higher costs applies to everyone. In comparison, if you are the only competitor in your sector paying more for materials and labor, you will raise prices and lose market share.

Just as a widespread misconception about price is believed, so is one about the quantity of supply. Many people believe that producers can force prices up by limiting the quantity of goods they deliver. This is ill-advised; consumers will simply buy from your competitors if you try to limit what you offer, meaning that you will lose market share by trying to artificially control the supply/demand equation. If you have a monopoly on a product, you are still limited as to how much you can raise prices. Consumers will buy less if the price is too high, even if they cannot find a similar product elsewhere.

Monopoly is a destructive force in economics because it circumvents the natural effects of supply and demand. If a company is the sole provider of an essential product, it can raise prices to any level it wants. Marathon Pharmaceutical developed a drug called *deflazacort* for the treatment of muscular dystrophy. A similar drug was available in Canada for between $1,000 and $2,000 per year, but Marathon charged $89,000 per year, an increase of 6,000%. Companies argued that the cost of research and development justified high prices, but was that legal? Yes. Under provisions of the Orphan Drug Act, developers of new drugs are granted a monopoly for seven years:

> Because this steroid had never been approved in the United States, the Food and Drug Administration considered it a new drug. That meant that not only did Marathon have to go through the process of getting it approved as a new drug, but that it got the benefit of the laws that Congress had passed to encourage drug companies to develop new medicines for rare diseases.[1]

In this situation, the law—which was intended to encourage development of new treatments—can be used to control the market and generate significant profits.

Other than this unusual situation, the more typical range of goods and services is subject to forces of supply and demand. The economic reality mandates that producers must consider the market forces on both sides. Economic theories analyze these realities endlessly and, to an extent, they are useful in helping to understand how those forces work.

THE IMPORTANCE OF CHOICE

Supply and demand does not operate as an isolated force. It is controlled by the choices that are made by producers and consumers. Producers offer products at a given quantity and price, and consumers can choose whether to pay that price, shop elsewhere, or forego the purchase.

For example, in picking a purse, a woman has a range of brands and prices to choose from. The cheaper versions will perform the same

function as the expensive one, so the consumer must decide how much importance is given to brand. A Gucci purse is available for $1,500, but a similar Coach brand purse can be bought for $250.

> Opportunity cost
> The benefit of one decision over another, given limited funds and the comparison of price and other attributes of a product.

> Relative price
> The price of two or more products, defining how consumers choose between one or the other.

In picking one over the other, or something in between, a choice must be made. Another choice can involve the decision to buy a purse versus spending money on new electronics, a vacation, or a different article of clothing. Every purchasing decision involves what is termed an *opportunity cost*, the benefit of one decision over another. It may be price, brand name quality, or the decision to save money rather than spend.

The opportunity cost has everything to do with levels of demand. Every purchase a consumer makes is a choice. It is based on the consumer's wants and needs of the moment, as well as on *relative price*. For example, a purse may cost either $250 or $1,500, yet both provide the same function. The relative price of the cheaper purse is one-sixth the price of the more expensive one—and relative price defines not only the price itself, but other attributes leading to the choice. Is it worth six times more to acquire a purse with the status of a recognized brand? Is the quality that much better? What other aspects go into analysis of relative price?

The selection of one product over another is not always a choice. For example, a family with a limited income cannot afford to buy expensive food and will invariably select cheaper food products to feed their children. The choice considers the need to also pay for rent, utilities, and clothing. In this case, *choice* is limited to the most affordable prices of necessities, rather than other matters.

DEMAND AND SUPPLY FUNCTIONS

The *demand function* is a combination of price, availability, and a market for goods and services. When consumers operate with a fixed budget,

some products are out of reach; even though they might want a product, it is not always possible to have it. The demand function describes the process of the choice that every consumer makes. Why does a shopper go to your store or your competitor's store? Why pick one provider over another?

Demand function
The combined motives for consumers of goods and services, a combination of price, availability, convenience, and service.

Most understanding of demand—notably from a business owner's point of view—is based on price. If you sell the same merchandise as a competitor, how does a consumer choose? Beyond price (which might be identical in every outlet in town), consumers also decide where to shop based on convenience (e.g., do you have a parking lot or easy street parking?), distance, and customer service. Demand function also varies with the availability of a product. The two economic constraints that affect how your customers buy are scarcity and choice. If a product is scarce, buying it requires research and patience; and if an alternate can be found easily, it usually will be taken. Choice is a combination of all attributes—not only price but every other motivation to buy or to not buy at your outlet. If your business sells products online, how easy is it to navigate your website? Are you often out of products due to scarcity (or simply due to poor planning for purchases)?

Demand is sensitive to price as a primary matter. If prices rise, consumers will either seek a substitute product at a lower price (and possibly, at lower quality); or they will buy less to avoid spending more than they can afford.

Why is all of this important? Chances are that you as a business owner have studied your market. You know what your competitors charge for the same goods that you sell, and you know how customers behave regarding price. But what about all of the non-price issues connected to the demand function?

Emphasis is invariably focused on price because that is a primary driving force of the demand function. If your price is too low, you will not be able to generate a gross profit or a net return. If your price is too high, you lose market share because consumers go to your lower-priced competitors. These forces of the demand function dominate how consumers

behave; but if prices are the same between competitors, those non-price considerations will be in play. The demand function is summarized as a demand curve, as shown in Figure 4.1. The curve slopes downward, indicating the relationship between price and quantity. This becomes important later when matters of surplus and shortage or increases and decreases in demand are examined.

> Supply function
> The willingness and ability of a producer to offer goods and services, based on the cost of goods and pricing considerations.

The opposite side of this discussion is the *supply function*, which is the relationship between a producer's willingness and ability to provide goods and services, and the economic factors affecting whether the producer can generate a profit in making goods and services available. For example, raw materials, labor, and

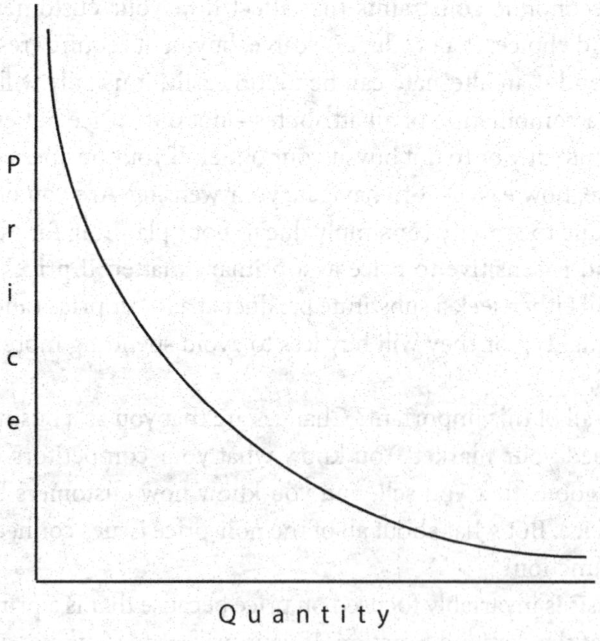

Figure 4.1 Demand curve

facilities costs could make some products too expensive to offer at competitive prices.

This supply function is affected by movements along the supply curve. This forces a producer to change the price. It's a simple economic reality: if your costs increase for products or components, you must pass along that increase or accept a lower margin of profit.[2]

The supply curve is graphically described as an upward-sloping line, as shown in Figure 4.2.

The demand and supply curves act and react according to principles called the *law of demand* and the *law of supply*. The first states that beyond price, when all other factors do not change, the higher a product's price, the lower demand will be. The second observes that a higher volume

<u>Law of demand</u>
The observation that the higher a product's price, the lower its demand will be.

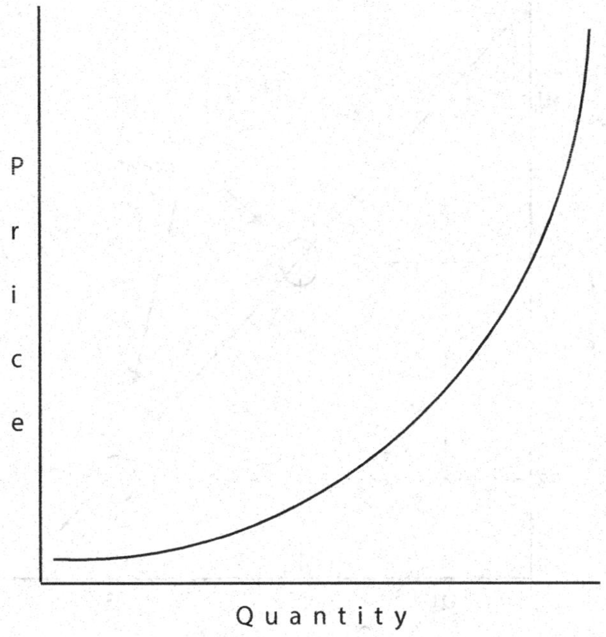

Figure 4.2 Supply curve

Law of supply
The observation that a higher volume of goods is offered at higher prices and a lower quantity of products is offered at lower prices.

of products are offered at higher prices, and fewer products are supplied at lower prices.

These laws can be represented graphically by demonstrating how various price levels affect each side of the demand and supply equation. Figure 4.3 shows that as prices are lowered, the quantity of production is reduced. The demand correlation between the sample price levels is a summary of how the law of demand functions.

The opposite occurs under the law of supply, as shown in Figure 4.4. As price increases, quantity of production also grows. These economic concepts have a practical side to them, and this is where every business owner can expand their understanding of the mysterious motivations

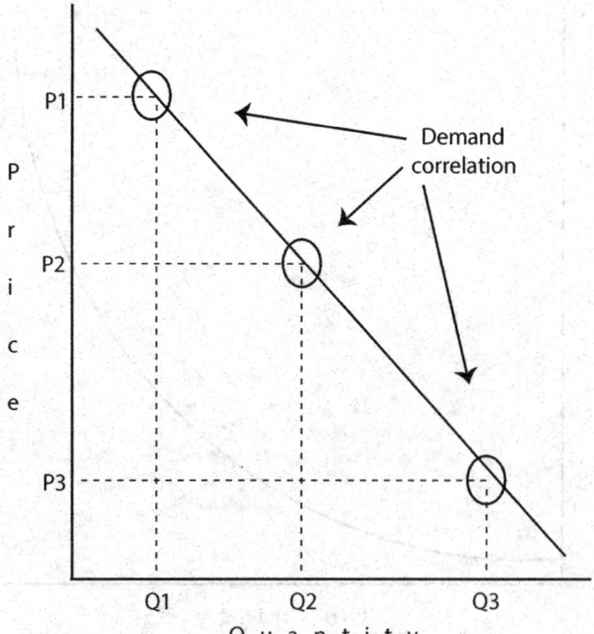

Figure 4.3 Law of demand

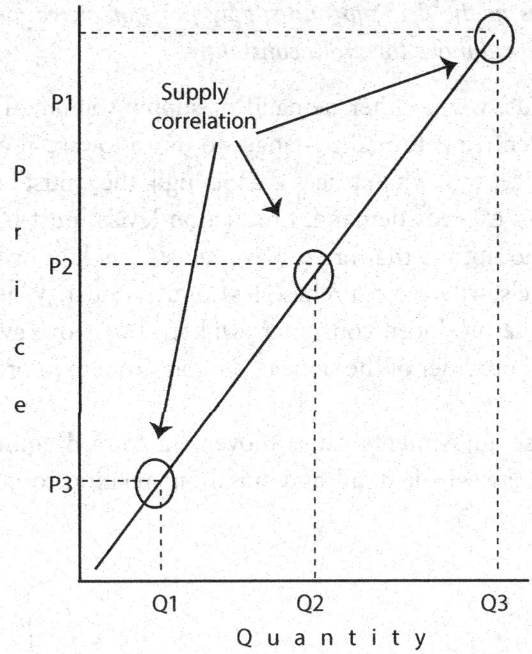

Figure 4.4 Law of supply

among customers and even among their competitors. The practical summary is this: when demand and supply meet at the same price and quantity, the demand and supply interaction achieves *equilibrium*. Goods and services supplied to the market are matched with demand for those goods at the quantity and price offered.

Why does this matter? First, it is impossible to maintain equilibrium for very long. It occurs, but almost immediately, one side or the other moves away from this "perfect" relationship between the two sides. It is important, however, due to another observation:

Equilibrium
The point where goods and services provided at a given price and quantity perfectly match the demand among consumers.

> *Both sides in the demand and supply function strive for equilibrium and will move toward it constantly.*

In other words, when either demand or supply wanders from equilibrium, the incentive is to make changes to move toward it again. A producer recognizes that when prices are too high, they must be lowered; or when quantity exceeds demand, production levels must be reduced. A consumer who notices that prices have moved too high will either seek lower prices elsewhere or purchase less of a product. When prices are lowered by one producer, consumers will tend to move away from the higher-priced provider of the same or similar product in order to get the lower price.

All of these adjustments cause movement toward equilibrium. The relationship between demand and supply in relation to equilibrium is shown in Figure 4.5.

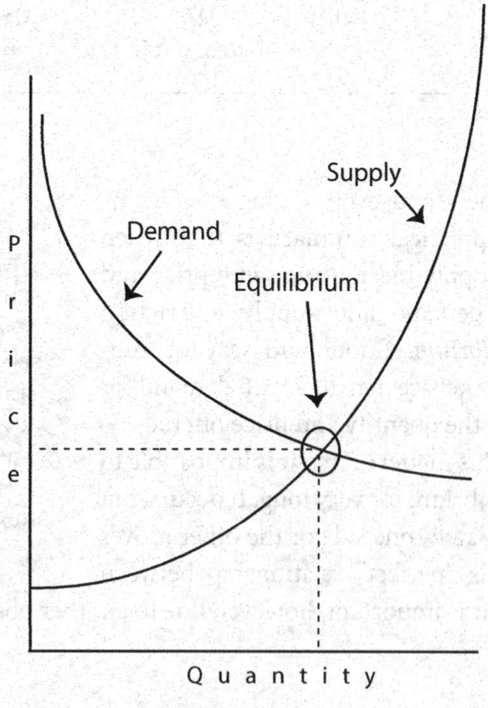

Figure 4.5 Equilibrium

A business owner can benefit by being aware of how the demand and supply functions affect both sides and by how equilibrium is a motivating force for both producer and consumer. As price and quantity evolve and shift, supply must adjust to the other side, shifting demand. Any business owner who does not recognize how these forces interact is doomed to failure; those who understand the demand and supply functions and how equilibrium works have an advantage over competitors who may not understand these realities.

Many economic texts devote a good deal of space to further analysis of the forces of equilibrium (and disequilibrium) and how shifts and movements in demand or supply appear on a graph. But it really comes down to a simple overall rule: prices and quantity cannot simply be adjusted by producers to improve profits; consumers have more to say about these matters and demand will affect profits. When a business does not recognize how these forces work, market share is lost—and that means that profits are lost as well.

STABILITY AND THE EFFECTS OF EQUILIBRIUM

Every business owner desires stability in markets. The regular purchases by the customer base, acceptance of reasonable prices, and consistent profits are all desirable outcomes for a skillfully managed business.

How is this accomplished? Prices and quantity will move toward equilibrium, either by choice or by market forces. Why does a competitor lose market share, while another gains? The answer may be given in many forms, but it comes down to the operation of equilibrium. By knowing that price and quantity continuously move toward equilibrium, you can compete well and even anticipate changes in your customer base. For example, when Eastman Kodak failed to recognize the revolution in digital camera technology, it lost market share. Management saw only that they had always been the leading company in the film industry. They did not recognize that most forms of film and film cameras had become obsolete. Consequently, they entered the digital camera market late, and it led to their bankruptcy and reorganization in 2012. In business since 1880,

the company ignored equilibrium and did not recognize that demand for film was disappearing and being replaced by digital technology.[3]

EXCESS DEMAND OR SUPPLY

When demand exceeds available supply, equilibrium is thrown into disarray and the result is a shortage. This is seen repeatedly in the economy. For example, whenever a major hurricane approaches Florida or the Gulf Coast, items like plywood (to cover windows), gasoline (to leave the area), and even bottled water become scarce. Demand rises to a level unanticipated by producers of those goods. This may involve price gouging as a response to heightened demand, or the basic unavailability of goods.

Excess demand also has been seen when popular products are released. A new electronic device made available by Apple, for example, is accompanied by long lines forming the night before and many who are unable to get the new product on day one. In many cases of excess demand, stores have seen angry consumers trample one another and start fights to get the last item on the shelf. It all may seem irrational, but it recurs often enough so that an observation must be offered: the level of demand, once it rises, overcomes common sense, the holiday spirit, and common courtesy.

For example, here is a description of one incident on Black Friday in 2011 that is not at all uncommon:

> In 2011, a woman used pepper spray "to gain preferred access to a variety of locations" in a Los Angeles Walmart . . . A captain from the fire department described it as "competitive shopping." The woman injured 20 people, including children. That year, the deals included $5 Bratz dolls, $10 Wii video games, and $29 tricycles. . . .[4]

Excess demand can lead to irrational and even violent behavior—and not just for necessities. Low supplies of toys, video games, or bicycles can create as much irrational behavior as a shortage of water or gasoline.

The opposite phenomenon is excess supply, also known as surplus. Although excess supply is the opposite of excess demand, both are

movements away from equilibrium but in the extreme. In some forms of surplus, the producers will reduce prices even below their net cost, in order to free up capital to be used elsewhere, when greater demand may provide a more robust outcome. However, excess supply is a difficult condition to overcome, because it may be persistent over time. A business owner may be able to avoid the situation by tracking the buying trends among consumers. For example, if you are increasing investment in products as demand rises over time, look for early warning signs that demand is beginning to flatten out. The slowing of demand levels could be a change foreshadowing a big move away from current demand levels, possibly leading to a surplus.

Supply and demand are logical forces in the economy; without these opposing forces, the economy could not work. Supply and demand set prices and quantities and define value. For every business owner, tracking the ever-changing effects of supply and demand and developing awareness of how each side strives for equilibrium leads to developing an edge over competitors.

There is much more to the study of supply and demand, but beyond the points examined here, it becomes more a matter of theory and less one of practical application. The primary point to be kept in mind is: consumers cannot be controlled by producers simply by increasing prices. The popular belief that producers hold all the power can only lead to trouble later. A business owner who respects the forces of supply and demand will be able to compete effectively and provide the market with the goods and services that it needs and wants—and at prices that consumers are willing to pay.

ENDNOTES

1. Herper, Matthew. (February 10, 2017). "Why did that drug price increase 6,000%? It's the law." *Forbes*, https://www.forbes.com/sites/matthewherper/2017/02/10/a-6000-price-hike-should-give-drug-companies-a-disgusting-sense-of-deja-vu/#117084e071f5.
2. Melvin, Michael and William Boyes. (2002). *Microeconomics*. 5th ed. New York, NY: Houghton Mifflin. pp. 56–62.

3. Rees, Jasper. (January 20, 2012). "The end of our Kodak moment." London, UK: *The Telegraph.*
4. DiGangi, Christine. (November 25, 2015). 7 Horrifying Moments of Black Friday Insanity. *WHIOtv7*, https://www.whio.com/lifestyles/holiday/horrifying-moments-black-friday-insanity/ridWk1JxpJeN4b0yOcuo0N/.

5

THE MICROECONOMICS BUSINESS CYCLE

Abstract

The business cycle usually is applied to national or regional trends. This chapter focuses on the immediate attributes of microeconomics and how companies and consumers operate and interact with one another. Decision making—within a context of competition among producers and decisions among consumers—defines the microeconomic business cycle. Behavior on both sides of the supply/demand relationship is based on the cyclical changes that affect the pricing and availability of goods and services.

Markets are created by the exchange of goods and services between producers and consumers. How do producers determine what to offer to the market and what prices to place on their goods and services? How do consumers decide whether to buy from one outlet or another and what price is acceptable?

In previous chapters, the point was made that some consumer decisions are based on non-price attributes. Brand loyalty or perceived status of the brand might motivate a buyer to pay significantly more for an item with identical utility to a cheaper alternative. Company reputation, customer service, location of outlets, even small matters like convenient parking areas, all contribute to the non-price decisions that consumers make.

Producers must be aware of these often fickle or impulsive decision points. In most economic analyses, price is the most important criterion for consumer decisions. However, if a producer focuses only on price and does not consider the non-price attributes of goods and services, opportunities may be lost—or worse yet, markets may be lost. Consumers have many choices, and widely available goods are marketed in many outlets. Some grocery stores also sell patio furniture and grilling equipment. The thinking behind the decision to expand product lines is complex and deserves analysis. For some producers, offering second and third product lines beyond the primary ones is a way to capture markets and market share that might be difficult through other means. If a consumer must visit the store to buy milk and eggs, that same consumer might be drawn to patio furniture and grilling equipment. The one-stop shopping model makes sense, but in recent years has been made more complex by the trend toward online shopping for a variety of products—including not only books or toys, but food, patio furniture, and grilling equipment.

The point is that the microeconomic business cycle has changed. Consumers no longer must leave home to shop. This means that non-price considerations like convenience of parking, distance between home and store, or basic customer service have all been replaced. Today, online shopping choices often come down to ease of navigation on a website.

THE BUSINESS CYCLE AND E-COMMERCE

The small business owner contends with the competitive web, especially if a store is opened at a physical location. Shopping must be personal and convenient in order to compel the buyer to visit that store rather than the less personal alternative of making purchases online, the relatively new e-commerce market.

In the second quarter of 2017, for example, Walmart (the world's largest retailer) saw sales up 1.8% year over year (YOY):

> That boost in revenue is largely due to the retailer's strong performance at its U.S. e-commerce arm, which saw net sales and gross merchandise

> volume (GMV) grow 60% and 67%, respectively, YOY. This marks the second straight quarter in which Walmart saw 60%-plus growth in U.S. e-commerce sales . . .
>
> Brick-and-mortar retailers are caught on the wrong side of the digital shift in retail, with many stuck in a dangerous cycle of falling foot traffic, declining comparable-store sales, and increasing store closures. Over 8,600 retail stores could close this year in the U.S.—more than the previous two years combined . . .[1]

The trend reflects not only where consumers shop, but how. In 2017, most consumers preferred buying groceries in a physical location; by 2018, the trend had shifted and many competing in that market (such as Walmart, for example) saw significant growth in online groceries sales. Consumers used to express clear preference for picking groceries in person. Other items, notably clothing and shoes, were rarely considered for online or mail-order purchase. Today, that has changed.

No company knew better than Sears & Roebuck that a consumer would buy goods from a catalog, even clothing. The first Sears catalog was published in 1887, aimed primarily at rural consumers who could not easily travel to a brick-and-mortar store. Sears dominated the mail-order business through to the 1920s. Even though consumers had greater mobility by that decade, Sears continued selling an array of products through mail order, and there was little if any resistance to buying from a catalog and a picture only, including clothing sight unseen. The Sears guarantee and no-questions-asked return policy promoted remote buying. Today, even with Amazon.com dominating the e-commerce space, larger competitors like Walmart and Alphabet are moving into the space and taking market share.

The historical model of a physical store is becoming obsolete. Shopping patterns are no longer limited by geography. Concepts like market area and merchandising floor plans no longer matter when compared to website design and ease of navigation for an array of products once belonging solely to the local store and later to the shopping mall.

The microeconomic business cycle is evolving and changing as a result. E-commerce has become dominant in a new business cycle that is

populated by consumers who are willing to buy online without any personal interaction. In the past and before the Internet even existed, part of the shopping experience was social. Shoppers met other shoppers, hunted for bargains by looking through many stores, and struck deals one-on-one. Today, negotiation is not a give-and-take matter like it was in the past; sellers offer bargain discounts and other deals online, and this generates a higher volume of sales for targeted products.

EQUILIBRIUM IN THE MICROECONOMIC SYSTEM

The business cycle is affected by the ever-changing face of the market. The emergence in recent years of e-commerce, for example, is making old-style brick-and-mortar marketing less attractive and in some cases, obsolete. For example, how can bookstores compete with the Internet (notably, the domination by Amazon)?

In a traditional bookstore, you roam the aisles and look at titles, occasionally picking up a book and leafing through it. This pleasurable shopping experience has become rare with more and more people buying online. A physical bookstore, even a large one, can place a finite number of books on their shelves. Online, you can explore the universe of books in print and buy as many as you wish with a click of a button. Discounted pricing takes online costs below the retail cost of bookstores, where overhead demands that prices be set higher; and with free shipping, it's impossible for brick-and-mortar bookstores to compete.

The same trends are seen in how consumers buy toys, electronics—even automobiles and food. The whole retail space is changing.

How does this affect the microeconomic business cycle? More to the point, how do these trends create a new business cycle? Anyone who has considered starting a business in the traditional way has to study the cost of rent, inventory, insurance, employees, utilities, and so much more. But if you have a product to sell, you can avoid many of these costs by selling online. Even the wholesale business has changed. Today, businesses are more likely to offer products at wholesale prices on online shopping outlets like Amazon and others and avoid the expense of marketing

and sales. It can all be done online, combining direct product sales with affiliate-based selling, volume discounts, and other changes that are never available with physical stores.

There is a cost involved in setting up a website in order to sell your wares, of course. But the business cycle is evolving rapidly and the criteria of success have changed as well. In the past, the economic consideration was to figure out how many sales you had to make in your store in order to cover your costs and expenses and, hopefully, to generate a net profit. Today, if you sell from your website and combine retail and wholesale, the new criteria for success include average costs of customer acquisition, markup from your cost to retail, cost of shipping, licensing fees you earn or pay, and the level of discount that you must provide to online outlets like Amazon.

For most small businesses that are operating from a website, the past economic tests of success and even of *breakeven* no longer apply. It appears at first glance that the cost of business online is much lower than in a physical store. This is true to an extent, but competition has expanded along with the expansion of technological convenience. You will have much more competition today and in the future. This comes not only from other individuals trying to grab market share through a new website, but also from large concerns dominating the space with high volume and big discounts. The microeconomic business cycle moves quickly and looks much different today than it did in the past.

Even the basic questions about your online presence are different today. In the past, a potential investor or lender would want to know your gross revenue and net profit from month to month as a means for deciding whether your business was a good risk. Those issues defined your business cycle of the past: cost, markup, sales volume, and profits.

Today, even while the same issues are of concern, the questions are different. Potential investors and lenders want to know the cost of customer acquisition, markup and volume, and the mix of wholesale and retail. For many, even thinking about moving into wholesale by placement in big stores is out of the question; money is made through direct sales online, licensing agreements, and website-to-website marketing.

DECISIONS AND THE MICROECONOMIC BUSINESS CYCLE

The business cycle affects individual small businesses in a few ways. Most critical today is the rapidly changing three-part environment:

1. *Products and services*: the types of products and services offered for sale have evolved rapidly as the Internet has created new markets and new demand. Looking over the range of products available for sale (on Amazon or eBay, for example), many of today's products did not exist 10 years ago. A business looking at the long term must be able to expand its range of products and services into the future in order to remain relevant for a changing market.
2. *Economic concepts*: in the past, new business owners focused on location and foot traffic, advertising, and store design. Today, the focus has shifted to web placement, online traffic, and website design. This opens the potential to offer many more products than in the past when the square footage of a physical store limited how much merchandise could be offered to the customer base.
3. *Delivery systems*: selling online opens many methods for delivering goods to the public view. Arranging the website with drop-down menus allows customers to navigate your website easily. This new *floor plan* of your home page should be designed so that a visitor can go immediately to the category they want. Just as physical store layout determined whether visitors bought or just left, website design is the new delivery system and the level of ease of use determines the level of sales.

All the economic concepts, including the business cycle, have changed. There remains a basic and cyclical attribute in every form of business, but it has changed in how customers are attracted and encouraged to buy. A business owner identifies a market niche, product sources, methods of promotion, price setting, and actual marketing. Within that cyclical process, the owner must understand the cost of goods sold (merchandise costs, direct labor, shipping, and other direct costs) and control expenses. If volume is adequate within these constraints, the total revenue generated,

minus cost of goods sold and expenses, will yield a profit. It may take time to get the word out, making the first year of a new business the most critical. About one-third of new businesses fail within the first two years, and one-half fail by the end of the fifth year, according to the Small Business Administration.[2]

Why does this occur? There may be many reasons for the high rate of business failures, but it usually comes down to inadequate planning, inexperience, and poor management. Other reasons include strong competition, poor merchandising, or lack of understanding of how to generate traffic. In the past, *traffic* referred to visitors into a physical store. Today, in many cases, *traffic* means visits to a website. Or, if you have a physical store also, it could be a combination of physical and online visits.

For example, many years ago, a would-be business owner started up an antique business. His specialization was large furniture—bureaus, tables, bedframes, etc. Unfortunately, he signed a lease for a very small store in which only about six pieces would fit. He failed to run the numbers and was not able to produce a net profit. He would have needed to sell two to three pieces per day just to cover overhead before generating any profit. When his accountant asked him why he chose that store (off the main road, by the way), he said it was "affordable."

The store was too small for his product, and it would not be reasonable to expect enough foot traffic to justify opening in the first place. Even if there was foot traffic, he would need a high volume of sales. Anyone who has investigated the antique business will point out that, as a rule, the larger and more expensive the item, the lower the volume of sales. This is true not only for antiques, but for most merchandise. There was no way for this store to succeed.

Today, the same observations can be applied to brick-and-mortar stores. It is a universal truth that you need enough floor space and traffic to set reasonable expectations for sales; and that at a minimum, the sales volume must be enough to cover your cost of goods sold and expenses. It must be higher than this breakeven if you expect to earn a profit.

Today, there is more to consider. If you run an operation online as well as through a store or even if you are operating only online, you must consider website ease of use and design just as you do with a physical store.

A visitor must be able to navigate and must find prices attractive enough to move an item to the shopping cart. What will you charge for shipping? You compete with big online stores like Amazon in several ways. They have a broad product range; their prices usually are discounted below retail prices; and on many items they offer free shipping or low-cost shipping.

With all of this in mind, the modern business cycle is a difficult path for any business owner. You need an easily identified niche market for products or services because competing directly with the big online store is not possible. The big online store has so much flexibility that the pricing and cost of shipping alone is insurmountable, not to mention the broad range of products and prices offered. But you need to be online, even if your product is unique, patented, priced well and attractively packaged.

For example, on the television show *Shark Tank*, most of the successful products that attract investors are online. These include Scrub Daddy, Tipsy Elves, Breathometer, Bubba's Boneless Ribs, Ten Thirty One Productions, Wicked Good Cupcakes and Bombas, to name the top success stories.[3]

By the way, Amazon.com announced in October 2018 that it launched a collection of products featured on *Shark Tank* through the Amazon .com website. Even if you design your website well and raise capital successfully, amazon.com remains likely to control a big segment of the overall market.[4]

BASIC DECISIONS AND THE BUSINESS CYCLE

The previous example demonstrated that some decisions make no sense, economically. Picking an "affordable" storefront that is located on a poorly traveled street and is too small to expect a net profit is not thrifty—it is suicidal. Basic decisions concerning various ways to control costs and expenses must be made with an eye to net profits.

For example, a store was run by two people who marketed handmade ceramic pots, plates, and other household items. The two owners were artists and their designs were unique and of exceptional value. Their store was designed with two rooms. The front room was the first one to be

seen when people walked into the store; and the back room was about the same size, but people needed to travel from one room to the other to visit the second area. In this back room, the owners marketed cheaper quality ceramics that they purchased from others, while their handmade ceramic products were in the front room.

Sales were far too low to cover costs and expenses, and they did not know what to do to solve the problem. A consultant advised them to place the expensive, handmade goods in the back room because these were significantly more expensive than the mass-produced items, which as a rule, caused sales to be lower. By placing cheaper merchandise in the front room, more sales were likely to take place. The owners resisted this suggestion, pointing out that their handmade ceramics were their own, and they wanted them featured. The consultant told them, "You are losing money and one reason is the arrangement of merchandise. You need to decide whether you want to be successful merchants or starving artists."

This was a harsh piece of advice, but it was also true. The store needed more sales in order to survive. The owners knew they needed the cheaper products to make ends meet, but this was at conflict with their artistic prices and the desire to showcase their handmade products.

The owners were not willing to make the suggested change and ended up going out of business. This was unfortunate, but it demonstrated a fact of life for business owners. Even when your product is exceptional, you must be able to generate sales in order to cover your costs and expenses.

Another relevant example is when a group of four friends decided to open a natural foods café. The idea was to sell organic meals in a comfortable setting. The business failed after only a few months. The four owners made several mistakes:

1. *Convenience of location*: even though the café was large enough to accommodate 12 tables with chairs, the volume of traffic was not high enough to cover the cost of food. Why? There was no parking available on the street where the café was located. Relying on foot traffic or expecting customers to park two or three blocks away were both impractical.

2. *Inexperience*: none of the four owners had any food business experience. They did not know the costs and expenses they would face and assumed that everyone would want organic and tasty food, just as they did. As it turned out, this was not the case.
3. *Basic cash flow and need for income*: four owners cannot always expect to earn enough profit for all of them to make a living. It is difficult enough in any business for one owner to generate enough profit to draw money out. Margins were too small to support four people, a basic reality that was evident; but the owners had never bothered to run the numbers.
4. *Spoilage of food*: the food business is vulnerable to spoilage. From the day the café opened, the owners bought too many vegetables, and because traffic was too low, much of the food went bad within a few days. Vegetables have a very short shelf life, so their true cost of goods sold was much higher than expected when they set up their menu and assigned prices. They ended up having to increase prices to cover their losses from spoilage.
5. *Cost of menu items*: the last straw for this business was the high cost of items. Costs were raised due to higher-than-expected spoilage, but this meant the café could not compete with others that were in locations with greater convenience and parking close by; were operated by people with food business experience; had well-planned levels of cost and expenses with fewer owners requiring draws; had better planning for the timing of food purchases; and featured less expensive items on the menu.

Many people think businesses fail due to fierce competition. It certainly is true that competing online with big companies like Amazon is impractical, just as a small storefront cannot compete with big box stores in the role of anchors for large shopping malls. But businesses do not fail solely due to strong competition. Poor management and planning are more likely to be the underlying cause for failure. The inexperience of a first-time business owner, setting impractical goals or failing to analyze the numbers at all, and not knowing the facts about basic business operations are more likely to contribute to failures.

The initial research phase should be the starting point in the micro-economic business cycle. What is the competition? What prices are going to attract customers? Will you have a physical location or sell exclusively online? What initial costs are required? How long will it take to get to breakeven? How much money do you need for initial investment and to carry through beyond the point of breaking even? Do you have those funds, or do you need lenders or investors? Perhaps most important of all: do you have experience in this business?

Starting out with a realistic understanding of the hurdles you will need to overcome increases your chances for success. If you conclude that your chances for failure are too high, the initial analysis can help you avoid an expensive mistake. If you identify the potential problems that a new business will face and address them effectively, you improve your likelihood of creating a successful business. Finally, remain flexible in the products or range of products you intend to sell.

For example, the well-known company—Mattel—was started in 1945 by Harold Mattson and Ruth and Elliot Handler. When it was first formed, the idea was to build and sell dollhouse furniture. They soon realized that by using scrap wood to make toys, they could expand their product base. In 1955, the company became the primary sponsor of a new television show, the Mickey Mouse Club. Their sponsorship gave them the exclusive right to market Disney toys. In 1959, the company introduced the Barbie doll, which became the best-selling toy ever made.[5]

The point to this story is that the company became a huge success in the toy business, even though it stumbled into that as an afterthought. Their success resulted from flexibility in what was manufactured and how it was marketed. The Mattel business did not appear promising at its inception. However, timing was critical. With World War II ending, returning soldiers married and began having children, the well-known Baby Boom. The market for toys exploded and by the mid-1950s, Mattel was well positioned to be a major marketing company for a business with greater demand than ever.

The business cycle followed by Mattel was modest at first, but it expanded rapidly and found its niche.

ENDNOTES

1. Keyes, Daniel. (August 18, 2017). "Walmart's online sales continue upward trend." *Business Insider*, https://www.businessinsider.com/walmarts-online-sales-continue-upward-trend-2017-8.
2. Small Business Administration (SBA), https://www.sba.gov/sites/default/files/Business-Survival.pdf.
3. Real Simple, https://www.realsimple.com/work-life/entertainment/shark-tank-products.
4. Canal, Emily. (October 16, 2018). "Why Amazon is making it easier to buy 'Shark Tank' products." *Inc.* https://www.inc.com/emily-canal/shark-tank-amazon-retail-site-online-store.html.
5. Companies History, http://www.companieshistory.com/mattel/.

6

PRODUCTION AND OUTPUT

Abstract

The microeconomic business cycle operates within restrictions of production and output. Production is the process of creating goods—most often associated with manufacturing but applying to every form of operation. Output is the range of finished goods offered to the market, which is restricted by the costs of raw materials, labor, and other factors of production. Every business owner contends with the limitations of production and output, and must skillfully determine the most advantageous levels of production and pricing to maximize profits.

The methods of operation developed by a business owner are termed overall as operating within the *theory of production*. This is the means of developing an understanding of the most appropriate quantity to produce, given the constraints of raw materials and their cost; labor and its cost/benefit study; and other necessary attributes of production (capital, facilities, technical skill or talent, and management capability).

> Theory of production
> The process of determining how many goods to produce and at what cost, given the constraints of raw materials and labor, as well as other production investments.

The combined cost of raw materials and labor defines most product-based production operations as the *cost of goods sold*, those expenditures

Cost of goods sold (also termed "direct costs")
The expenditures of a business associated directly with the production of revenue, as opposed to expenses that cannot be assigned to the revenue produced by one or more products.

related directly to the generation of revenues. Although other investments are required to establish a productive environment, the recurring commitment to buying materials and paying workers represents most of these direct costs.

The interaction of the volume of revenue generated, the cost of goods sold, and the expenses of an operation define whether a company can produce net profits. The volume of revenue can be studied to determine the dollar value that is necessary to break even after paying for costs and expenses. This analysis is further influenced by levels of demand, prices offered by competitors for the same products or similar ones (substitutes), and any changes in levels of direct cost. For example, if raw material costs are raised, a producer must raise prices to pay for higher costs; however, the margin also must be set with awareness of competitive prices.

THE FACTORS OF PRODUCTION

As a producer you must address three categories of decisions: identifying the methods and strategies you devise to meet standards of production; determining the best possible level of supply required to maximize price; and analysis of how to create profits for a product or range of products (based on assumptions about future levels of demand and price levels).

Factors of production
The four attributes required to generate a profit within the constraints of the market.

These decisions are based on how you employ the *factors of production*: land, labor, capital, and entrepreneurship. Together, these factors of production describe what is needed to make a profit under the constraints of the market.[1]

The four factors work together as part of the producer's process. The first factor of production is *land*. This encompasses natural resources plus actual territory: water, air, fuel, and lumber, for example.

The second factor is *labor*. You hire people based on skills, education, and the type of requirements involved. For basic factory work, you might require unskilled laborers for repetitive functions; and these may eventually be replaced with robotics. Another type of labor is a skilled worker with defined skills or technical expertise.

The third factor of production is *capital*, the resources that are created to facilitate production. This includes constructed plants and factories, offices, and other facilities; and tools, equipment, and machinery used in a production process and for delivery to markets. These necessary elements must be paid for, so the use of *capital* includes equity and debt brought together to capitalize an operation.

The fourth factor is *entrepreneurship*, the risk-taking aspect of starting and operating a business. An entrepreneur has a vision and is willing to take the necessary risks to accomplish that vision. This individual combines the other factors of production (land, labor, and capital) to create net profits in a going concern.

PRODUCTION ACTIVITIES

Production activities are viewed for the most part as the creation of physical goods that are intended to meet demand at a specific price and quantity. Raw materials are applied in the process and—with the application of labor and the use of machinery or equipment—transformed into finished goods and marketed, advertised, and delivered to the market.

The functions of raw materials, labor, and capital (such as equipment and machinery, facilities, and more) are the factors of production. They define how the production process works in the transformation and combination of these resources to create output or the finished supply of products for the market.

The analysis of how much is required in the quantity of output, labor, and the amount of capital required can be reduced to a formula that describes the production function, also known as technical efficiency:

$$Q = f(L, K)$$

Where Q = the quantity produced
f = the production function
L = labor
K = capital

This relationship between quantity produced and the two key factors of production (labor and capital) defines *technical efficiency* and can also be visualized graphically, as can be seen in Figure 6.1.

The chart identifies the most advantageous conditions in which quantity and labor intersect—a concept like equilibrium between supply and demand. At these points, a producer is operating at the most efficient level possible. When quantity falls below these levels, it is operating inefficiently and will earn less profit.

Why does anyone need a chart to understand how this process functions? Every producer knows that resources must be maximized in order to create the best possible margin of profit. The chart (and the formula) summarize what a producer might know instinctively, especially when the ideal levels of quantity are not being reached. These tools help to visualize the challenge of production: ensuring that the maximum utility is gained from labor to meet output goals and generate the best possible gross profit at a given price. This concept is called the *cost of production theory*—stating that price itself is ultimately set by labor, materials, and capital. If the price is too high, demand will go elsewhere; and this would be the result of inefficiency in the operation of a production process.

> **Cost of production theory**
> An economic theory observing that the price of goods is determined by the combined application of labor, materials, and capital.

In the market economy, price ultimately is controlled by consumers. Observing the cost of

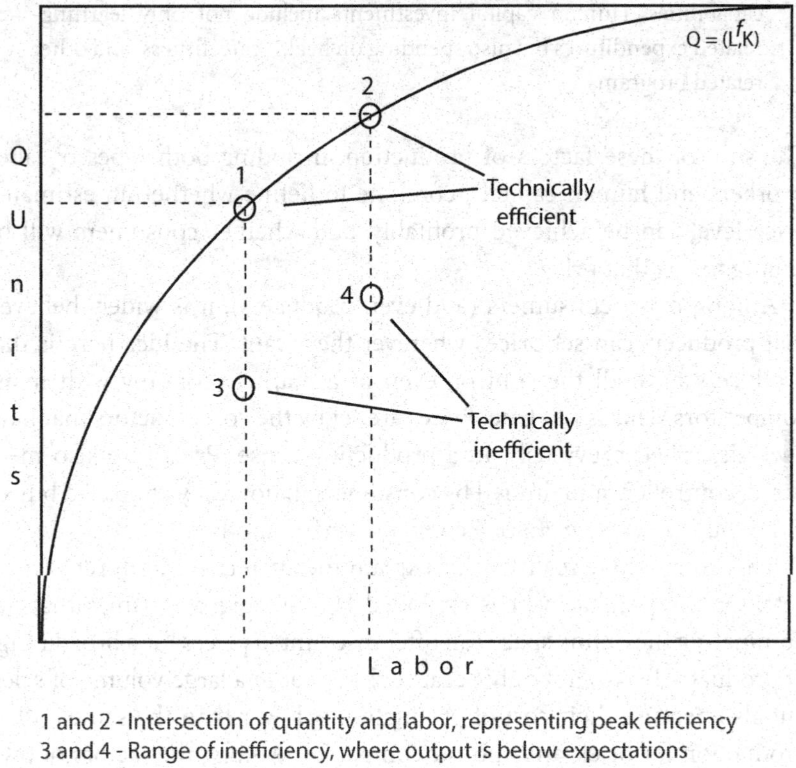

Figure 6.1 Technical efficiency

production theory at work, if a company is inefficient, it must raise prices or lose money. If prices are too high, consumers will buy less, and demand will migrate to competitors. The analysis of cost of production is not always clear, either. It is not always easy to separate the differences between workers in the production process and what often is termed *human capital*—the specialized knowledge and the technical skills needed to create products and processes:

> The expenditures of time, effort, and money to gain an education and improve a person's productivity are called human capital investments. Just as a business can invest in machinery and equipment, human beings can invest money and time in improving their own productive

capabilities. Human capital investments include not only learning-related expenditures but also spending on health care, fitness, and other related programs.[2]

The sum of these factors of production, including both types of labor (workers and human capital), combine to define whether an estimated price level can be achieved profitably, and whether consumers will be willing to pay that price.

Among many consumers (and even producers), it is widely believed that producers can set prices wherever they want. The idea here is that producers have all the control, even in a market economy with many competitors. This is not true. Prices are set by the cost of factors that have been described previously, in a production sense. Prices are also measured, controlled, and limited by consumers in how they choose to buy or to not buy products from one company versus another.

This competitive reality helps explain the current trend in retail markets. Online purchasing has exploded because big companies that are dominating the online space can offer discounted prices for a broad range of products. This is not only because they deal in a large volume of sales, but also because their cost of production is lower than the same cost of production for brick-and-mortar companies. Among the factors of production are facilities and the associated rent, utilities, and maintenance needed to run a company, produce goods, store them, transport them, and operate logistics for the entire operation. In comparison, a large company such as Amazon.com does not produce books from inception (hiring authors, editing text, hiring printers and binders, moving books to bookstores). The online bookstore buys finished products from publishers *after* these production costs have already been expended. All the online company must do is advertise the product, buy books from the publisher, and ship them to purchasers.

DEFINING THE PRODUCTION FUNCTION

The varying costs of production among different companies describe the workings of the *production function*, which varies based on levels of costs and expenses, as well as whether a company has exclusive control

over a product. For example, when a product is unique and produced by a company that owns the patent, that company has an advantage. Competitors may offer substitutes, but assuming superiority of a patented product owned by a single company, the production function will not be defined in the same way for all producers.

<u>Production function</u>
The cost of production and level of competition based on efficiency and application of unique properties, such as utility patents.

Can a producer compete efficiently? The cost of quantity and labor (inputs) may translate to desired levels of quantity (output) at a price needed to yield a net profit. This is determined by the efficiency of production described earlier. However, the equilibrium between labor and quantity is simplified when those are the sole considerations of profitability. The production process is usually more complex and involves many variables.

For example, the cost of fixed assets (such as equipment used in production) will vary based on age and maintenance costs. At what point is it economically efficient to replace older equipment and commit capital in order to offset growing maintenance costs? Another variance is found in logistics and other supply chain costs. How much does warehousing cost, including insurance, security, and loss from theft? How much does it cost to move goods to market, based on changing fuel costs? Are raw materials purchased from a sole supplier or from many? What happens when the cost of raw materials is raised? Of the indirect costs, how much is assigned to a product line in the cost account process, and how does this assignment affect margins of profit?

The degree of profit is determined by the producer in identifying the most efficient levels of quantity in consideration of two factors. First, what will the market bear in terms of demand and how does a company fit into the competitive landscape? Second, what is the most efficient level of quantity, based on all the factors of production and variables?

These variables describe how the fixed costs of production are efficiently reduced as quantities are increased. For example, maintenance of a production facility, equipment insurance and maintenance, and management compensation, are all fixed costs. This means that as output is increased, greater efficiency is achieved; but even this is limited. Producers

Profit maximization
The process of determining the level of output, given fixed and variable costs of production, required to generate maximum profits.

must decide the quantity at which maximum profit can be earned, based on analysis of fixed and variable costs of production. This process of analysis is called *profit maximization*. Cost efficiency is possible at maximum levels, and if this is achieved, it is a *perfect market*. It is part of the idea of equilibrium when the quantity supplied by producers is perfectly matched with the quantity of demand by consumers at an agreed-upon price.[3]

Perfect market
A theoretical condition in which equilibrium between supply and demand are achieved, in which producers operate at peak efficiency and generate the exact level of supply and price demanded by consumers.

THE LAW OF DIMINISHING RETURNS

Profits, as desirable as they are, cannot continue growing indefinitely. Anyone following the stock market realizes this. Successful companies tend to generate profits rapidly, but at some point, those profits plateau. There is a finite market share in every industry. The consumer pool of buyers not only splits among competitors, but also grows at a limited rate.

Law of diminishing returns
The point where the cost of gaining higher profit is greater than the profit itself.

Another key to this is that at some point, generating additional profits becomes too expensive. That is the point where the cost of gaining higher profit is going to be greater than the profit itself. This is called the *law of diminishing returns*. Every entrepreneur and business owner eventually must face this reality. Growth in any economy is finite.

A consequence arising out of this economic law is that growth is limited by attributes of the factors of production. Gross profit declines as output increases while factors of production remain the same. This inhibits growth and presents the finite nature of how much profit can be earned realistically.[4]

> **Negative return**
> The reduction in gross profits caused by increasing factors of production.

Eventually, when a business attempts to increase profits, a discovery is made: increasing factors of production in order to increase earnings (such as labor and raw materials) will not maintain levels of gross profit but will create a decline. This *negative return* is unavoidable.

Why does this have to occur? Consider this case of a furniture company. When they opened, they were selling products that had been purchased from a well-known distributor. Meeting initial success, the owners decided to add their own manufacturing plant and produce furniture themselves. The initial number-crunching forecast exhibited better gross margins as a result of this effort. However, the company ended up *losing* money over the next six months. After adding workers to manufacture furniture, the original factory they had leased was not big enough. Material costs were higher than the original estimates had indicated and several personnel issues came up—such as a demand for health care and other benefits.

The higher output looked like an initial success story, but that soon proved a false assumption. The higher-than-expected costs and expenses cut gross margins substantially. If the company raised its prices in the competitive retail furniture business, it would lose market share, making matters worse. The company ended up closing its manufacturing operation and trying to retreat to its previous profile. They broke the lease on the manufacturing space and lost a great deal of money in legal fees and the final judgment against the company.

All of the added factors of production caused a snowball effect. Adding space led to having to buy more materials in order to meet demand, which also required hiring more people because the original space was not large enough. The cost of goods sold continued to rise to the point that it was impossible to maintain gross margins or net profits. The initial idea of taking manufacturing in and cutting out the supplier was not a profitable move. The owners did not understand the law of diminishing return.

There is much more to the economic questions of production and output. However, as a broad introduction to this topic, the points

introduced before summarize the key issues that must be addressed by every business owner. No one can control price without considering the effects on demand—and when a business reaches a growth plateau, further expansion is possible only by coordinating the factors of production, by considering demand levels and competitors' prices, and by realizing the threat of diminishing returns. Far too many new businesses have failed because the concept of expansion—more outlets, employees, and products—was not understood well enough to accomplish expansion profitably. Many first-time business owners do not know these economic realities. Those who succeed understand the dangers of expansion and the irony of it all: expansion itself may present the greatest threat to a new enterprise.

ENDNOTES

1. Friedman, Milton. (2017 ed.). *Price Theory*. New York, NY: Routledge. Chapter 11.
2. Welch, Patrick J. and Gerry F. Welch. (2016). *Economics, Theory and Practice*. 11th ed. Hoboken, NJ: John Wiley & Sons. p. 403.
3. Debreu, Gerald. (1972). *Theory of Value: An Axiomatic Analysis of Economic Equilibrium*. New Haven, CT: Yale University Press. p. 26.
4. Samuelson, Paul A. and William D. Nordhaus. (2009). *Microeconomics*. 19th ed. New York, NY: McGraw-Hill. p. 110.

7

PRICE AND ELASTICITY

Abstract

An understanding of prices and how they move or change is essential for every business owner and entrepreneur. Levels of elasticity affect price but may be poorly understood even among business owners and executives. Both demand and supply experience elasticity, and this explains the often mysterious adjustment to price. Consumer demands and preferences are perhaps the greatest driving forces in price, even more so than levels of competition; however, prices may change even without changes in quantity or cost, and this is worthy of analysis by every business owner.

Why are prices adjusted periodically? Many people believe that a producer or seller of goods raises prices arbitrarily and will exert the greatest profit possible, not due to internal changes but only to gain as much as possible from the consumer. In fact, the nature of price setting and changing is more complex, and changes in price are not determined at random or in isolation from other economic forces.

PRICE AND ELASTICITY

The price of any goods may be adjusted without changes in quantity produced, or when the cost of goods has remained unchanged. Quantity produced may also be adjusted even if prices remain unchanged. There

> **Elasticity**
> Changes in price or quantity even without corresponding changes in cost that occur within the economy often due to perception of overall economic trends. The elasticity related to price is only one form; demand may also be elastic, and this affects how producers will be able to raise prices or quantity of supply. When both sides—supply and demand—move through periods of elasticity, price and quantity policies are more complex.

is no hard and fast rule for the relationship between price, cost, and quantity. Although restrictions and limitations always apply, there is room for change in one element even when there is no change in the other. This is termed *elasticity*. The changes experienced by consumers reflect broad economic trends. Regardless of whether people view current trends as favorable (at which point price increases are acceptable) or unfavorable (when price increases would not be acceptable), elasticity is continually present.

Demand elasticity occurs when other variables change, notably the current price and the consumer's income. The higher the demand elasticity is, the more sensitive the consumer will be to price changes. The trend in this is difficult to articulate but easy to observe. From a business owner's point of view, it can be simplified as the observation of the consumer's level of resistance to changes in price.

Demand elasticity often is described as a negative attribute within the economy. It implies volatility in equilibrium and may point to emerging friction between producers and consumers. In other words, as one or both sides move away from equilibrium (overall agreement as to price and quantity), instability is the result. This instability works against equilibrium—or the tendency for producers and consumers to move toward agreement on quantity and price of goods. Demand elasticity may lead to prices being raised in order to increase income; ironically, higher prices are likely to reduce income as consumers either buy less or move to a competitor.

Classifications of goods may be classified as elastic or inelastic. Elastic goods are those with abundant substitutes. For example, consumers may purchase over-the-counter drugs with brand name recognition or generic

and store-labeled substitutes. They also may substitute organic food for less expensive offerings.

Inelastic goods tend to have no suitable substitutes. As prices rise, demand remains the same, and consumers have no choice. For example, the price at the pump for gasoline may rise, but drivers still need to fill up their tanks. They can drive less to a degree, but necessary use of autos (for commuting, taking children to school, or shopping, for example) are forms of inelastic demand. The reduced usage of goods is the only way consumers can react to price increases for inelastic goods. This is not the same as behavior for elastic goods. Lower demand in response to higher prices translates to lower revenues.

This reality—producers earning lower revenues due to raising prices—contradicts a commonly held belief that producers and retailers have all the power to raise prices as high as they want and that consumers cannot do anything to change this. Going to a different outlet is one possible response, but another belief is that producers and retailers collude and raise prices together, so that consumers end up with no choice. However, in practice a competitor may react to higher prices by keeping their prices at the same level or even reducing prices. This elasticity on the supply side leads to higher revenues—if the adjusted price remains higher than the cost of goods sold. A producer must continue to earn revenue that is adequate to cover costs and provide for expenses, at a minimum.

When a business raises prices, another consequence will occur. Increased prices for elastic goods (most of what consumers buy) will result in fewer sales, so the increased price causes lower demand for the quantity of goods. In extreme cases, a producer may see weakened demand to a degree that producing the quantity required to cover the costs and expenses cannot be met; demand falls too low for the producer to make a profit.

CROSS-PRICE ELASTICITY

Demand changes whenever prices are raised and when consumers pick substitutes. In other words, rather than paying a higher price for one brand, consumers select a cheaper brand. Another form of this change in

Cross-price elasticity of demand
The lower demand of a product with price increases versus higher demand for a substitute available at a lower price.

behavior is substituting one product for another. For example, if the cost of broccoli is raised, a family may decide to buy peas and carrots as a substitute. This is called *cross-price elasticity of demand.*

This concept matters to every business owner. Many first-time entrepreneurs have gotten into trouble because they did not appreciate the nature of elasticity or the cross-price changes it may cause. They end up on the losing side of cross-price elasticity (as the producer who is raising prices) when the better position is to be on the winning side (as the producer who is keeping prices the same or lowering prices, especially for a product that is working as a substitute). The producer of peas and carrots will benefit from an increase in the price of broccoli because the lower-price revenues and profits will be higher.

The degree of cross-price elasticity may be quantified by comparing the percentage of change in demand between products. However, from the producer's point of view, this is basic supply and demand analysis. The percentage of change does not matter as much as the realization that demand has changed in response to changes in price. If you are the producer who raised prices, your profits will decline; if you are the producer offering a lower-priced substitute, your profits will increase (assuming your price is adequate to cover costs and expenses and still yield a net profit).

This cross-price elasticity of demand can be seen in every industry. For example, in 2018, auto manufacturer GM announced its plans to close some U.S. production plants following a weak quarter and a decrease of 11% in revenue over the previous year:

> The moves reflect the stark consumer shift to SUVs, crossovers, and pickups. All of the GM plants on the chopping block make passenger cars. The company will also discontinue the Chevrolet Cruze and Volt in North America as well as the Buick LaCrosse, Cadillac XTS, and Cadillac CT6.[1]

This announcement, resulting from weak revenue and profit results in the third quarter of 2018 contrasted with Tesla, which reported earnings per share for the same quarter of $2.90, versus expectations from analysts of a 19-cent loss. Tesla announced it would be willing to consider buying closed GM plants, a move it has taken in the past:

> Back in 2010, Tesla bought NUMMI, a car factory jointly owned by General Motors and Toyota in Fremont, California, for just $42 million shortly after it was shut down.
>
> The company gradually built the workforce back, including many former NUMMI workers, and now, 8 years later, Tesla Fremont employs more employees than the original factory and it produces electric vehicles at a current rate of over 300,000 units per year.[2]

This comparison—between GM, a company existing for more than a century, and Tesla, a relative newcomer—is stark. GM is losing market share and appears unable to figure out how to change direction. This is like what happened to Eastman Kodak, also existing for over 100 years but was unable to shift to digital camera technology until years after film had become obsolete. Another example: Sears continued with its failed big box store model, while newcomer Amazon and other online alternatives took an ever-larger market share.

Both Kodak and Sears filed for bankruptcy—largely due to their inflexibility toward making changes as the products consumers demanded change. The cross-price elasticity of demand was accompanied by the inability of each company to make economic adjustments while their competitors offered products with better prices and convenience. In the case of Kodak, old-style film was all but obsolete after the digital revolution, and the company did not recognize this in time. In the case of Sears versus Amazon, the brick-and-mortar store of the past no longer met the needs of the modern consumer.

The experience of this century-old company reveals something else about elasticity. There are times when this refers not only to prices or changing demand, but about *where* and *how* consumers shop. They may prefer the convenience of online shopping over going to a mall even

when prices are in the same range in both venues. In the modern era, with e-commerce dominating the scene, elasticity also must be redefined.

PRODUCT SUBSTITUTES AND COMPLEMENTS

Substitute
A product bought by a consumer as an alternative to another product, due to obsolescence, quality, convenience, or price.

A *substitute* is any product that is selected by consumers as an alternative. This occurs due to obsolescence (for example, Kodak's film sales replaced by digital technology). It may also occur because a more reliable, higher quality, or cheaper product comes to the market. Price may be similar or not—consumers are likely to select a substitute for convenience and other features, more than just for price.

> For example, Tesla developed a solar roofing product in 2016, but it is expensive. The Tesla solar tiles are a premium product. Constructed of thin layers of quartz—they are virtually unbreakable. While price estimates may eventually vary depending on location and installation costs, Tesla insists that their solar roofing tiles will sell for a price of $21.85 per square foot. The cost of regular roofing materials is between $1 and $2 per square foot for asphalt shingles.[3]

A consumer might select the solar roof in the interest of reducing climate change, if the consumer can afford to spend nearly $55,000 on a new roof. If a family spends $2,000 per year on energy expenses, it will take nearly 28 years to offset the added cost of solar.

The decision would not make sense on a strictly economic basis. There must be another factor or combination of factors in play to justify the significantly higher cost. This decision is not made objectively, either. If a family cannot afford to spend $55,000 for a 28-year investment in solar power, the desire to reduce climate change will not justify the substitute.

This means that the substitute must contain several attributes. First, the benefit in addition to cost must be important enough to justify the substitute. Second, the consumer making the choice must be able to afford the

product. Third, the long-term perceived benefits must be worthwhile (for example, solar energy may add to the market value of the home, so it will be worth more on the market when the family sells).

The same analysis of substitutes applies when a consumer buys a $3,000 pair of shoes, a purse, or a dress. A similar product of equal quality would accomplish the same purpose, and can be bought for $400, or even for $50. However, the substitute of a $3,000 article of clothing may be justified on the same three criteria: the status of the brand name is compelling, the consumer can afford to pay $3,000, and the more expensive article is expected to last longer. To this final point, it would require substantial years of use to justify the added cost, and with clothing, resale is not usually an issue. An alternative rationale is that the quality of a status brand is far superior to a less expensive item. However, this is not always true; or the difference in quality may be slight in comparison to the difference in price.

A substitute is not always selected rationally or economically. Beyond obsolescence, substitutions may be bought based on many factors beyond price—and they may not all be rational. As a theory in economics, products may be substitutes based on many factors. The most often cited factor is similarity in price—but this is not always the case. A business owner might discover that some consumers will pay much more for a substitute based on reputation and brand, perceptions of higher quality, and other criteria. A substitute replaces another product, and the decision to pick the substitute might be the result of exceptional marketing, claims of higher quality (true or not), or superiority. This theory of substitution is usually simplified as a price analysis. As the price of one product rises, demand for a different product (the substitute) rises in response. However, substitutes often involve more than price.

For example, consumers may purchase frozen food rather than fresh, even if the cost is much higher. This is a substitute of convenience. It is easier to prepare frozen food in a microwave oven and it only takes five or six minutes. Buying instant coffee costs about one-half compared to buying the beans and grinding them yourself. However, the second choice produces a superior cup of coffee in the opinion of many consumers. In that case, price does not matter, even a much higher price; what matters is quality in this form of substitution.

Compared to substitutes, *complements* (or, complementary goods) lack elasticity of demand. The demand grows because the price of a similar product rises; consumers pick the complementary product based on price comparison, assuming both products provide the same benefits and are of comparable value and quality.[4]

When the price of goods is increased, quantity tends to increase as well. Supply must be increased to meet higher demand. These relationships between price and quantity on one hand, and demand and supply in response, are shown in Figure 7.1.

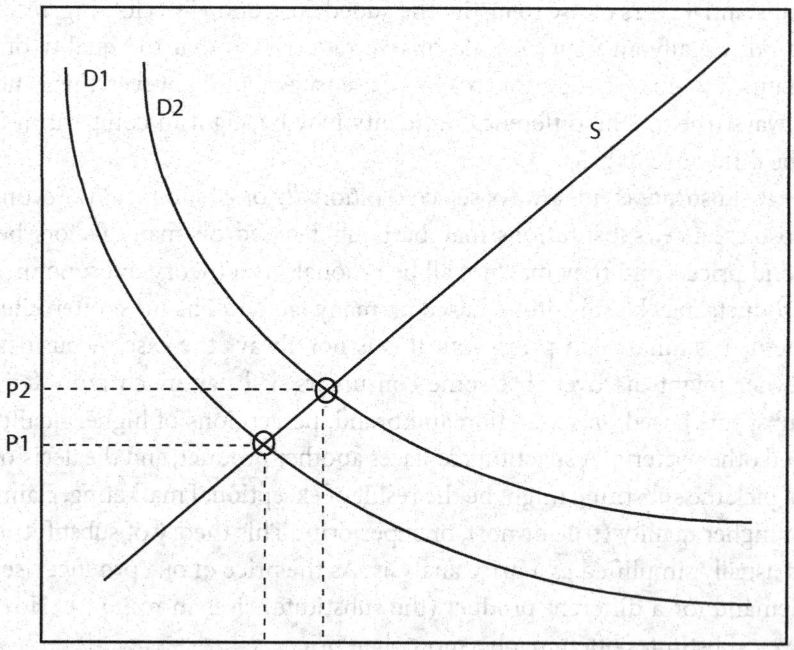

D1 Initial demand
D2 Increased demand
S Supply
P1 Initial price
P2 Increased price
Q1 Initial quantity
Q2 Increased quantity

Figure 7.1 Complements and the demand and supply curve

This is where complements enter the picture. As an initial price rises and the producer offers more goods at the higher price, an opportunity arises for a competitor. By offering a complementary product at a lower price, the competing producer will be able to take greater market share from the initial producer.

Assuming prices remain similar for complementary goods, consumers are likely to pick the one that is lower (even if only slightly lower) unless other factors are involved, such as brand loyalty. For example, in a grocery store, a name brand of canned vegetables costs three cents more than the store brand. Even if the vegetables are canned in the same factory and contents of the can are the same, some consumers will pay an extra three cents due to the brand. Many believe the product is superior, and this belief is persistent. Even when shown that the contents of two cans are identical, the consumer might continue buying the higher-priced can of vegetables solely due to the brand.

The theory of complements applies when price is the sole consideration for which product a consumer picks. However, the decision is not always rational. Despite all of the economic theories pointing to price as the ruling factor between complementary goods, consumer behavior does not always conform to the model.

INCOME ELASTICITY

Price elasticity can be analyzed and understood by most business owners. However, in thinking about long-term growth, it also is very important to know about *income elasticity* among your customer base.

> Income elasticity
> A measurement of demand based on rising income; divide increases in demand by increases in customers' income.

This is a way of measuring changes in demand based on the trend in income. A customer is likely to spend more or buy more of a product when income rises. This is a calculation: divide increase in demand by increase in income.

For example, over the past year, let's say that the average customer in your city had a 3% increase in income. Over that same year, demand

increased by 8.5% (measured by the quantity of products sold year over year). Income elasticity is:

$$8.5\% \div 3\% = 2.83\%$$

This reveals that your customers (assuming the entire population represents the customer base) have had an increased elasticity of 2.83%. The growth in income has led to growth in demand.

Elasticity can also be negative. If customers experience a net decline in income or if demand falls, that decreased elasticity will lead to lower demand. Customers will either buy less or turn to an acceptable substitute. When negative elasticity appeared, a business must either reduce prices or offer other incentives. For example, providing a free extended warranty for products or discounting the price for buying more than one (buy two, get one free, for example).

Normal goods
Those products with demand likely to increase as consumers' income elasticity is positive.

Inferior goods
Products likely to experience a decrease in demand even when customers' income elasticity is positive.

It often is seen that positive income elasticity is associated with *normal goods* and negative income elasticity is related to *inferior goods*. Normal goods are those whose demand grows along with positive income elasticity. Inferior goods experience decreased demand even when income elasticity is positive. For any business owner, this is of great interest and importance. If your products are inferior goods, you cannot expect to experience growth, even when your customers' incomes rise.

Figure 7.2 illustrates how the demand for inferior goods falls as income rises. The use of the term *inferior* does not mean that goods are of lower quality, but rather is in reference to affordability. Inferior goods are affordable when income is at one level; but as incomes rise, consumers tend to seek out products with more status, better health benefits, or that provide greater satisfaction.[5]

For example, goods offered based on rent-to-own are considered inferior. It is necessary to enter into an agreement for goods that are not otherwise affordable; but as income rises, that same consumer is more

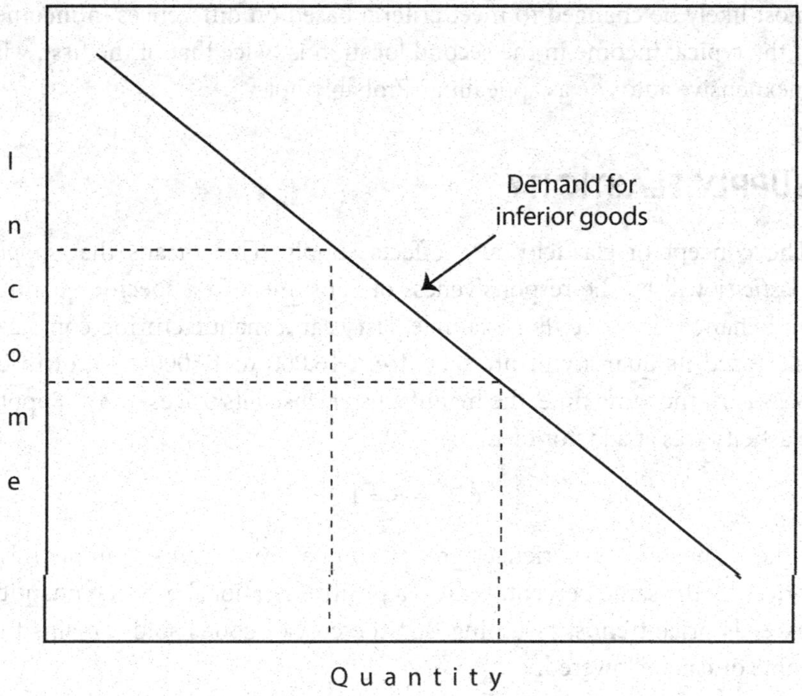

Figure 7.2 Demand for inferior goods

likely to enter into an outright purchase agreement. Another example is the selection of a low-priced automobile with the decision being made based on affordability. The next purchase might be made after an increase in income, meaning the same consumer can afford a more expensive auto. Yet another example is the payday loan business. It is targeted to lower-income neighborhoods. Consumers pay exceptionally high interest to get cash needed to buy food or pay rent. In middle- and higher-income neighborhoods, consumers are more likely to have credit cards and savings accounts and will not need payday loans.

A business owner must be aware of the demographics in an area in order to ensure that products and prices are a competitive match. For example, a used car dealership that is located in a low-income neighborhood will tend to offer very inexpensive autos. If the owner decides to open a second location in a different neighborhood, the business model will

most likely be changed to meet criteria based on differences in income. If the typical income in the second location is twice that of the first, will inexpensive autos be as appealing? Probably not.

SUPPLY ELASTICITY

The concept of elasticity also affects supply. This means that *supply elasticity* will be the responsiveness of consumers to a specific quantity and changes in price. For example, last year a manufacturing company increased its quantity of products from 16,000 to 17,000—a growth of 6.25%. At the same time, the manufacturer raised its prices by 4%. Supply elasticity was at a factor of 1.25:

$$6.25 \div 5 = 1.25$$

When a business experiences growth in quantity, it cannot simply raise prices by the same percentage. It is a positive relationship when quantity exceeds price trends, assuming that the cost of goods sold remains the same or can be lowered.

> <u>Utility maximization</u>
> The tendency among consumers to seek products they need and want, given the limitations of income and conflicts between spending decisions.

This is one aspect of economics in which consumer behavior is revealing. A business owner who understands the concept of *utility maximization* will be able to plan and adjust as income levels change. Utility maximization describes consumer behavior in the environment of changing demand, supply, and income. The consumer will tend to buy products that meet their needs and wants. But this cannot be accomplished in every instance. This maximization is limited by a consumer's income and by competition between needs and wants.

For example, a family wants to purchase a new car and can afford a range of prices based on current income. The same family would like to take a one-week vacation this year. They cannot afford both. Utility maximization can be accomplished in several ways:

1. Select a new auto or a vacation, but not both
2. Select a less expense auto or a cheaper vacation, or both
3. Use savings or finance both choices

These are typical versions of how consumers deal with their decisions. Elasticity on all levels matters because as income rises (income elasticity), normal goods become more affordable (supply elasticity), and consequently, consumers want more (demand elasticity).

The business owner must coordinate these attributes of the economy and be able to anticipate how changes in demographics will affect changes in revenue and profits. Too often, successful businesses have experienced a gradual decline in revenue because the owner was not aware of how elasticity affected the entire product line. Awareness of the difference between normal and inferior goods, changing local income levels, and customer preferences all define why some businesses thrive and continue to grow each year while others offering the same products eventually go out of business. It depends on how well the owner anticipates changes in elasticity.

ENDNOTES

1. Bomey, Nathan. (November 26, 2018). "GM poised to close plants in Michigan, Ohio, Maryland, will cut 15% of salaried workers." *USA Today*, https://www.usatoday.com/story/money/cars/2018/11/26/gm-general-motors-plant-closures-job-cuts/2113275002/.
2. Lambert, Fred. (December 7, 2018). "Tesla would consider buying shuttered GM factories [again], says Elon Musk." *Electrek*, https://electrek.co/2018/12/07/tesla-consider-buying-shuttered-gm-factories-elon-musk/.
3. Sendy, Andrew. (November 6, 2018). "Are Tesla solar roof tiles worth it?" *Solar-Estimate*, https://www.solar-estimate.org/news/2018-11-06-are-the-tesla-solar-roof-tiles-worth-it.
4. O'Sullivan, Arthur and Steven M. Sheffrin. (2003). *Economics: Principles in Action*. Upper Saddle River, NJ: Pearson Prentice Hall. p. 88.
5. Mankiw, N. Gregory. (2012). *Principles of Economics*. Boston, MA: Cengage Learning. p. 70.

8

SUBSTITUTES AND COMPLEMENTS

Abstract

Every business owner must be aware of the role they play in how consumers select what to buy. Substitutes are available for most goods and services, so the big question remains: why should anyone buy your product and not a substitute? In a similar vein, a complement represents different goods and services selected by consumers but which represent two or more choices, including how consumers allocate income between the two when they need both.

The last chapter introduced the basics of substitutes and complements in the context of elasticity. However, in any economic system, these factors play an expanded role, representing how consumers choose, and how elasticity works in making decisions.

To business owners, consumer behavior often seems random. Why pick one product over another? This is a mystery for which there often is no answer.

THE NATURE OF SUBSTITUTES

Consumers will prefer one product over another, often when there is no significant difference in price. This may appear random, but when studied, the reasons often become obvious. For example, a brand of jam might

be wildly successful, but a competing jam a complete failure. Is it due to better marketing, label colors, company reputation, brand loyalty, or something else? It often is due to a combination of factors.

For example, how do devoted video game players pick one game over another? Some games have been huge market successes, such as Fortnite, Minecraft, Grand Theft Auto, Wii Sports, and Player Unknown's Battleground.[1]

At the same time, several games have been huge flops. They were adequate substitutes for what gamers want, but whereas some succeeded, others never caught the imagination of consumers. The biggest example was *E.T. the Extra-Terrestrial*:

> Several video games have failed over the years, but arguably none as spectacularly as *E.T. the Extra-Terrestrial.* The video game was created/developed shortly after the release of Steven Spielberg's classic film. With only five weeks spent in development—games typically take months, if not years, to program—the game was notoriously difficult and sold miserably. Atari spent $21 million to purchase the rights to the franchise and $5 million on promotion of the game. The company made 4 million copies of the game, but sold only 1.5 million. Atari buried the leftover copies in a landfill.[2]

Another example is a famous case of consumers rejecting a product for no obvious reason. When Ford Motor Company introduced its Edsel model, the consensus opinion at the time (the initial launching date was September 4, 1957) was that the new car was overpriced and overhyped; it was a big disappointment. Ford offered 18 different Edsel models, and none succeeded. Ugly and poorly made according to many, it endured for only two model years:

> The Edsel fizzled. It flopped. It tanked. It became a national joke, the car that launched a million punch lines. By November 1959, when Ford finally mercy-killed the Edsel, it had lost an estimated $250 million—nearly $2 billion in today's dollars.[3]

The Edsel (named after Henry Ford's son) was a worthwhile substitute of the day, based on design and appearance. But based on price and

perception, it was an utter failure and became synonymous with any type of commercial failure, even a joke.[4]

Why are some products wildly successful while others fail? To address this, business owners must examine the nature of substitutes. These are goods believed to be comparable and similar to one another. Under this theory, consumers should not make any distinctions between substitutes based on the same levels of price and quality.

For example, canned peas may source their product from California and Mexico. But they are mixed together, processed, and canned in the same facility. There are no differences. The two products are substitutes in every sense of the word. The difference arises once the peas are canned. Although the same plant is involved, different labels are placed on cans based on orders received. Although these differently labeled products are identical, perception, brand loyalty, and price all play a role in why consumers favor one over the other.

Although this example is not always applicable, it makes the point that in some instances, substitutes result in varying levels of market success, at least partially, on perceived differences in quality. The added cost of two or three cents is considered worthwhile to some in order to get the favored brand; to others, cheaper is always better, even if quality is not the same.

In the case of canned peas, without the distinction of labels, the value of the two is identical. However, for many products, substitutes are seen in degrees. For example, if one airline offers discount ticket prices, it is perceived as a bargain even if they charge for carry-on as well as checked luggage, food and beverage service, and everything else. The cabin is packed and the flying experience is uncomfortable. In comparison, flying a full-service airline and selecting first class or business class provides a more comfortable experience.

Both get passengers to their destination, but the cost of each is considerably different. These degrees of substitution exist because they address a different population of consumers. Some want price economy, and others want comfort. Some use accumulated miles and others will be reimbursed by an employer. All these markets account for the degrees of substitution.

Perfect substitutes
Products that compete within the same market and are priced the same, for which the selection of either represents the same quality but experience difference preferences among consumers.

Some products are described as *perfect substitutes* because they are equivalent to one another in terms of price and quality. Examples may include toys that are the same in every respect except color. They are priced in the same range and sold in the same store. Another example is the selection of a soft drink. Some prefer Pepsi and others swear by Coca Cola. There are varying degrees of difference in taste, but they are priced the same and provide the same general value sought by consumers.

Business owners cannot afford to assume that their product will be better received than a competing product that is a perfect substitute in every way. Both products will get some market share, but the ultimate winner will be the product better advertised and marketed. For example, comparing Coca-Cola and Pepsi is complicated because they both sell not only soft drinks but a variety of other products as well. In 2016, Coca-Cola booked $35.4 billion in revenue and $1.2 billion in profits; the same year, Pepsi reported $63.5 billion in revenue and $4.9 billion in profits. In the same year, Coca-Cola spent $3.96 billion in marketing and advertising, but Pepsi spent only $2.4 billion.[5]

The distortion between these results is caused by differences in overall product lines. However, it remains true that a perfect substitute—such as Coca-Cola versus Pepsi—is difficult to articulate. In cases of product differences based on price or quality, substitution does not apply. Each product addresses different markets. However, any business owner who is competing in a well-defined market must be aware of how substitution affects overall success or failure of products. Whether you market an Edsel or a soft drink, your markets are likely to act and react in ways that are difficult to understand.

How can you distinguish your product from a perfect substitute? Many methods have been tried beyond the most obvious, a price war. As producers each undercut one another, the point of breakeven or net loss eventually is reached. Can you afford to offer products below your cost?

Perhaps a business can do this for a while, but at some point, they must either offer something else (extended warranty, customer service, higher quality) or lose market share. They might even have to switch to an entirely different product.

For example, Andy Grove of Intel is known as the genius who recognized a market opportunity when the company was failing. At the time, Intel was in the memory chip business, but competitors undercut prices and were destroying Intel's competitive ability. Intel could not match competitor prices, but Grove suggested the company abandon that market and instead go into the microprocessor industry. The now famous *Intel Inside* dominated the market and enabled Intel to survive after near failure and become today's #46 on the *Fortune 500* list.

This was accomplished by switching to an entirely new business, upon realizing that the company could not compete in the memory chip industry. In this case, substitution proved impossible based on price alone, and the switch of industry not only saved Intel, but allowed it to thrive and dominate the microprocessor industry. This was based on Grove's familiarity with semiconductor technology, learned during his time as assistant director of development at Fairchild Semiconductor.

THE NATURE OF COMPLEMENTS

Complements (complementary goods) have cross elasticity, meaning that as the price of one product rises, demand for a different product falls. The two products are related directly in some manner, meaning a joint demand relationship is created.

For example, a store sells battery-operated flashlights. They also sell batteries. At the beginning of carrying these products, prices for both were stable. However, one year the cost of batteries rose significantly and the retailer noticed an immediate decline in the sale of flashlights. Consumers chose a more expensive flashlight—the kind that were rechargeable and solar powered. In this example, the original battery-operated flashlight and batteries were complementary goods.

A business owner offering complementary goods might take satisfaction in knowing that a consumer needs to buy both (jam buyers also buy

bread, razor buyers also buy blades, and auto owners need to buy gasoline and oil). However, as the price of any product increases, demand falls, and consumers seek alternatives. The solar powered flashlight is one example of this.

Perfect complement
The combination of two products in which both must be acquired for the intended purpose to be achieved.

A *perfect complement* is one in which consumers must buy both products. Few perfect complements exist, but there are examples. These include a pair of shoes; people need both in order to dress properly. Another example is a printer and a supply of ink.

The problem with some perfect complements occurs when manufacturers adjust prices to exploit the need for consumers to buy both. For example, a manufacturer of printers sells one model at an attractively low price—and sales are robust. However, the same manufacturer sells ink cartridges at a much higher price than other brands. Consumers face several choices when they discover that the cost of operating the printer is high:

1. Abandon the printer (and the brand) and look elsewhere for a new printer, shopping not only the price of the printer but also the price of ink.
2. Buy ink from one of many cartridge refill services, bypassing the more expensive cartridges being sold by the printer manufacturer.
3. Use the printer less, saving money on ink cartridge replacement costs.

In all of these choices, consumers lose faith in the manufacturer upon realizing that the manufacturer took advantage of them by charging so much for ink. This is likely to destroy any brand loyalty that might have existed in the past, driving consumers to a competitor.

Any business that is selling complementary goods must be aware of the destructive nature of price exploitation. Consumers will make choices in their best interest. Throwing away a printer that is expensive to operate, and buying one with cheaper ink replacements, is an example of how the complementary goods issue is managed. The more important

outcome is the loss of customer loyalty to the brand—and perhaps to the retailer as well.

Beyond the obvious connection between complementary goods, consumer behavior will also be influenced by non-price comparisons. These affect the degree to which consumers will pick one set of complementary goods over another:

1. *Personal preference and tastes*: consumers follow fads and may purchase a newly released gadget or a new design of clothing. But the complementary nature of two products does not ensure success. For example, in 2012, Google developed *Google Glass*, an optical, head-mounted display that looked like glasses. The device required Internet access, and the two together represented complementary products. Google Glass was hands-free and operated on voice commands.[6] The product cost $1,500 when first released. Since its release, criticisms have included safety concerns (users wearing the glasses while driving, for example) and the threat of privacy violations. Google has become controversial due to accusations of control over what users see in their searches and how the company uses information. The high price tag of Google Glass has run into market resistance.[7]
2. *Income*: the level of consumer income also affects a decision. As incomes rise, the tendency is to buy more expensive goods; but if incomes are reduced, demand follows the same path immediately.
3. *Expectations and concerns about future costs and income*: consumers are concerned with how their future income will affect today's decisions for complementary goods. For example, an expensive car with poor gas mileage will be appealing on one level; but what if gas prices rise in the future? That will affect today's decision.

The roles of substitutes and complements in the economy can be analyzed on a theoretical basis, which provides little value to the business owner trying to make choices that appeal to consumers. The practical application of these ideas may affect the decisions made and lead to a more informed strategic marketing plan.

For example, a seller of flashlights cannot take comfort in increased markup for batteries. The assumption that this translates to higher profits

defies the basic truth about economics: higher prices lead to lower demand and *less* profit, not more.

Awareness of the role played by substitutes and complements affects how any producer or retailer acts. The greatest danger is being unaware of consumer attitudes, opinions, and behavior, along with the consequences of raising prices. With substitutes, consumers will go to a lower-priced competitor. This demonstrates why consumers are in control of price and quantity, in opposition to the commonly held belief that producers have all the control.

With complements, consumers will buy less of both products and seek other products to meet the need. An example is that of the solar-powered flashlight as an alternative to battery-operated models. Higher battery prices result in lower battery and flashlight sales and replacement with a model that does not rely on a complementary product with a higher price.

Producers must be keenly aware of consumer behavior and preferences. This applies to the producer as well. In the factors market, the producer is also a consumer, as demonstrated in the next chapter.

ENDNOTES

1. Wynne-Jones, Jonathan. (June 6, 2009). "Computer game Tetris celebrates 25 years." *The Daily Telegraph*, https://www.telegraph.co.uk/technology/news/5460283/Computer-game-Tetris-celebrates-25-years.html.
2. Sauter, M., E. Comen, T. Frohlich, and S. Stebbins. (July 11, 2018). "When product launches go awry: 50 worst product flops of all time." *USA Today*, https://www.usatoday.com/story/money/2018/07/11/50-worst-product-flops-of-all-time/36734837/.
3. Carlson, Peter. (September 4, 2007). "The flop heard round the world." *The Washington Post*, http://www.washingtonpost.com/wp-dyn/content/article/2007/09/03/AR2007090301419.html.
4. Dicke, Tom. (2010). "The Edsel: Forty years as a symbol of failure." *Journal of Popular Culture*. 43(3):pp. 486–50.

5. Sources: https://www.statista.com/statistics/286526/coca-cola-advertising-spending-worldwide/ and https://www.cheshnotes.com/pepsico-advertising-and-marketing-budget/.
6. Newman, Jared. (April 4, 2012). "Google's 'Project Glass' teases augmented reality glasses." *PC World*, https://www.pcworld.com/article/253200/googles_project_glass_teases_augmented_reality_glasses.html.
7. Arthur, Charles. (March 6, 2013). "Google Glass: Is it a threat to our privacy?" *The Guardian*, https://www.theguardian.com/technology/2013/mar/06/google-glass-threat-to-our-privacy.

9

FACTOR MARKETS

Abstract

Every business deals with the *factor markets*, which broadly describes the elements needed to market goods and services. To the extent that a business relies on outside products (e.g., labor, raw materials, and facilities) every producer is also a consumer. For a manufacturer, reliance on suppliers of raw materials and on labor dominates the factor markets; for the retailer of products, suppliers are the most important factor market; for those providing services, the factor markets most often rely on intellectual or technical labor, or on the owner's own labors.

The *factor markets* include all of the elements required by a business to create the goods or services offered to consumers. This includes raw materials and labor; facilities, equipment and other capital assets; and in many cases, the hiring of people with specialized technical skills.

<u>Factor markets</u>
The elements that every business needs in order to create and market its products and services, including raw materials and labor in a manufacturing environment; facilities and capital assets; and technical or intellectual skills in production of specialized products or services.

FACTORS OF PRODUCTION

The overall factor markets are described in many economics books or courses as *factors of production.* This goes back to the days when manufacturing dominated economic life in many countries and regions. Even though this is not always the case today, the term is applied even when no physical production of goods takes place. *Production* has taken on an expanded meaning referring to production of a supply over a broad range of products or services.

> Derived demand
> Reference to the producer's need to purchase materials and labor, facilities, and capital assets in order to produce goods demanded by consumers; the scope of a producer's role as a consumer.

The business (the *producer*) purchases resources and pays a factor price. This applies to raw materials, labor, rent of facilities, purchase of specialized equipment, and even to the owner's entrepreneurial ability. The process of making factor payments to create a marketable product or service is termed *derived demand.* This refers to the demand for resources on the part of the business and is derived from the demand for a final product by the consumer. The business owner (producer) is also a consumer who operates under the terms of derived demand.

The demand generated by a business owner is based on a need for these productive resources. Very few entrepreneurs can operate without derived demand. For example, an attorney or accountant may open a service and offer to provide expertise for a fee. Working from a home office initially, there is very little requirement for the factor markets. However, in addition to needing to purchase furniture, the professional entrepreneur will need case law books (attorney) or tax regulations (accountant) and eventually will need to hire other experts as the service business expands. Adding more employees means the professional will need to rent an office, not only to provide room for employees, but also as a place for clients to visit.

As expansion occurs, the attorney or accountant will need to purchase furniture, equipment, and other capital assets. The investment in assets, cost of facilities, and payments to employees are all forms of the factor

markets. Even as far removed from manufacturing as a service business may be, the need for factor markets is unavoidable. Even a service provider faces a derived demand in one form or another. The traditional definition of *production* is the transformation of raw materials, labor, and capital investments into a finished product. For a service business, production is the transformation not into products, but into services. This applies to professional services such as those offered by attorneys or accountants, as well as contractors, landscapers, real estate brokers, or home inspectors. Everyone who starts a business must address the derived demand associated with production.

Labor represents a major part of this derived demand, both for goods and services. A question faced by every business owner is how many people to hire. A mistake often made by new business owners is hiring too many people too soon, which erodes profits. When derived demand is responded to excessively, it destroys profits and cash flow. The formula for properly addressing the need for labor may not be expressed specifically on the idea that a business owner somehow knows when to hire new people or when to expand other factors. In fact, however, the timing is properly based in analysis:

> A firm will hire another worker when the marginal revenue product of that worker exceeds the marginal factor cost of the worker. In exactly the same way, a firm will decide to rent more building space or more equipment if the *marginal revenue product* of the additional capital exceeds the *marginal cost factor*.[1]

Just as the producer must set prices for consumers based on the realities of supply and demand, the factor markets also operate based on supply (by the labor or materials market) and demand (from the producer). In the theoretical *perfect market*, a producer can buy as much as needed, either materials or labor, at the going rate in today's market. However, competitive markets affect price. As a producer demands more materials or more labor, the prices rise. The perfect market may exist in the moment but will not endure.

Economic theories aside, this is the reality. The factor markets are as responsive to changing supply and demand as are the consumer markets.

This is easily overlooked by new entrepreneurs, who may project assumptions of future revenue, profits, and cash flow based on today's known prices of the factor markets *and* on today's prices paid by consumers for finished goods. Both assumptions could prove to be misguided, especially if the factor market and its forces are overlooked.

In some economic systems outside of the market economy, this reality may be challenged but history has revealed that other economic systems, notably socialism, do not work. The idea under socialism is that factor markets can be replaced when prices rise, usually by some form of state-operated planning. The notorious failures of the USSR's five-year plans were due to several factors, including the *closed distribution* associated with state control:

> Closed distribution was meant to protect the working population from the worst consequences of shortages and link rations to employment. But it also quickly developed another function, which was to provide privileged supply for certain categories of privileged people. Special closed distributors were established for various elite categories of officials and professionals, supplying them with much higher-quality goods than were available in the normal closed stores and enterprise cafeterias.[2]

The failure of state-planned economic ideas like socialism make the point that at its core, economics is not so much an idea to be controlled (especially by an inefficient mechanism such as the state), but one that operates on these two basic, logical principles: (1) consumers have specific wants and needs, which can never be fully satisfied and (2) producers have a desire for maximum profits, which also can never be fully satisfied. These two opposing forces represent the economy, both in producer-to-consumer marketing and in the factor markets. The entire matter is competitive in nature.

THE COMPETITIVE FACTOR MARKETS

Every producer presents a *resource demand* for the factors it requires—capital, facilities, labor, materials, and technical expertise among them. As buyers (consumers) in this form of demand, producers act as consumers.

Marginal analysis must come into play. This is the study of labor and materials, revenue and profits.

> **Resource demand** The form of demand presented by producers for its factor markets and the goods and services that it requires to generate finished products or services.

A comparison between inputs (factors) and outputs (finished products) determines prices needed and quantities produced to meet and exceed a breakeven point—the level at which revenues are equal to direct costs and expenses. Most business owners understand this breakeven intimately and are likely to monitor it constantly. A diligent business owner must be aware of this breakeven point where marginal revenue resides. A recurring goal exists in the mind of the business owner, concerning the dollar amount of revenues that must be generated to experience a profitable month, quarter, or year. This diligence is based on the knowledge that failing to meet this minimum marginal revenue will result in business failure.

In some economics publications, this analysis is expressed in complex terms and formulae, but the simple truth and *bottom line* remains the same: the business must generate at or above the marginal revenue that is required for breakeven in order to stay in business. It is the difference between success and failure.

The math does not need to be complex. The owner knows the current cost of sales and expense levels. If, for example, direct costs are 45% of revenue (so that gross profit is 55%), then a given level of revenue will be adequate to pay expenses. If expenses average $4,800 per month, how much revenue is needed to break even? Divide the dollar value of expenses by the gross margin to find this point:

$$\$4,800 \div .55 = \$8,727$$

This business needs to generate a monthly revenue of $8,727 to reach the breakeven point:

Revenue	$ 8,727
Cost of goods sold (45%)	– 3,927
Gross profit (55%)	$ 4,800
Expenses	– 4,800
Net profit (breakeven)	$ 0

This simplified calculation explains everything the business owner needs to know about marginal analysis. It is the identification of the level required in revenue to create adequate funds for payment of costs and expenses. When this analysis is applied to factor markets, the business owner knows what is affordable in terms of material and labor. If the price is raised for these factors of production, then the price offered in the market must be raised as well to maintain margins.

If this price is greater than the price asked by competitors, customers will purchase less and abandon the business for a lower-priced substitute product. This becomes a point of competition at the factor market level because the business cannot simply raise prices charged to consumers without losing market share.

The business owner also contends with *resource supply*, the level of price and quantity that a resource provider offers to the business. For example, material costs tend to rise when the supplier faces higher costs; and labor prices rise when workers are scarce and able to demand more for their services.

Resource supply
The cost and quantity of factors of production charged to a business, based on past and current costs.

The interaction between price and quantity at the resource level is like the interaction between producer and consumer. In terms of factor markets, however, it refers to the interaction between the supplier and producer. On both levels, prices and quantities do not remain the same indefinitely. As a supplier's costs rise, they increase their price. Just as consumers have choices in where they make purchases, the producer (now in the role of consumer) may also compare prices among several suppliers. It may be possible to find a more favorable price with an alternate supplier. Adjustments may apply. For example, quality might be compromised or a supplier may impose minimum purchase-quantity levels.

The same is true for labor markets. Going offshore for production is likely to reduce the costs of labor, but producers need to analyze the entire picture in order to determine whether moving production to a foreign

country enables control over quality as it does when production is closer to home. In other words, the savings in labor could be accompanied with higher costs elsewhere (in quality of products, safety, use of materials, and more).

This is a complex matter in the globalized economy. Trade policies and agreements, plus trends in migration between nations, affect the factor markets in terms of labor, in several ways:

1. The composition of labor markets is not the same everywhere. Restrictions in the movement of goods and people within a nation or limitations on migration complicate the decision to move labor to a different country.
2. Trade agreements may restrict the use of foreign labor or migration, and other requirements might also be imposed. For example, as of 2017, China has required U.S. firms to locate research and development activities in China, and to favor China-based firms for licensing and intellectual property partnerships. This has led to an estimated $600 billion in annual losses:

    > Increasingly, China is also forcing U.S. companies to localize their research and development—the seed corn of future IP—on Chinese soil. Further, China is coercing American firms into providing its state-owned enterprises with below-market acquisition and licensing terms while asserting ownership over any improvements made to the licensed technology.[3]

3. Migration may lead to the imposition of tariffs and other secondary costs not known at the time a business owner decides to move production to another country. Beyond the national policies involved, workers making the decision to migrate are also affected by income, skill levels, cultural differences, language, cost of living, and the cost of migration.[4]

The decision to move suppliers to a different country is more complex than the initial comparison of labor costs. Much more becomes involved when also considering trade policies, cultural and income differences, and much more.

PRODUCTION FUNCTION AND PROFITABILITY

The analysis of resource demand and supply is essential for every business owner. Everyone must know their factor markets if they want to survive. For example, if you manufacture a product like jewelry that requires buying gold and silver, what happens when the price per ounce goes up? Or down?

Precious metal prices change all the time, based on demand for coinage, jewelry, medical, and automotive technology. In a sense, as a manufacturer, you are at the mercy of the market. There are no substitutes for specific precious metals, so you face a squeeze between your factor market costs and the price the market will bear.

This is the reality of running a business, whether manufacturing, wholesale, retail, or service. Everyone contends with the production function, which defines competition in terms of the cost and availability of input factors (notably labor, materials, capital, facilities, and when applicable, intellectual or technological property). Expanding on this, if a company holds an exclusive control over a market, it has a clear competitive advantage.

The competitive advantage created with exclusive ability to market a product arises in several instances. For example, a utility company is granted exclusive rights to provide electric, water and sewer, or gas power to a defined area. This is a monopoly, but the prices a utility may charge often are controlled by the government granting the utility the rights.

Another example arises when a company or principal in the company owns a patent to a product or process. The patent gives its owner the right to prevent competitors from manufacturing, selling, and copying the property being protected without permission. This protection lasts for a specified period; during that period, there should not be any competition unless the patent owner sells licensing rights to a competitor.

A monopoly, whether granted by a government agency or by way of a patent, is the exception to the rule. Most businesses must deal with production functions under the rules of supply and demand. If one competitor raises prices above others, customers will purchase less and go to another provider; if a competitor lowers prices but can still generate a

profit, others must also lower their prices or abandon the market. If they do not, customers will select the lower-priced offer (assuming other factors, such as identical quality, no brand loyalty, and availability of products in a reasonable market area).

In a market that is not constrained by monopolistic control, a direct relationship exists between labor and capital; in other words, a given maximum quantity of output is possible with a given quantity of available labor. A producer cannot demand higher output from a workforce without adding labor expense to the equation. That relationship is shown in Figure 9.1.

If quantity is increased, labor must also be increased. If a business attempts to add quantity without adding labor, the effort will fail. For example, in a restaurant, the owner has initial success in both food quality and service. After a few weeks, the restaurant is full in peak hours. But over time, profit margins slide, a common occurrence in this business.

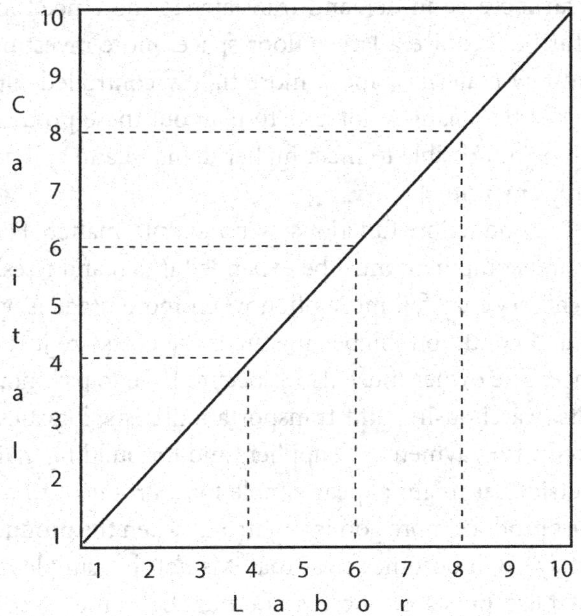

Figure 9.1 Output and labor

The owner makes a common mistake: the server workforce remains unchanged, and servers are expected to take care of a higher number of tables. This is assumed to save money, but customer service suffers as a result. Customers stop coming to the restaurant because customer service is negative. In this situation, the owner failed to realize that restaurant customers expect the best of both worlds—good food and good service. If either is lacking, customers will stop coming.

This owner also failed to understand the unavoidable relationship between output and labor. It is not realistic to expect more work from a labor force (servers, for example) without a corresponding decline in output (service). This also applies in a manufacturing environment. If the owner demands higher productivity without adding more workers, the result will be more defects and a failure to meet quotas of finished goods.

The dilemma every business faces in the production function is the need to change the environment. Success (meaning higher demand) may easily lead to failure if production functions do not keep up. For example, in a plant, an increase in demand translates to more need for workers. This may further require a larger floor space, more investment in machinery and raw materials, and a more tightly controlled supply chain. If the owner of this plant is not able to plan out these production functions, it will be impossible to meet higher demand and still generate the required profit margin.

Adding to production functions is no simple matter. For example, machinery and equipment must be expanded if demand rises. Currently owned machinery may fail more often when more usage is applied, and due to age and condition, higher maintenance costs are just one aspect of the change. The owner must also expect to have to pay more for labor and benefits, warehousing and transportation costs, logistics, and cash flow involved with payments to suppliers and for building maintenance.

To an outsider, it might appear simple for a producer to meet higher demand. Just produce more goods, right? But when the production functions are analyzed, it becomes clear that it is not that simple. A producer cannot just raise prices or increase output. Even the basic restaurant model fails if the owner does not increase the number of servers; but this is only the beginning. The success of the business, based on excellent food and service, also requires a higher volume of food orders (and higher

chances of spoilage), and likely, expansion of floor space. Is it possible in the area currently leased? It often is not. This means opening a second location, which introduces a new range of greater management problems and expenses.

When a business expands by opening new locations, the production functions become more complex as well. For example, a restaurant owner has two locations. Are they both profitable or is one carrying the other? The cost of goods sold is easily identified by location; for example, food purchases are related directly to sales. But profitability involves expenses as well as costs, and these are not as easily defined.

For example, if the owner draws a salary, how much is assigned to each location? How is the cost of advertising, telephone, office supplies, insurance, and accounting services divided between two locations (or more)? A business owner might believe that having a set of fixed and variable expenses is efficient, but the outcome often is different. Success in a single location is difficult to duplicate in a second location. Hiring a manager to provide the oversight the owner provides in the original location often fails and the second location ends up being closed. Expansion is not a simple matter, because the production function is more complex with two or more locations.

THE THEORY OF PERFECT COMPETITION

Economics is populated by many theories. The theory of *perfect competition* is one of these. This describes conditions in which supply and demand are in harmony and equilibrium exists.[5]

The producer contends not only with the quantity and price of goods produced, but also the quantity and price paid for factors of production. This is not simply a matter of setting prices for consumers based on costs; the producer also must understand how to create optimal profits while remaining competitive. The pricing that

> **Perfect competition**
> A theoretical condition of equilibrium between producers and consumers (or between producers and suppliers), in which optimal profits are created by the best possible use of factors of production.

goes into this effort is twofold: prices set for consumers of finished goods and prices paid for the factors of production.

DIMINISHING RETURNS

Expansion is not an easy matter for business owners. The inexperienced sees expansion in highly simplified terms, as if a directly managed single outlet can be expanded to two or more with expectations of the same results. This is not likely. By the same argument, adding people to a labor force expands capability, but it also expands administrative expenses, personnel problems, and numerous indirect expenses that might be anticipated in the original expansion plan. The same is true of materials, facilities, and other factors of production; expansion and its originally perceived benefits are not as straightforward as they seem at first glance.

The comparison between two different forms of labor or materials brings up a related topic. It is possible that in the pursuit of production efficiency, a producer will suffer *diminishing returns.* This occurs, for example, when the business owner assumes that quantities of output can be increased without adding costs. It might be true to some extent, but without adjusting for factors of production as an aspect of expansion, costs eventually outpace the required breakeven or profitability state.

> Diminishing returns
> The tendency for increased factors to yield less per-unit returns in the long run, notably when a single factor is increased but others remain unchanged.

This diminishing return can be experienced when a business increases its labor to deal with higher output, but does not increase other factors, such as floor space. For example, a production plant receives orders for an exceptionally large number of monthly units. The owner adds more people to the labor force but fails to recognize how higher output will affect other factors. Floor space is inadequate; machinery will be used at higher volume, creating higher maintenance costs; and the greater demand for raw materials could lead to higher costs. Increasing only the labor portion of factors but failing to anticipate the other costs leads to problems later.

This tendency reveals that the long-run average cost (LRAC) will decline, but only to a point. The ultimate outcome will be increased costs and lower margins. This is summarized in Figure 9.2.

The chart in Figure 9.2 shows what happens when a single factor of production is increased. The initial effect is a reduction in costs per unit. However, once maximum efficiency has been reached, costs begin to rise and—unless further adjustments are made—profitability declines as costs climb on a per-unit basis.

The initial benefits, the economies of scale, are limited. This benefit is the cost advantage gained when the cost per unit produced falls as the volume of production grows. Eventually, however, without adjusting all of the factors, costs rise and create diseconomies of scale. This is what creates diminishing returns.

The negative returns that can result from uncontrolled movement along the LRAC curve is a common cause of net losses even as the volume of the business grows. If a manufacturer adds to a labor force without

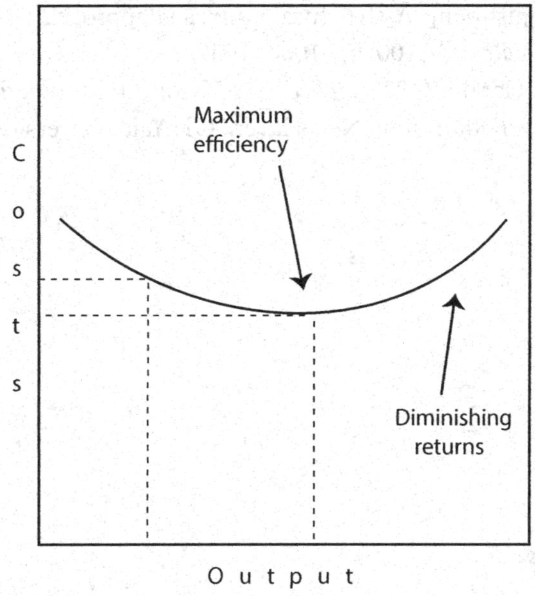

Figure 9.2 Diminishing returns

expanding the factory floor or investing in upgraded equipment, the overall picture eventually is one of finite volume with increasing costs—in other words, a declining level of profitability because of growth.

ENDNOTES

1. Boyes, William and Michael Melvin. (2015). *Microeconomics*, 10th ed. Boston, MA: Cengage Learning. p. 344.
2. Fitzpatrick, Sheila. (2000). *Everyday Stalinism: Ordinary Life in Extraordinary Times: Soviet Russia in the 1930s*. Oxford, UK: Oxford University Press. p. 56.
3. Navarro, Peter. (August 14, 2017). "China must stop forcing U.S. firms to share intellectual property: Trump trade official." *USA Today*, https://www.usatoday.com/story/opinion/2017/08/14/china-must-stop-forcing-us-firms-share-intellectual-property-peter-navarro-column/563151001/.
4. Artuc, E., S. Chaudhuri, and J. McLaren. (2010): "Trade shocks and labor adjustment: A structural empirical approach." *The American Economic Review*. 100. pp. 1008–1045.
5. Debreu, Gerald. (1972). *Theory of Value: An Axiomatic Analysis of Economic Equilibrium*. New Haven, CT: Yale University Press. p. 26.

10

MARGINAL ANALYSIS

Abstract

The study of scarcity demands that choices be made; and every business contends with this study, which includes an understanding of marginal analysis. This is the observation of optimal behavior. The consumer seeks the best possible price and product utility; the producer seeks the optimal level of profits and sustainable brand loyalty. The producer also acts as a consumer in the factor markets, getting the best price for labor, materials, and other factors while being able to produce goods at the lowest possible cost.

The concept of marginal analysis applies to all segments of the economy. It is the study of benefits derived from an activity (such as production or purchasing) versus its cost.

This choice is always based on scarcity. If a product is not scarce, it cannot have economic value. Consequently, every producer applies marginal analysis to every decision, including the selection of factors of production, pricing, quantity produced, and changes to the price of goods and services based on how competitors behave.

In the same manner, consumers apply marginal analysis. This is best understood in the comparison of price. A consumer is likely to select the lower-priced item, assuming all other features are identical. However, perceptions of different quality, safer or better products, and brand loyalty all affect the marginal analysis by consumers. Previous chapters have

included examples of how this marginal analysis works. Some consumers seek out the lowest prices or substitute products in every case; others are loyal to a single brand or are willing to pay much more for the status of a brand, notably in the selection of status items (fashion, automobiles, vacation destinations, hotel selection, etc.).

MARGINAL BENEFITS AND MARGINAL COSTS

The description of producer and consumer behavior as *optimal* describes how marginal analysis controls decisions. Price and utility by consumers versus optimal profits by producers is the guiding force behind decisions. The benefits and costs are determined marginally in most instances. The savings of two cents in the selection of one brand over another is decidedly marginal on the part of the consumer. The selection of one supplier over another with a raw materials savings of less than 1% is also marginal.

It is more complex than marginal cost savings. A business owner might select a marginally more costly service provider based on past experiences and knowledge of reliability. The vendor will deliver the promised quantity by the promised deadline in every case, for example. A different supplier might offer a lower price but not be as reliable. This is a related marginal decision. The producer is willing to pay more for raw materials because the supplier is reliable. The producer also knows that receiving the wrong material or suffering a delay in promised delivery time translates to higher costs elsewhere. Labor sits idle while waiting for materials, and this more than offsets the small savings the producer would have gained by selecting a lower-cost alternative and sacrificing that reliability.

When the producer sets a price for a given quantity of goods produced, it matters that demand is finite and market share is variable. If the price is too high, consumers will seek lower-priced alternatives. The increase in price causes lower profits or even losses. If the producer sets the price too low, it will not be possible to meet or exceed the cost of goods sold. This also sets up a loss. In between is the thin margin where the best possible (optimal) price resides.

The producer's pricing decisions involve small incremental changes, and the consumer's decisions involve marginal cost and benefit

comparisons. Both sides operate under the requirements of marginal analysis. The producer is continually striving to maintain market share and competitive advantage while earning a profit; market constraints define this profit level as marginal. The consumer is constantly comparing benefits and costs marginally, to make the best purchasing decision.

The following case is an example of the producer's marginal behavior. In order to reduce the cost of labor, a producer decides to assign a portion of its manufacturing process to an outside vendor. This leads to a small reduction in quality and removes the producer's ability to exert oversight in the process. The producer believes that the differences are justified by the lower cost factor and believes that consumer perceptions will not be affected by these small changes.

Here is an example of how benefits are added when price is increased. A producer must increase the price of goods because labor and material costs rose. However, aware that this could lead to loss of market share, the producer adds an extended warranty to the product without extra cost. In the past, the extended warranty had required an additional payment. Consumers accept the marginally higher price in exchange for the free extended warranty.

Incentives are offered to consumers in many industries. Auto rebates, furniture discounts, and all forms of *buy one, get one free* are incentives that were designed to help consumers make favorable marginal decisions.

MARGINAL REVENUE

Revenue inevitably changes in a marginal way. *Marginal revenue* is a theoretical value equal to the added revenue booked when sales are increased by a single unit. It may also be defined as the amount of revenue that the company earned with the last unit sale.[1]

> Marginal revenue
> The additional revenue earned when the current level of sales is increased by a single unit; or the revenue earned with the last unit sold.

Why is it important to analyze marginal revenue? Transaction levels rarely jump higher or lower in a volatile manner. The tendency of change in economic value is usually marginal,

representing small changes resulting from interaction among competitors, consumers, and producers. Marginal revenue also is a starting point for understanding why one competitor gains market share while another loses. If marginal costs rise but marginal revenue does not (often the result of competition), then the assumed outcome (reduction in marginal costs with higher production volume) does not occur.

If the market is perfectly competitive, the equilibrium theory applies (producers and consumers are both content with current levels of quantity and price). Supply equals demand. This condition does not last and exists only in passing, but it is a model worth understanding in order to also understand marginal analysis.[2]

In conditions of perfect competition, the producer will always receive the same price for every unit, no matter how many units are sold. The producer cannot change the price if equilibrium holds. This is a theory alone, of course, but it makes the point that things change when levels of revenue change. If revenue increases, costs will also increase. If marginal revenue and marginal costs maintain a consistent relationship, then marginal revenue is maintained on a per-unit basis—but this simply does not occur.

As revenue increases, costs also increase, and margin of profit is likewise adjusted. A business owner can control the cost of goods sold and maintain gross profit, but with higher revenue and costs, variable expenses also increase. Even if gross margin can be maintained, net margin cannot keep pace without adjusting price. Every business owner who has experienced increased revenues understands how this can become a problem. The balance between higher profits and strong competition is difficult to accomplish. It's not impossible, but it does require management skills and the ability to manage the factor markets as well as the consumer markets.

<u>Marginal benefit</u>
The willingness of each participant in the economy to pay a price for the products or services offered; or for the producer, for the elements in the factor markets needed to produce products.

MARGINAL BENEFITS

The producer needs to break down a series of decisions in order to identify the willingness to pay for a level of activity. The *marginal benefit* of

this effort applies to the producer as a consumer in the factor markets and in setting quantity and price for consumers; it also applies in the way that consumers decide which products to buy and what prices to pay.

For example, any decision to make a purchase goes through a marginal benefit. A child craves candy, and the first candy bar is highly valued; as the child buys more candy, the value declines. Eventually, the value of yet another candy bar is marginal and may lead to a decision to not proceed with a purchase.

The same marginal benefit applies to both producers and consumers. For example, a consumer is focused on buying a pair of jeans. Having seen a commercial, she is convinced that she will look great and feel even better. The first pair of jeans is so important that this consumer is willing to pay more than for a second or third pair of jeans. The marginal benefit declines with each additional pair of jeans. The same declining marginal benefit applies to other clothes, potato chips, cocktails, and all other purchase decisions.

Consumers make decisions like this every day. A two-part rule of thumb applies to all decisions. When benefits are perceived as greater than the cost, the decision to buy makes sense. When the cost is perceived as higher than the benefits, the decision to buy does not make sense. The *marginal net benefit* of a decision matters more than the cost. Retailers understand this, if only intuitively. Therefore you often see promotions such as "buy one, get one free" or "half-price sale" in stores, online, and in ads.

> Marginal net benefit
> The perceived value of a decision to buy; when the benefit is perceived to be greater than the cost, a decision to buy is more likely to be made.

Every business owner must understand marginal benefits and how these lead to decisions to buy one product over another—or to not buy at all. For the business owner, the same observation applies. Do you use a trusted supplier for your raw materials or wholesale goods? A cheaper substitute is also available, but quality is not the same. What are the marginal benefits of one supplier's goods over another—your price, quality, or reliability? And how does a selection affect the price that is passed on to the consumer?

In this example of how marginal analysis affects a business owner, an airline charges $858 per passenger for a flight from Chicago to Hong Kong. If a plane holds 125 passengers, and 115 tickets have been sold, the cost of adding a 116th passenger is extremely low; as a result, the airline might offer an attractive discounted price of $375 for the same flight. At that price, added costs are marginal but almost all of the ticket price represents profit.

Many business models fit this description. Guided tours of a city, shared Uber or Lyft rides, or admission to a motivational speaker's presentation all have fixed costs and must have enough customers to cover those costs. The cost of adding more attendees is marginal and moving from breakeven to full participation generates nearly 100% added profits.

MARGINAL COST

> Marginal cost
> The added cost of producing the latest added unit.

The cases of business models with fixed costs or marginal added costs for adding more people are examples of *marginal cost*. Economists like to describe this as the cost of producing one additional unit (passenger on a flight, rider in a shared car service, or attendees at a speech). This means that marginal cost is the difference between a known quantity and one more unit:

$$MC = Q + 1 - Q \text{ (where } MC \text{ is marginal cost, and } Q \text{ is quantity).}$$

The efficiency of producing a higher volume of units (or serving a higher number of customers) further describes how marginal cost declines as more units are produced. For example, if a financial planner offers a seminar about retirement planning and includes a free meal at a local restaurant, the charge for each meal is set at $17 for up to 20 people, and $13 per person for attendees above 20. Attendance costs nothing, but the speaker expects to gain at least two new clients out of every 20 attendees (based on experience), and the average client generates commission income to the planner of $185. If 20 people attend, the cost is $340 (i.e., $17 × 20 attendees). However, on average, the planner will gain two new

clients; each one generating added commission income of $185 for a total of $370. This is close to breakeven, with costs of $340 and added income of $370. The charge per meal above 20 attendees is reduced to $13, but benefits remain fixed for the planner. If 30 people attend, total cost is $470. Total benefit to the planner is estimated at *three* new clients, for total added income of $555. The margin now is $85, versus only $30 for 20 attendees.

In this example, marginal costs are lower for more participation, leading to a greater profit for a higher number of people in attendance. The marginal cost is reduced as well:

Attendees	Cost	Average
20	$340	$17
30	470	15.67
40	600	15
50	730	14.60

The profit margin climbs with the number of attendees as well. With an estimation of one new client per 10 attendees and an average of $185 in new commissions earned:

Attendees	Revenue	Cost	Margin
20	$370	$340	$ 30
30	555	470	85
40	740	600	140
50	925	730	195

Any business that benefits when average cost declines with more volume of production will benefit from marginal cost adjustments. The relationship between marginal cost and average cost is illustrated in Figure 10.1.

Related to marginal cost is the concept of *marginal utility*. A decision to buy one unit of a good provides a specific utility. This declines as more goods are purchased, to the point that the last unit purchased provides only marginal value, or utility.

For example, a homeowner buys a pair of garden gloves. But because he tends to go through

<u>Marginal utility</u>
The utility gained from the last item purchased, which is lower than the utility for buying the original unit.

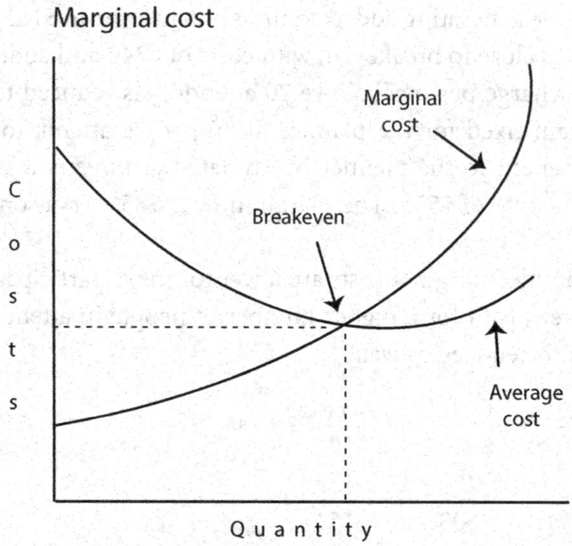

Figure 10.1 Marginal cost

them rapidly, he takes advantage of a discount offered by a local nursery of 20%. The purchase of two or three pairs makes sense for one season, but why would the homeowner buy 10, 15, or 20 pairs of gloves? It would not make sense.

THE BUSINESS VALUE OF MARGINAL ANALYSIS

As an economic theory, marginal analysis validates and explains much of the behavior of consumers. However, it also serves as a decision-making tool for business. Owners use marginal analysis to measure the initial benefits and also the benefits of increasing output. Will it be profitable? Marginal analysis allows you to uncover the essential requirements of profitable growth.

The cost-to-benefit analysis relies on incremental changes in volume and ultimately determines whether changes in quantity or price will be profitable. A preliminary observation misleads many to believe that by adding a few cents to the price and increasing output, profits will follow. This more often is not the case. Increasing price leads to less volume; and

higher output places downward pressure on price, even when producers may be raising prices. This can be observed repeatedly in the market.

For example, in late 2018, General Motors announced it would increase the price for the 2019 Chevrolet Volt Premier by $3,900, to $38,120. This price increase was occurring even as the Volt market was shrinking.[3]

At the same time as the announced higher price for the next year's model, GM also announced it was closing several U.S. factories while continuing to manufacture cars overseas. It appears irrational to raise prices of a car model while shutting down plants:

> General Motors is poised to end production at five plants in the U.S. and Canada . . . The moves reflect the stark consumer shift to SUVs, crossovers, and pickups. All of the GM plants on the chopping block make passenger cars. The company will also discontinue the Chevrolet Cruze and Volt in North America as well as the Buick LaCrosse, Cadillac XTS, and Cadillac CT6.[4]

The story demonstrates what happens to companies that fail to develop products wanted by consumers. The desire for popularity of electric vehicles was just that, a desire. It ignored the reality—consumers clearly wanted larger vehicles such as SUVs and trucks.

Even so, the failure of GM to understand its marginal analysis (demonstrated by the announcement to raise retail prices even as the Volt was failing in the market), makes the point that raising prices ignores reality. It seems that GM had two rational choices: (1) figure out a way to lower the cost of producing this model or (2) discontinue it altogether. Instead, they raised prices and closed domestic production in the belief that overseas manufacturing would solve the problem. When companies take this approach (ignoring market forces), any savings are invariably eaten up by tariffs and supply chain costs.

Marginal analysis by GM before this problem emerged would have pointed to the futile effort of raising prices. Even with the justification that the company's costs had been raised, was this a logical move? Perhaps a more fact-based form of marginal analysis would have revealed that a $38,000 electric vehicle could not compete with more popular models of traditional automobiles or more impressive electric cars; that increasing

the price would not lead to higher sales, but would actually cause lower sales; and that it would make more sense to *lower* the price and find ways to also lower costs.

The variables of production costs and consumer demand affect how decisions must be made. Marginal analysis involves a study of how much each unit's costs will increase by the production of additional units. In moving production overseas, it may be assumed that labor costs decline; but other costs rise. These include tariffs, cost of transportation, warehousing, logistics, taxes, and more. The initial problem in the case of GM—higher raw material costs—might be reduced by a move overseas, but probably are not. The company attempted to offset higher material costs with lower labor costs but may not have considered these other factors.

What did GM's marginal analysis reveal? Was the analysis even performed? If so, did it consider all of the variables that go into the cost of production? Given GM's huge investment in the Volt ($1.2 billion in development costs, or an average of $56,000 per car sold by 2012) it appears that marginal analysis was not performed or even basic cost accounting. The auto was introduced in 2004 to prove that:

> GM still had a bright future as it was about guzzling less gasoline. "This isn't about science projects," [CEO Rick] Wagoner said after unveiling the Volt. "This is about creating cars and trucks propelled in an efficient manner that people really want to own. And that's the way we're going to win."[5]

Clearly, this prediction was not true. It was based on a belief rather than on logic and analysis.

Performing a marginal analysis before spending billions in developing the Volt could have been accompanied by market studies, enabling GM to avoid an expensive mistake. The analysis would have revealed the added cost for producing more vehicles, and could have pointed to problems needing to be addressed when sales were not impressive.

It is the same process as a hotel. Assume the hotel has 200 rooms but breaks even when 75 rooms are occupied. Typically, it rents out just over 50% of rooms, or about 105 rooms per night. The 30 rooms rented out above the breakeven amount represent marginally higher profits than the first 75 rooms, which only cover the hotel's costs and expenses. Renting out more rooms increases expenses (free breakfast, electricity and water usage, front desk staffing, laundry, and increased housekeeping, for example) so it is not all profit; but costs are marginally lower when more rooms are rented out.

An automaker can apply the same analysis in comparing costs at various levels of production, but GM seems to have not performed this function. The assumption was clearly stated that the Volt would be a best seller and if it had, there was a chance that profits would have been possible with a volume of production. Unfortunately for GM and its lack of market testing in advance of its developmental investment, the car failed in the market. The announced plan in 2018 to close U.S. plants but continue production elsewhere ignored the fact that the product itself had weak demand.

Marginal analysis might have helped anticipate this, but it would not have solved the problem of poor market research (research that would have informed GM's management that raising prices was not a solution to weak sales).

ENDNOTES

1. Nicholson, Walter and Christopher M. Snyder. (2014). *Intermediate Microeconomics and Its Application.* 12th ed. Boston, MA: Cengage Learning. p. 254.
2. Debreu, Gerard. (1972). *Theory of Value: An Axiomatic Analysis of Economic Equilibrium.* New Haven, CT: Yale University Press. p. 74.

3. Loveday, Steven. (August 27, 2018). "2019 Chevrolet Volt slight price increase." *InsideEVs*, https://insideevs.com/2019-chevrolet-volt-price-increase/.
4. Money, Nathan. (November 26, 2018). "GM poised to close plants in Michigan, Ohio, Maryland, will cut 15% of salaried workers." *USA Today*, https://www.usatoday.com/story/money/cars/2018/11/26/gm-general-motors-plant-closures-job-cuts/2113275002/.
5. Bunkley, Nick. (January 2, 2017). "GM's journey from Volt to Bolt. A troubled vehicle paved the way for more audacious bets." *Automotive News*, https://www.autonews.com/article/20170102/OEM05/301029932/gm-s-journey-from-volt-to-bolt.

11

MARKET EQUILIBRIUM

Abstract

The concept of equilibrium—an agreement between producers and consumers on the level of supply and its price—is not complicated. However, *when price or quantity changes, or when supply or demand shifts,* the analysis of market equilibrium takes on a new appearance. Understanding how these changes affect behavior among producers and consumers clarifies the otherwise mysterious operations of the economy.

As explained in Chapter 4, equilibrium is the point where the price of goods or services is equal to the demand level in the market. Both sides (producers and consumers) constantly move toward equilibrium. For producers, this requires finding the best possible quantity and price in order to compete in the market while still earning a profit. For consumers, this translates into finding the most acceptable price possible. If one source's price moves up, consumers are likely to go elsewhere; if the price moves down, the tendency is for consumers to purchase more of that product.

EXTERNAL FACTORS

Although equilibrium is a theory and is not likely to remain fixed indefinitely, there are usually no compelling reasons for producers to change prices or for consumers to change their purchasing habits. It is only when

external factors appear that prices or quantities change, disrupting the delicate equilibrium in the market.

Market equilibrium changes when external factors come into play that affect supply or demand and change the interaction between producer and consumer.

The external factors that influence *demand* include:

1. *Income*: when the consumer's income rises, the consumer can afford to buy more goods and to pay higher prices. This is seen in several examples. After receiving a raise, a consumer might choose a new car costing much more than the previously purchased car. The same applies to selecting a residence and the area where it is located.
2. *Quality*: a change in the quality of available goods leads to more purchasing by consumers. This may result from imports, technology, or new ideas. For example, when digital cameras were made available, consumers abandoned traditional cameras and film, preferring the easier and more advanced technology. Many were willing to pay more in order to obtain higher quality.
3. *Substitutes and complements*: when one product's price moves up, demand is likely to move to other, more affordable products.
4. *Expectations of the future*: consumers may expect future prices to rise, so buying today makes more sense.
5. *Brand loyalty*: consumers may hold a brand loyalty, even when prices rise. A well-known brand of food, for example, costs a few cents more than a comparable store brand, but brand loyalty leads to the consumer choosing the recognizable brand.

The external factors that influence *supply* include:

1. *Lower production costs*: when producers can reduce their cost of goods sold (for materials or labor, for example), it becomes possible to increase the level of supply at the current cost.
2. *Greater production capacity*: when producers add space, it increases the ability to make goods. For example, expanding a factory's floor space enables the addition of machinery and labor.

3. *More active producers*: competition means an increase in the supply of comparable goods. As more producers enter the market, supply inevitably increases.
4. *More efficiency*: this comes in many forms. Supply grows when robotics are used, when technological advances are applied in production, or when a company invents a new process and holds the patent to it.

Equilibrium is affected when any of these demand and supply external factors become part of the equation. This does not mean that equilibrium is lost; it does mean that equilibrium changes and finds a new level.

When price moves above equilibrium, a surplus results; supply is greater than demand as consumers slow down their buying activity. The producer then needs to reduce the prices of those goods in order to remove the surplus. Producers that are facing a surplus will have to slow down or cease production until the supply numbers move back to equilibrium. This condition is summarized in Figure 11.1.

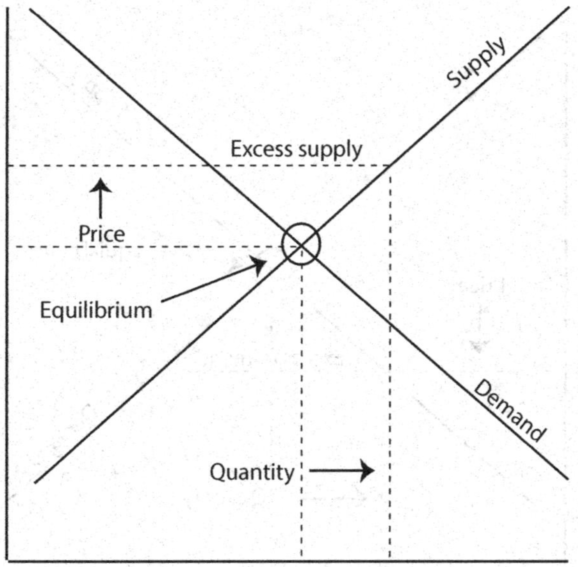

Figure 11.1 Surplus

When price moves below equilibrium, it causes excess demand, more commonly known as a shortage. Consumers will be willing to pay more for goods and services that have become more difficult to find. Producers react to this situation by increasing production. The initial goal may be to sell more of a product at a higher price. However, the effect of these opposing forces will stabilize, and equilibrium will be established once again. This situation is summarized in Figure 11.2.

Whether price is higher or lower than supply, the situation is referred to as disequilibrium. It is not desirable and motivates both producers and consumers to take steps to establish equilibrium once again.

For example, in 2010, as Japan-based Toshiba was experiencing increasing demand for its NAND flash chips, a power blip at its factory damaged the complex machines that make the chips. Toshiba, in partnership with SanDisk in California, was at the time responsible for one-third of the entire market for chips. The power disruption, Toshiba estimated,

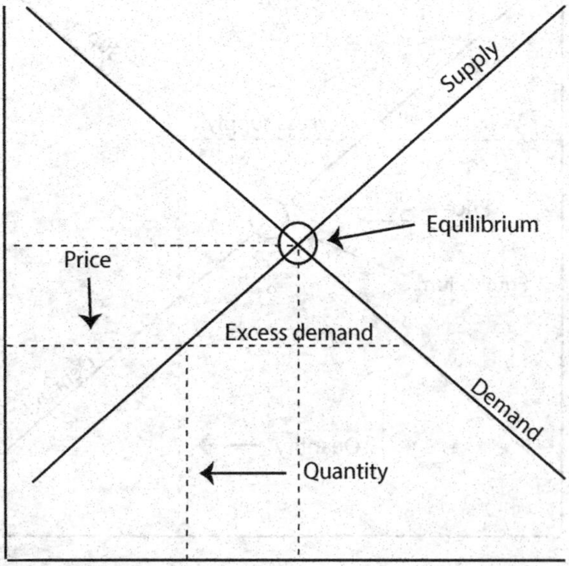

Figure 11.2 Shortage

would cause a 20% reduction in shipments for the next two months. Although the expected problem was only temporary, it could not have happened at a worse time (when demand was increasing). This would be classified as a short-term disequilibrium as demand grew but supply was curtailed.[1]

THE EQUILIBRIUM SHIFT

Equilibrium is not a fixed event. When supply and demand are matched perfectly, the situation will not last. However, a move away from equilibrium and then back toward it is not the only way that supply and demand are adjusted.

When demand and supply change over time, an *equilibrium shift* is also likely to occur. This may be an increase or a decrease in either demand or supply.

There can be four versions of an equilibrium shift: increase in demand, decrease in demand, increase in supply, or decrease in supply. Because these cause a change in the level of equilibrium, any business owner experiencing a shift must be aware of how it affects both sides of the equation.

An increase in demand, like that experienced in 2010 by Toshiba, sounds like a highly desirable situation. It would be, unless events like power disruptions and other unexpected circumstances (caused by technology, natural disasters, political unrest, labor strikes, piracy, or any number of other events) create new problems even as demand grows.

> Equilibrium shift
> A move of equilibrium to a new level, caused by increases or decreases in levels of either demand or supply.

The increase in demand moves the demand curve to the right, so that equilibrium will occur at a higher price point. This shift is illustrated in Figure 11.3.

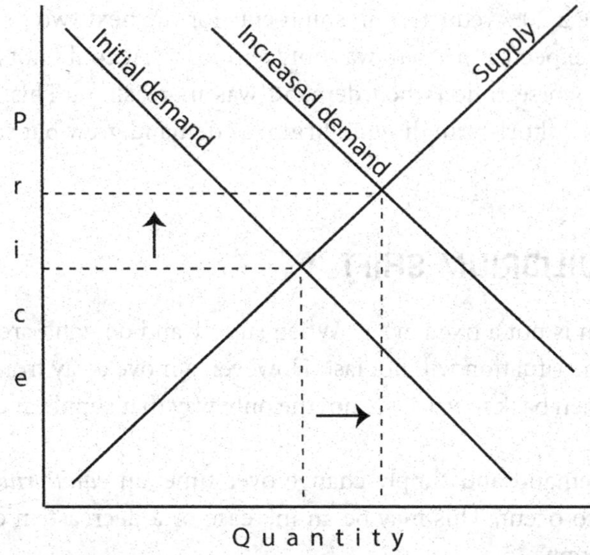

Figure 11.3 Increase in demand

A decrease in demand would see the demand curve move in the opposite direction, to the left. The chart in Figure 11.3 would be identical, but demand would decline along with a decline in price and quantity. For example, in 2017, Home Depot reported a decline in revenue but an increase in net income. The revenue decline was caused by a combination of store closures and declining demand in the company's business solutions division. The increase in net income was the result of increased gross margins, creating greater efficiency and cost savings.[2]

Home Depot was fortunate in being able to reduce costs during a year when revenues were falling. This situation cannot be sustained indefinitely, however, and the concern in this situation should be with the decrease in demand.

An increase in supply appears in a similar manner to shifts in demand, except that the supply curve moves to the right. This is shown in Figure 11.4.

With an increase in supply, price is reduced as quantity increases. The opposite occurs with a decrease in supply. Reviewing Figure 11.4, a decrease would cause the supply to move to the left, accompanied by higher

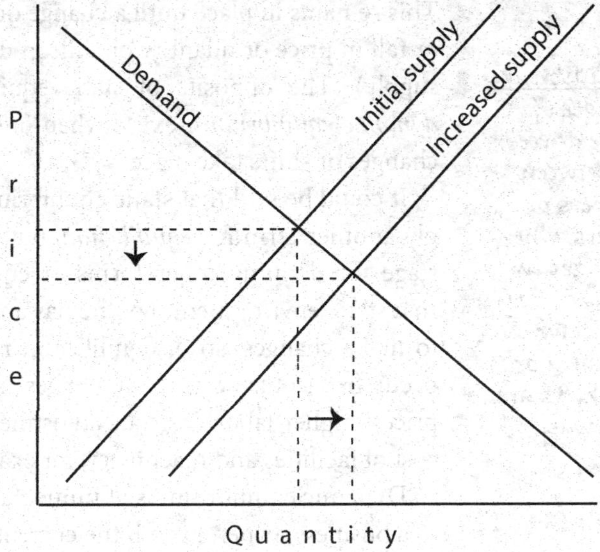

Figure 11.4 Increase in supply

prices and reduced quantity. For example, in 2017, BMW suffered a supply shortage in steering components that were supplied to the company by Bosch. The quantity of autos that were being manufactured had to be reduced as a result. This situation points out the importance of supply chain diversification; relying on a single source supplier can lead to lost revenue and potentially higher prices—in other words, a decrease in supply so that the producer must reduce quantity and, eventually, raise prices to make up the difference.[3]

MANY FORMS OF EQUILIBRIUM

Disruptions to equilibrium are caused by changes in either supply or demand. It is wise to expect constant possible changes on either side; and in fact, one symptom of a vibrant economy is the frequent adjustments needed to maintain interactions between the sides.

In some situations, *static equilibrium* is found. This is when no changes are underway in supply or demand *and* no shifts are taking place presently.

Static equilibrium
The state of complete agreement between producers or consumers, when no changes in price or quantity occur and when no demand or supply shifts are underway.

Dynamic equilibrium
The condition when one or more changes or shifts take place, disrupting the agreement between producer and consumer, or shifting equilibrium.

Walrasian equilibrium
A theory that equilibrium can exist for the entire competitive market, rather than observed in some markets but not in others.

This remains in place until a change occurs (rise or fall in price or quantity or shift in demand or supply). The opposite of static equilibrium—*dynamic equilibrium*—exists when one or more changes or shifts take place.

It could be said that static equilibrium is simply another term for *equilibrium*, but it sets the stage for defining other forms of equilibrium. In a static environment, no one has an incentive to make changes, so disequilibrium is likely to occur from outside forces (changes in supplier prices, higher labor costs, or adjustments in the cost of facilities and machinery, for example).

Dynamic equilibrium is of immediate interest to a business owner. Even if the current situation is at equilibrium or close to it, you cannot expect it to last. Dynamic equilibrium is the analysis of economic conditions over time and the observation of constantly changing levels of price and quantity for goods and services. In a period of dynamic equilibrium, a business owner must expect to constantly see shifts and conflicts between demand and supply.

Many forms of equilibrium are theories only and cannot be applied practically. Even so, there are brief moments in time when complete equilibrium can be seen. For example, *Walrasian equilibrium* (also called *competitive equilibrium*) is the belief that in a competitive environment, all goods and services are marketed in equilibrium at the same time. It is the ideal standard.

This economic theory is named for Léon Walras (1834–1910), a French economist who was credited with developing the general equilibrium theory, based on the study of the entire economy rather than of individual markets within the economy.

It is an interesting theory, but in fact, most business owners are more concerned with their market, not the overall market. However, this idea is worth keeping in mind because the condition and balance (equilibrium) of the entire economy affects all sectors.

Competitive equilibrium
An alternative description of Walrasian equilibrium.

Another theory is *Nash equilibrium*, an idealized view of economics in which individuals make decisions representing the best decisions for everyone. If no one changes their contribution to equilibrium, Nash equilibrium can (in theory) generate perfect harmony in all markets. Named for mathematician John Forbes Nash, Jr., Nash equilibrium assumes that every participant in the economy is fully aware of the strategies of all other players; and no one will gain an advantage by adjusting their strategy.[4]

Nash equilibrium
A theory where everyone is fully aware of everyone else's strategies and no gain will be achieved by changing a strategy.

Nash equilibrium is interesting in game theory, but when applied to economics, it is unlikely that perfect conditions can exist in a competitive world where many people constantly look for an advantage. Despite its impracticality, Nash equilibrium often is cited by economists as a theory that is worth striving for.

The concept of equilibrium is not complex: prices rise and fall—and quantities of output rise and fall. Either demand shifts or supply shifts. At times, all of these events take place together and may be difficult to sort out. But the idea itself is not more complicated. However, entire books have been written about equilibrium, mostly textbooks. For example:

- *The Theory of General Economic Equilibrium: A Differentiable Approach*, 392 pages
- *Equilibrium Analysis: Variations on Themes by Edgeworth and Walras*, 310 pages
- *Macroeconomic Theory: A Dynamic General Equilibrium Approach* (2nd ed.), 616 pages
- *Economic Dynamics and General Equilibrium: Time and Uncertainty*, 396 pages

These books serve a purpose and have value in an academic setting, but what does the business owner or entrepreneur need to know? A basic appreciation for the real-world tendencies of supply and demand, a study of consumer behavior, and appreciation for how and why shifts occur all serve as a sound footing for understanding this idea.

Equilibrium is part of the daily life of every business owner. It might not always be described using the term itself, and a business owner is not likely to debate the merits of Walrasian or Nash equilibrium, but awareness of how it affects profitability and competition is a worthwhile skill to develop. A business owner might ponder why consumers do not buy as much product as desired or why a competitor enjoys a larger market share. These questions are not puzzling but go to the core of how equilibrium affects everyone.

Equilibrium is not any single or unified idea. It describes a variety of outcomes based on behavior and choice. For the academic professor or student, equilibrium is represented by a series of equations, graphs, and expected outcomes. For the practical business owner, it is a fact of life and a reality to struggle with daily.

> Best response dynamics
> The tendency for producers to react to conditions to maximize profits and for consumers to select price and quality to find the best bargain.

Of added interest is the *best response dynamics* of equilibrium. This is an observation that the reaction to current conditions by a producer will be designed to provide the highest level of profits (best response). For consumers, the best response to different prices will be based on the best bargain or the perceived better quality of one brand over another.

This is a restatement of the basic economic idea that was previously presented. When equilibrium is added to the idea, it makes sense in the real-world application. Why do producers raise or lower prices or change the quantity of goods offered? Why do consumers change buying habits based on prices or brand perceptions? The answers to those questions are the engines of decisions, and collectively, agreement by both sides is equilibrium.

For the business owner, a problem with equilibrium analysis is that it does not always address the realities of a competitive world. The analysis of rising or falling demand or supply or of shifts does not consider some realities faced by business owners. These include:

1. Business owners do not always understand their markets adequately enough to study the demand and supply curves.
2. The owner might have an intimate knowledge of the market, but a poor or incomplete understanding of the demand curve at a given price or quantity of goods.
3. Some business owners analyze supply and demand but do not consider their own production costs and how these influence equilibrium.

The business owner attempting to understand the behavior of the market may take some comfort in the study of equilibrium, assuming this study is restricted to practical observation and does not get lost in the tall grass of theories. However, it should be all-inclusive. The owner needs to observe not only consumer behavior (i.e., why don't customers buy more or why do they buy more from my competitors?), but their own behavior as well.

A business owner may benefit from studying his or her own behavior as a producer and supplier. Why do we set prices at a specific level and how do we determine the most profitable quantity? How do we act in the role of consumer, in other words, how do we deal with suppliers and vendors? Are we acting as a rational and informed consumer in this role?

These are worthwhile questions to ask, not only to better understand equilibrium, but to better understand the behavior of producers and consumers in setting the equilibrium model.

ENDNOTES

1. Clark, Don and Juro Osawa. (December 10, 2010). "Power blip jolts supply of gadget chips." *The Wall Street Journal*, https://www.wsj.com/articles/SB10001424052748703766704576009071694055878.

2. Sleter, Greg. (May 9, 2017). "Office Depot Q1 sales down, net income rises." *HomeWorld Business*, https://www.homeworldbusiness.com/office-depot-q1-sales-net-income-rises/.
3. Hauschild, Marc. (May 30, 2017). "Supply shortage sees BMW production plummet." *The Manufacturer*, https://www.themanufacturer.com/articles/supply-shortage-sees-bmw-production-plummet/.
4. Osborne, Martin J. and Ariel Rubinstein. (1994). *A Course in Game Theory*. Cambridge, MA: MIT Press. p. 14.

12

ORGANIZATIONS: PERFECT COMPETITION

Abstract

No markets are ever perfect, and the concept of perfect competition is not intended as a goal, but as a benchmark for measuring today's conditions and changes in competitive environments. Ideal conditions are described by a series of situations, all of which will rarely, if ever, exist together. In any market, perfection is further inhibited by barriers to entry and to exit. A business owner seeks the best possible set of conditions based on *normal profit*, an economic term describing a fiscal breakeven point where revenue and costs are equal.

The *ideal* condition of a market is not a practical goal. However, understanding the features of the conceptual existence of *perfect competition* sets a standard for measuring the realistic condition of the market today. This model observes that when competition is completely in balance, and all aspects of the market are in equilibrium, all participants are happy; and no one can improve their situation without causing harm to someone else.[1]

IDEAL CONDITIONS

An examination of ideal conditions in a perfectly competitive market displays how such a market will appear. This does not mean any business

owner should expect to function in perfect competition; in fact, the skills of a business owner are best observed in less-than-perfect markets and in how effectively the owner is able to move closer to equilibrium.

The problem with theories like perfect competition is that they make it all too easy to proceed in analysis on the assumption of perfection:

> The assumption that is constantly made, tacitly or openly in most economic textbooks, of perfectly competitive conditions, has tended to obscure its workings. When we say, for instance, that price is equal to marginal cost, or that marginal net productivity of labor is equal to wages, or that marginal utility is equal to price, we are tacitly assuming perfectly competitive conditions.[2]

This points out the dangers of relying too heavily on the ideal conditions that, while possible, provide only a benchmark and not a goal in and of itself. A set of conditions make up this idealized market. These include:

1. *Many participants*: both buyers and sellers are abundant, making the market an efficient market. This facilitates the robust supply-and-demand activity that is required for a market to function well; an inadequate population on either side would impede the ability of all participants to accomplish desired price and quantity levels.
2. *Perfect information*: an assumption is made in the perfect model, that everyone—producers as well as consumers—possesses all prices and utility of products. This idea is found often as a part of game theory when every player has observed all preceding events and shares an equal understanding of conditions. Examples include card games and board games such as chess. In the reality of economic study, too many variables are introduced, impeding a business owner's ability to benefit from perfect information.[3]
3. *Perfect substitution among products*: the theory requires homogeneous products, in which the characteristics of each are identical among several suppliers. This is possible when a sector offers a range of identical products (such as a grocery store or auto parts outlet, for example).

4. *Clearly defined property rights*: what can be sold by a business owner? What rights are granted to the buyer? These conditions include a warranty of merchantability or other promises that sellers make to buyers and may be applied between a business owner and consumer or between a supplier and a producer.
5. *No barriers to entry or exit*: a barrier is a condition impeding the ability of someone to enter or exit a market. This topic is explored in greater detail in the following section.
6. *Participants are price takers*: no one participant in a perfectly competitive market can set and control prices; each is a price taker, meaning they have no market power. Having market power enables a seller to raise prices without the risk of losing customers to competitors. These price makers are rare and usually exist only in a government or a monopoly. Most businesses and consumers are price takers.
7. *Factor mobility*: all factors of production (materials, labor, facilities, and capital) are mobile, so that producers can adjust to market conditions without losing competitive edge or pricing themselves out of the market.
8. *Profits are maximized*: this means that producers are free to sell where profit is highest. Equilibrium is controllable and, in theory, unending.
9. *Buyers are rational*: all purchases will increase the utility of products, and consumers will not make purchases that do not improve their economic utility. This is a concept that originally meant that buyers make choices to improve their satisfaction; in a more general sense, economic utility is a measurement of value. Buyers are assumed to act in a rational manner and this can be anticipated.
10. *There are no external influences at work*: this includes actions by anyone beyond the seller and the buyer, and often refers to government control or intervention.
11. *There are no transaction costs*: the buyer and seller can complete a transaction without having to pay added costs.
12. *The number of producers is perfect*: in ideal conditions, the number of producers is stable or changes only to meet changing populations of consumers.

13. *Regulations protect participants against anti-competitive activity*: the ideal market includes a regulatory environment to prevent any market activity working against competition.

Most business owners recognize that all of these conditions are impossible to meet. Some may exist to a degree, but others clearly are impractical. The model is a fair benchmark, however, to understand how competition may be made more robust with a focus on these attributes.

Among the list of attributes, one deserves more explanation. The removal of barriers to entry or exit is especially important in a competitive market. Activities by governments, regulatory agencies, and others to establish barriers prevent not only perfect competition but, at times, reasonable competition as well.

BARRIERS TO ENTRY

Barriers to entry
Conditions preventing or limiting the ability of a business to enter and participate in a market.

Whenever a business is prevented from entering the market, it is due to one or more *barriers to entry*. Barriers to entry are established to benefit those companies that are already in the market. By restricting new competitors from entry, the limited number of existing competitors can limit new competition and enjoy greater control over their own profits.

Typical barriers to entry include the need to reach an *economy of size* in volume of production. A relatively small competitor may not be able to sell profitably without volume. A well-known example is small retailers going out of business when Walmart opens a store and offers lower pricing.

Closely related is the need for *capital investment* that is demanded for output. A new manufacturer is limited when it comes to entry into the business, while the established, larger manufacturers have adequate capital to produce at a profitable level. For the new competitor, the cost of borrowing money to buy equipment and rent facilities may be so inhibitive that entry is impossible. Buyers may also resist moving from one product to another. The new business must figure out how to promote

their product to an existing customer base. The *high switching cost* of reaching out to customers cuts into profits and makes it difficult to enter the market. The *brand identity* of products and companies in business for many years is also difficult to overcome.

Within most communities, *zoning* restrictions may limit what types of businesses can exist within an area of the city. For example, zoning may prevent gas stations from operating on the same block as daycare centers. Other zoning restrictions may limit the number of businesses of one type from opening in a city or county. For example, a city may deny a permit to a business based on concerns about high traffic volume that is already caused by others in that business—with a desire to prevent further traffic congestion.

Some businesses also require *permits* or *licenses* to operate. In many cities, a limited number of licenses are granted to taxi drivers, for example, and the expense of a license can be very high. The same is true for someone who wants to open a bar and faces a huge licensing fee. In 2005, for example, in San Francisco a liquor license cost about $15,000. By 2015, the cost had skyrocketed: "A Type 47 liquor license—one that will allow a restaurant to sell hard liquor in addition to beer and wine—can cost $250,000 in San Francisco."[4]

Another barrier to entry is seen in *restrictive practices* in some industries. Limited entry may be based on standards preventing new entry. For example, the Federal Aviation Administration (FAA) limits runway slots at airports in order to limit the volume of air traffic. A new airline would have difficulty obtaining slots at high-volume airports as a result. For example, runway slots at John F. Kennedy, LaGuardia, and Ronald Reagan airports are very difficult to get for new airlines—and even existing airlines are restricted from adding more due to high volume. The FAA also imposes a stringent approval process at ORD, LAX, EWR, and SFO, where the process of getting new slots can prevent a smaller airline from participating in major high-volume travel routes.[5]

In some industries, retailers, wholesalers, and distributors may hold exclusive *distributor agreements* that completely exclude competitors from entering the market. Likewise, *supplier agreements* limit the ability of new manufacturers to enter markets. A similar range of limitation can be imposed by governments through *taxes* and *tariffs* imposed on imports.

A monopoly can be created when a business holds *intellectual property*, notably patents that prevent other businesses from duplicating a product design or utility for a limited period. Although patent protection is intended as an encouragement for the development of new ideas, it also presents a barrier to entry for competitors.

BARRIERS TO EXIT

On the other side of the barrier world is a *barrier to exit*. This is a condition preventing a company from leaving a market.

Barriers to exit
Conditions preventing or limiting the ability of a business to exit from a market.

For example, in some markets a company must make a sizable *investment in capital assets*. Manufacturing companies must buy the equipment and machinery that is used in the production process and may also need to invest millions to build factories. To exit that business, it is possible that recapturing the cost of this investment will be impossible. Many forms of capital assets are *nontransferable assets*, meaning that it would be difficult to find a buyer for machinery and equipment or to take over a long-term lease on a factory.

Some labor agreements also have high *redundancy costs*. Employees holding contracts may cause very high costs if the company tries to leave the market. In considering changes to an existing market, the contractual agreements, notably through labor unions, can act as inhibitors. This includes not only benefits for current employees, but also legacy costs for retirees. This was one reason that General Motors was forced to file for bankruptcy protection in 2009:

> GM maintains hourly and salaried benefit plans that provide post-retirement medical, dental, vision, and life insurance to most U.S. and Canadian retirees and eligible dependents. The cost of such benefits is recognized in the consolidated financial statements during the period employees provide service to GM.[6]

Many companies have entered *contingency agreements* with suppliers or buyers, calling for payment of penalties in the event that contracts are ended. This provision may restrict a business from being able to exit without incurring large net losses.

Perfect competition is affected by barriers to both entry and exit. Aside from the ideal theory of a perfectly competitive market, economists study the effects of how economic profits are created and the role of normal profits.

NORMAL PROFITS

Barriers to entry and exit are often necessities. For example, FAA oversight of airports and restriction of runway slots is unavoidable in high-volume locations. However, barriers also impede business from pursuing profits—and this is a fact of life in any economy.

If barriers did not exist, businesses would face no external restriction on profits. Every business owner knows that this is not possible because perfect markets do not exist; and having competitors is one barrier that's unavoidable. Getting back to the theory of perfect competition, a goal for the typical business is to generate *normal profits.*

Normal profits
A level of revenue equal to its total costs; the breakeven point required for a business to compete in the market and avoid losses.

There is no surplus profit when normal profits are achieved. This might seem like a pointless exercise. Why break even when the true goal is to earn profits? However, normal profits represent the *minimum* level of revenue needed to function. Naturally, a business owner wants to perform above that level, but that same owner must know the normal profit level as a line in the sand. If revenue falls below the level of normal profits each month, it's only a matter of time until the business fails. The owner must take steps to improve the situation.

For example, a small business that was supplying filtered and bottled water operated in the San Francisco Bay Area several years ago. Drivers visited businesses and residences to fill large bottles regularly. This model

worked if tap water quality was the only alternative. However, over time, new technology was developed enabling homeowners to filter tap water at an affordable price. Faucet-mounted treatments today are available in home improvement stores like Home Depot, and online from outlets such as Amazon.[7]

These alternatives made home delivery of bottled water impractical for most homeowners and small businesses. In addition, rising fuel costs and maintenance made home delivery expensive and costs rose, thus revenue volume fell. Normal profits were not being achieved and eventually, the owner realized the situation was not going to change. The owner wanted to switch to the sale of purification systems, but there were two problems with this idea. A barrier to entry was stiff competition, notably online and via home improvement stores.

A barrier to exit from the existing business was the investment in delivery trucks and inventory. These would not be transferrable to the faucet-mounted purification systems, which would be sold through mail order or online. The competition was too great, so the business owner faced the prospect of either continuing to lose money or shutting down the operation and selling assets for whatever was possible.

This example demonstrates that obsolescence of a product or service may be a key element of declining normal profits. While the business had been profitable at one time, it was no longer a viable enterprise. On a larger scale, this is what has happened to numerous companies, including Eastman Kodak. Founded in 1888 by George Eastman, Kodak dominated the film industry for over 100 years. By 1976, the company had 90% of film sales and 85% of camera sales. However, they failed to evolve quickly enough or to recognize the digital revolution away from film. Business declined and normal profits became impossible. In 2012, the company filed for bankruptcy protection and reorganized.[8]

To achieve normal profits or better, a business—big or small—must be able to monitor conditions of the market. What do buyers want and at what price? What is the competition offering? In the case of Kodak, hubris prevented management from evolving and too many perceived barriers to exit got in their way. These included many film and camera patents that had value in a world of film cameras. Once digital came along, the market

changed dramatically and left Kodak behind. Ironically, the hand-held digital camera was invented by Kodak back in 1975. The engineer presenting his invention (Steven Sasson) offered the idea to Kodak management, but it was rejected as conflicting with the existing product markets:

> The main objections came from the marketing and business sides. Kodak had a virtual monopoly on the United States photography market, and made money on every step of the photographic process. If you wanted to photograph your child's birthday party you would likely be using a Kodak Instamatic, Kodak film, and Kodak flash cubes. You would have it processed either at the corner drugstore or mail the film to Kodak and get back prints made with Kodak chemistry on Kodak paper.[9]

Kodak has closed its mind to any new technology that threatened its dominance of film and film cameras. That was its downfall. By citing barriers to exit as the reason to not pursue a competing technology, Kodak was left behind, and the digital revolution was dominated by competitors.

THE VALUE OF THE PERFECT COMPETITION MODEL

The history of companies like Kodak, General Motors, Polaroid, and many others demonstrates that profitability for any company can erode and decline over time. The failure of companies to recognize changing trends is the flaw. For example, when the automobile began taking over the horse and carriage industry, thousands of blacksmiths and stable operators went out of business. The shrewd business owners recognized the trend and switched to become auto mechanics, which were in great demand in the early 20th century. Those who continued operating their shops under the old model eventually lost their ability to meet normal profit levels and were forced out of business.

Some business owners simply assume that their markets are perfectly competitive, even though this is a rare situation. In a perfectly competitive industry, 12 conditions exist:

1. Many participants, perfect information
2. Perfect product substitution

3. Clearly defined property rights
4. No entry or exit barriers
5. Participants acting as price takers
6. Factor mobility
7. Maximized profits
8. Rational buyers
9. No external influences
10. No transaction costs
11. A perfect number of producers
12. Regulatory protection against anticompetitive activity

These ideal conditions are rare, especially the assumption that everyone (producers and consumers) acts rationally. Decisions are made based on perception rather than reality, and not often with perfect information. For example, why buy a $150,000 car when you can accomplish the same utility with a $25,000 model? Status, brand loyalty, ego, ability to afford an expensive car, and similar irrational factors are more likely. Otherwise, everyone would buy the most economical model of car (or purses, shoes, handbags, and scarves).

The perfectly competitive model is useful, however, for two reasons. First, some markets do hold many features of perfect competition (notably, in many commodity markets where a limited number of producers are not able to control market price). Second, competitive forces can be measured accurately in some markets by using perfect competition as a benchmark and thus, acquire a better understanding as to how markets operate.

Too often, economic theories are misunderstood as standards that businesses are expected to achieve. This is not the case. In practice, perfect competition is the highest possible outcome in what would have to be a perfect world for businesses. It is like the standards of *Six Sigma*—the business system that is used to measure business processes and reduce errors or inefficiencies. In Lean Six Sigma, the purpose is to measure improvements against the standard of zero defects. As a statistical measurement, a six sigma process is 99.99966% free of defects, or as close as possible to perfect. No business expects to reach that level in its processes, but it sets a high standard to observe improvements.

Compared to a Six Sigma measurement of business processes, perfect competition is a measurement of the most idealized economic environment. All 13 of the conditions are not likely to be met permanently or even at all, especially the theory that everyone acts rationally. This is useful not as a standard to meet, but as an observable fact. A business owner may examine a set of assumptions about consumers, competitors, or barriers to entry and exit and recognize flaws in those assumptions. By re-examining the core beliefs and adjusting them, the owner moves closer to the ideal of acting rationally.

This is not likely to ever occur in all aspects of operations, but improvement in many core beliefs and removal of clearly false assumptions may be enough for most business owners. By maximizing the principles of perfect competition, it is possible to approach perfection in many areas. A 99.99966% error-free rate is a standard and not a goal; and perfect competition offers the same benchmark for a business owner, a standard by which attitudes and beliefs can be measured.

ENDNOTES

1. Machovec, Frank. (1995). *Perfect Competition and the Transformation of Economics.* New York, NY: Routledge. pp. 11–12.
2. Robinson, Joan. (1965). *The economics of imperfect competition.* London, UK: Macmillan. p. 230.
3. Osborne, M. J. and A. Rubinstein. (1994). *A Course in Game Theory.* Cambridge, MA: MIT Press. p. 89.
4. Sciacca, Annie. (November 17, 2015). "Here's one cost to opening a restaurant that might surprise you." *bizjournal*, https://www.bizjournals.com/sanfrancisco/blog/2015/11/cost-liquor-license-restaurant-open-san-francisco.html.
5. Federal Aviation Administration (FAA), https://www.faa.gov/about/office_org/headquarters_offices/ato/service_units/systemops/slot_administration/.
6. General Motors Corp., Securities and Exchange Commission Form 10-K for the Year Ending December 31, 2006, note 19. p. 153, http://www.sec.gov/Archives/edgar/data/40730/.

7. Home Depot, https://www.homedepot.com/b/Kitchen-Water-Filters/N-5yc1vZarmz; Amazon, https://www.amazon.com/s/ref=nb_sb_noss_2?url=search-alias%3Dgarden&field-keywords=water+purification+&rh=n%3A1055398%2Ck%3Awater+purification.
8. De La Merced, Michael J. (January 19, 2012). "Eastman Kodak files for bankruptcy." *The New York Times*, https://dealbook.nytimes.com/2012/01/19/eastman-kodak-files-for-bankruptcy/.
9. Estrin, James. (August 12, 2015). "Kodak's first digital moment." *The New York Times*, https://lens.blogs.nytimes.com/2015/08/12/kodaks-first-digital-moment/?smid=pl-share.

13

COMPETITION AND ECONOMIC GAME THEORY

Abstract

Game theory, the science of strategy, often is viewed as merely an interesting analysis of circumstances and how people react. However, it is more. As a useful economic force, game theory analyzes interactions among producers and consumers and studies behavior to better understand how strategic decisions are made and how seemingly irrational choices make sense on both a logical and mathematical basis.

People are continuously running probability tests in their heads, even if they do not call this process a test or mathematical calculation. For example, toward the end of the month, consumers must think about paying the rent by the first, putting food on the table, and paying other bills. Is this a wise time to buy that new hat or a ticket to this weekend's game?

Some people impulsively make decisions that contradict their best interests, while others will be prudent in delaying *wants* in favor of *needs*. In order to make these kinds of decisions, consumers may either calculate the outcome and consequence of a decision or satisfy their immediate needs without thinking about the consequences. This latter action is itself a decision. The consumer who decides to buy something that ruins this month's budget, calculates the outcome, and decides that the impulse is more important than the result.

Game theory
A set of analyses by consumers and producers, both individually and with one another, to better understand how rational people make strategic decisions.

Game theory is a series of *what-if* analyses that studies the choices consumers make as well as interactions among consumers and producers, in order to better understand how strategic decisions are made—assuming that the individuals are rational in how they make those decisions.

The qualification of *rational* people sets aside any irrational behavior. A consumer who cannot afford a piece of jewelry might decide to steal the item even though the store has security in place. Thinking it will be easy to out-run a security guard, not thinking about the probability of a security camera in the store, and ignoring the legal consequences of being arrested—all define the action of stealing as irrational. Given the total possible outcomes, stealing can be analyzed as a behavioral decision beyond the scope of rational decision making.

GAME THEORY AS AN ECONOMIC FORCE

Economics, broadly speaking, is the study of decisions and choices, given the fact that the wants and needs of consumers can never be fully met. Scarcity of products determines price, and choice about which wants and needs will be met in the immediate future leads to the study of game theory. How people act and why they make decisions is the core study in economics; without scarcity and the unlimited wants and needs of people, the concept of value would disappear.

Some products are widely available but have no economic value. The air people breathe, for example, cannot be given economic value in normal circumstances because there is no need to pay for it. Game theory applies only in situations where a product or service can be assigned a value because the consumer wants or needs it and is willing to pay to acquire it.

Other products have value because consumers want those products or need them. An automobile is a need for anyone commuting to work daily, taking children to school, and buying groceries. An expensive high-performance car meets that need, but the price tag crosses over and makes

the car a want as well. A family needs groceries on a regular basis, and needs to pay rent or mortgage, utilities, and insurance. At the same time, the family would like to buy a bigger home, take a luxury vacation, and buy an LG 55EG5SD-C 55-inch Dual Side In-Glass Digital Signage television costing $16,240. How does the family decide whether to make this expensive luxury purchase? This is where game theory comes into the picture.[1]

There are several participants in the decision to buy an expensive television. The manufacturer advertises its products to induce purchases that often are impulsive but responsive to what the advertisement promises. Your life will be improved so much that the decision to buy is rational. The quality of the picture is so exceptional that the buyer could never go back to a smaller, cheaper television. The manufacturer and the retailer promote these ideas about the television in the same way that a car salesperson tries to convince a visitor in the showroom that they *must* buy a new car, not only due to the desire for a new car but also with a list of good reasons, making the want more like a need.

Another participant is the buyer, of course. This buyer *wants* the television but knows it is not a need. Even so, the arguments presented in advertising by manufacturers and by salespeople in the store make it sound like a reasonable decision. The quality is so much better than on any other television you have ever owned—and it will last for so long that you will never have to buy another television.

Yet another participant is the potential buyer's spouse. If the husband stops at the store on the way home and decides to buy the expensive television, what happens when he gets home? The wife, who tracks the budget and pays the bills, will likely be upset if the husband did not consult with her before making an impulse purchase. The husband is likely to take this into consideration when deciding to buy the television. The interaction between all the participants—husband, wife, manufacturer, and salesperson—is complex and involves numerous interests. The manufacturer must find a market for this expensive television and must appeal to an impulse on the part of the buyer. The salesperson relies on commission, which is very attractive for expensive television sales, as part of a separate economic motive. The husband in this example is tempted by advertising and the quality of the product, but also must consider his wife's reaction

to buying something they cannot afford. The wife struggles every month to balance the budget, prioritizing purchases of necessities, savings, and some set-aside allowance for items that are desirable but not necessary. There is no room in this budget for a $16,000 television.

Applying the principles of game theory, all of the motivations among participants—the way decisions are made, arguments are presented, and decisions are finalized—can be studied and understood as economic forces. Game theory is a means for understanding how all of these rational participants behave and arrive at a decision.

One version of game theory that is applicable to economics and to other versions of deciding on a course of action is called the prisoner's dilemma.

THE PRISONER'S DILEMMA

The best-known example of game theory is called the *prisoner's dilemma*. The typical example of this involves two suspects caught and questioned separately. Each is offered leniency to blame the crime on the other. If neither agrees, both go free; if one agrees, the other is charged. And neither of them knows for certain that the other is keeping quiet.

<u>Prisoner's dilemma</u>
An idea in game theory that two suspects should both keep quiet when questioned; but each one is unsure whether the other is blaming him, so the tendency is to blame a crime on the other suspect, even without evidence.

The prisoner's dilemma is well-known by law enforcement and is used often to get a confession or testimony among partners in crime. It also applies in economics by describing how competition works and how business owners interact with one another.[2]

For example, two companies competing in the same market need to set a price. If both charge a higher price than they need to, both will make a nice profit. If one sets a lower price, it takes customers away from their competitor. If both set a low price, they both profit but those profits are lower. How does either competitor know what the other will do? Consider the case of a grocery

store owner selling a variety of produce. With a limited shelf life, setting the price too high results in higher spoilage—and the price can only be lowered to the point of normal profits (breakeven). But what will a competing grocery store do?

The study of the prisoner's dilemma as it applies to competing businesses explains how and why prices tend to be similar between two or more outlets. The choice, based partly on the prisoner's dilemma, is dictated by not knowing how a competitor will act. Just as a prisoner who does not know whether his partner in crime will turn on him is compelled to make an accusation first and gain a reduced sentence, a business owner, similarly, does not know how a competitor will act in setting prices. Should the produce seller lower the price to gain only a marginal profit, also gaining more customers from a higher-price competitor? Or should the owner go for higher profits, assuming the competitor will do the same?

Perhaps the two owners could get together and agree on a price. In some industries, this would be called conspiracy. Also, as a part of the prisoner's dilemma, how does anyone know that a competitor can be trusted? Would agreement be price-fixing? Many issues arise when this idea is considered. As Adam Smith observed in his famous book *The Wealth of Nations*, "People of the same trade seldom meet, even for merriment and diversion, but the conversation ends in a conspiracy against the public, or in some contrivance to raise prices."[3]

Adam Smith also spoke of the *invisible hand* in economics behavior. This is a force in the market that moves supply and demand toward equilibrium, whether participants engage in that effort or not. This works, according to the theory, even when individual producers and consumers work only in their own interests. If a producer raises prices too high, the invisible hand reduces market share; if prices are lowered too far, the producer suffers a loss.

> **invisible hand**
> A force within the economy moving supply and demand toward equilibrium, even when participants act only in their own self-interest.

The invisible hand addresses part of the prisoner's dilemma. Is business self-interest likely to lead to higher profits or to loss of market share? Like two prisoners who are unaware of what the other is telling the police,

two competitors cannot know what each other is deciding for prices in the market. A lack of trust prevents them from outright collusion (not to mention possible legal liability), so self-interest must consider not only normal profits and the cost of goods sold, but also a competitor's actions. The invisible hand observes that these competitors ultimately work for the good of the economy because to do otherwise would be detrimental.

When producers violate the principal of the prisoner's dilemma and act solely in self-interest, the results are disruptive, to say the least. In one infamous case, the head of a pharmaceutical company raised the price of a drug to a level never seen before:

> A dramatic increase in the price of a decades-old drug called Daraprim has sparked protest among infectious disease doctors and advocates.
>
> The rights to Daraprim were purchased in August by a new company, Turing Pharmaceuticals, which promptly increased the price from $13.50 per tablet to $750 per tablet . . .[4]

In this instance, the company's CEO, Martin Shkreli, was found guilty of securities fraud and sentenced to a seven-year prison term.

In the prisoner's dilemma, several aspects of game theory demonstrate how the idea applies in economics:

1. *The idea works in the economy only if cheating or abuse is detected and then punished.* The pharmaceutical example points out how that works. Raising prices by 5,000 percent is a form of cheating because consumers had no choice but to pay the price or go without.
2. *Abuse by one participant might lead to an equal level of abuse by another.* ("If you raise your prices, I'll raise mine, too.") Thus, the abuse and punishment appear rational, so that events like price wars are inevitable.
3. *Reward is instant, but loss is in the future.* Lowering prices today results in a higher volume of sales (and profits), but raising prices does not generate reward or punishment until later.

It seems rational for competing businesses to cooperate and maintain a level of reasonable profits based on price. However, businesses do not

always act rationally. The ultimate decision to act cooperatively or to pursue exceptional profits will often be based on another aspect of game theory, the distinction between *zero-sum* and *non-zero-sum* games.

ZERO-SUM GAMES

A *zero-sum game* is any situation in which one side's gain is the other side's loss. Taken together, there is no net gain. The opposite, a *non-zero-sum game*, describes interaction in which there is a net gain on one side or the other.

Zero-sum game
Any interaction in which gains on one side of a transaction are offset by equal losses on the other side.

Non-zero-sum game
Any interaction in which a net gain is realized by one side.

The distinction is important because it describes two entirely different methods of transaction. The zero-sum gain implies that there must be one winner and one loser (or a collective set of winners and losers). In practice, there may be only one set of participants, all breaking even. For example, thousands of people buy shares of stock in an initial public offering at $20 per share. A lock-up period of six months applies, meaning no one can sell shares for that period. After six months, the value of the shares has moved around but ends up at exactly $20. No one has gained, and no one has lost. The outcome: a zero-sum gain.

In a longer view of the stock market, in a growing economy, winners will outnumber losers. When the markets turn bearish, those who are holding shares will lose and those who short shares (sell) will gain. In either event, the long and short positions represent winners and losers trading in the same company's shares of stock.

Many economic transactions involve winners on both sides. A producer sells products expecting to earn a profit; a consumer wants the product and is willing to compensate the producer. They benefit from utility; for example, food is bought to feed the family and the price paid generates a profit for the retailer as well as for the farmer who grew the

Pareto optimal
A condition when resources are applied with maximum efficiency, and when any reallocation would harm one side or the other.

food or raised cattle. Unlike the gaming industry, which offers negative-sum games (the house wins more than it loses), or a board game for two, which offers only two possible outcomes (winner/loser or a tie), the example of food creates mutual benefit. In economics, this is called a *Pareto optimal* situation. This describes the use of resources with maximum efficiency. Any reallocation would adversely affect one side in the transaction. This theory is named for Vilfredo Pareto, a 19th-century economist who studied efficiency and other economic topics.[5]

The non-zero-sum game model is not healthy in an efficient economy because although there is always a winner, there also is always a loser. The example of a gaming establishment makes this point. The house usually wins and the customer usually loses. However, the comparison is understated. Because the gamblers return time and again to the casino even when they usually lose, they are gaining some benefit. There is the long shot of making a huge win; short of that, the enjoyment gained by gambling may justify the lost cash, making the casino example an imperfect example of a non-zero-sum game. One side (the house) benefits financially, while the other side (the gambler) might win in other ways. They hold onto the chance of making a lot of money but also pursue the excitement of gambling as a recreational pursuit.

COOPERATIVE AND NON-COOPERATIVE GAMES

Cooperative games
Forms of interaction based on two competing sides or teams with external rule enforcement.

Taking game theory to another level, interactions can be divided between *cooperative games* and *non-cooperative games*. The cooperative game involves competition between two sides with external enforcement of rules. A non-cooperative game lacks external enforcement and must be self-enforcing through threats that can be enforced.

In an efficient economy, many sectors operate in a cooperative game environment. For example, securities dealers are regulated by the external oversight of the Securities and Exchange Commission. If a dealer breaks the rules, it may be fined, principals imprisoned, or the entire organization banished. This protects the investing public from individuals and organizations that might break the rules except for the possible consequences imposed through the oversight function.

> **Non-cooperative games**
> Forms of interaction with no external enforcement of rules and based on credible threats by one side to the other.

An example of a non-cooperative game is the operation of a labor union. Members are instructed to behave in a particular manner. For example, lunch breaks are taken at an exact time and last for exactly one hour; members cannot start work early but must begin exactly at 8 am. Any member violating these and similar rules may be fined by the union and must respond to their union representatives. The collective power of the union keeps its members under control. This enforcement mechanism was originally intended to prevent management from exploitation but it also serves the purpose of providing a non-cooperative game. If a union member breaks the rules, the union has the credible threat available in the form of fines or other sanctions.[6]

Game theory can make distinctions to better understand and explain transactions. Concepts like zero-sum and non-zero-sum versus cooperative and non-cooperative games can articulate how the economy works. Game theory is a useful device for studying behavior. One popular game is exceptional in this regard. The *tragedy of the commons* explains behavior and self-interest among producers and consumers.

> **Tragedy of the commons**
> An economic theory based on a tendency to destroy common areas through overuse rather than preserving the resource through cooperation.

TRAGEDY OF THE COMMONS

The tragedy of the commons demonstrates how cooperative behavior is beneficial and at the same time, how self-interest can work against

cooperative action. The theory was developed by William Forster Lloyd, a British economist who published his *Two Lectures on the Checks to Population* in 1833. In his example, Lloyd described the behavior of ranchers sharing a common grazing area for cattle. He observed that human nature allows one or more participants to take more than their share of the common area, resulting in its complete destruction.

The tragedy of the commons is the ultimate *lose-lose* economic theory. The idea of sustainable resources assumes that everyone cooperates in protecting a particular resource by not overusing it. This is sometimes ignored under the theory due to self-interest. Even if only one participant violates the sensible rule, it provides an incentive for all participants to also violate the rule.

The theory is simple but elegant. A group of 10 cattle herders share a commons with each having access to it to feed his cows. Based on the available land, each herder can feed two cows. If all 20 adhere to this limit, the resource is renewable and sustainable. However, if any one herder adds an additional cow, the commons will be overgrazed. The violator receives greater benefit than his neighbors, but the entire group is negatively affected by the result of overgrazing. There will not be enough feed and everyone suffers.

If a participant is following the rules but observes that his neighbor has three cows rather than the agreed-upon allotment of two, his incentive will be to do the same. If one neighbor benefits, why shouldn't others? In terms of economics, the behavior of both neighbors is based on self-interest but also is irrational.

The herder who is abusing the rule should have known that others would also violate it, and that overgrazing would harm all 20 neighbors. But self-interest ruled, and the violator sought an advantage by adding more cows. The second herder also should have realized the negative impact of adding more animals, but also responded to self-interest.

In 1968, a published paper formalized the tragedy of the commons as a social and economic dilemma. The paper expanded on Lloyd's original 1833 publication and analyzed how some situations cannot be solved technically. These situations, according to the paper, can be resolved through awareness of consequences. The issue of overpopulation was

used to make the claim that if people have too many children, the result will be famine, climate change, and other disastrous results.[7]

It is a social reality that any variety of the tragedy of the commons (whether discussing cattle grazing or human population) ends up depleting resources. As an economic reality, however, people do not act in the common good but instead out of self-interest. And the 1968 proposal in the paper that people can and should recognize the limitations of resources and act accordingly is not simply rational. Social conscience does not necessarily translate into economic conscience.

The problem points out a need for economic *commons* to be regulated externally in many cases. For example, if fisheries can fish without limitation, some species of fish will be made extinct, just as overhunting has endangered many species of mammals. At one time, African safari activity did not consider the possibility of extinction. Many hunters, such as ex-president Theodore Roosevelt (applauded as a great conservationist), hunted with abandon, including killing many animals that today are on the endangered species list. Roosevelt and his son killed over 500 animals on one safari in 1909.[8]

If Roosevelt and other hunters had acknowledged that lions and elephants were becoming scarce, they might have agreed to limit their kills to one animal per safari. But it would take only one hunter to ignore that guideline to destroy its intention of protecting endangered animals. Due to a lack of regulation, similar problems cannot be solved.

A closely aligned concept in game theory is called the *Nash equilibrium*.

NASH EQUILIBRIUM

John Nash was the mathematician whose life was explored in the movie "A Beautiful Mind." But Nash was also known for developing an economic theory. This theory stated that when equilibrium is in force, no side in a transaction has a rational reason to change a strategy, even if all possible choices available to someone else are analyzed and understood. This idea is called *Nash equilibrium*.

A comparison between *Nash equilibrium* and the *tragedy of the commons* reveals the separation between rational action and economic

motivation. Equilibrium is supposed to work for everyone. A commons shared by 20 herders, with two cows each, is adequate to sustain everyone. There is an equilibrium between the demand (for grazing pasture) and supply (the resource). There is no rational reason for any herder to add more cows and try to take advantage of his 19 neighbors. However, upon doing so, the remaining 19 have an irrational incentive to also violate the rule, resulting in complete destruction of the resource.

Nash equilibrium is a comfortable theory, revealing that none of the herders will benefit by changing their strategy. But the tragedy of the commons contradicts this, pointing out that self-interest may not be rational, but it does exist. Even though overgrazing is a form of economic suicide, no one herder will want to pass up the chance to also overgraze the commons.

This is perplexing, but it demonstrates that economically, people do not always act in a rational manner and might even prefer to cite self-interest to act irrationally. ("I don't want to be the only one left out, so I will overgraze just like my neighbor.") The action of the first violator is purely selfish and fails to recognize the probable outcome. The action of subsequent violations is not only irrational, but also counter-productive. In these situations, some form of regulation is required. Either the herders themselves would need to prevent any one member from overgrazing or a government agency with regulatory authority is needed to prevent abuse.

The observation of game theory versus economic behavior points out that rational behavior may be assumed as the basis for choice, but it does not always work in practice. Because human beings are not always rational, economic theories have only limited value in analyzing how and why people behave as they do, and for the decisions they make.

ENDNOTES

1. *Office Wonderland*, https://officewonderland.com/listings/lg-55eg5sd-c-55-dual-side-in-glass-digital-signage/?gclid=Cj0KCQiA1NbhBRCBARIsAKOTmUsF851vYcry8eb-Rbq5et2beg3fmmCIpU8TN1Nkx3-LkDAAGiYJihUaAgXvEALw_wcB.

2. Kreps, David, Robert Wilson, Paul Milgrom, and John Roberts. (August 1982). "Rational cooperation in the finitely repeated prisoners' dilemma." *Journal of Economic Theory*. 27(2). pp. 245–252.
3. Smith, Adam. (1827). *The Wealth of Nations*. Edinburgh, Scotland: University Press, Book I. p. 54.
4. Seidman, Bianca. (September 22, 2015). "Drug price increases 5,000 percent overnight." *CBS News*, https://www.cbsnews.com/news/generic-drug-price-increases-5000-percent-overnight/.
5. Greenwald, B. and J. E. Stiglitz. (1986). "Externalities in economies with imperfect information and incomplete markets." *Quarterly Journal of Economics*. 101(2). pp. 229–64.
6. Harsanyi, John C. (1982). "A simplified bargaining model for the n-person cooperative game." *Papers in Game Theory*. Theory and Decision Library. Dordrecht, Netherlands: Springe. pp. 44–70.
7. Hardin, Garrett. (1968). "The tragedy of the commons." *Science 162(3859)*. pp. *1243–1248*.
8. Edwards, Phil. (February 3, 2016). "All 512 animals Teddy Roosevelt and his son killed on safari." *Vox.com*, https://www.vox.com/2015/7/29/9067587/theodore-roosevelt-safari.

14

MARKET STRUCTURES

Abstract

Concluding Part II about microeconomics are the topics of market structures and market failures. There are four general classifications of structure—and a comparison is both necessary and instructive. Competition involves two or more producers attempting to seize market share from the same finite group and the structure of a market determines how well any one participating producer will be able to accomplish this goal. Market failure refers to inefficiency and conflict of motives between individuals and a larger group.

The four market structures are: perfect competition, monopoly, oligopoly, and monopolistic competition. Each structure contains characteristics distinguishing the markets from one another and each contains clear advantages and disadvantages.

PERFECT COMPETITION

The concept of perfect competition describes conditions where many small producers compete. This leads to maximum possible output at the lowest possible price. Any one producer who raises prices will lose customers; and even with a higher price point, this leads to loss of market share and reduced profits. A producer who lowers prices will gain

additional customers from other higher-priced competitors for the same products or substitutes. However, lowering the price too far leads to net losses, and that cannot be sustained.

In some situations, lowering the price below cost is a strategy to gain greater market share. In the 1980s, Japan employed this strategy, called *dumping*, to dominate the computer memory chip (D-RAM) market at the expense of American companies. By 1986 the problem reached a peak and the United States imposed sanctions to end the practice:

> Commerce department officials argued that many memory chips were being sold at only 60 percent of their fair market value, based on the estimated production costs of the individual Japanese companies in the market. By June, that figure had risen to about 84 percent.[1]

Other than trade practices manipulating the market through dumping and other means, producers tend to see pricing as part of profit generation, rather than to unfairly seize larger market share. When one country imposes sanctions on another, it is a response to unfair practices. On a more localized level, the interaction between producer and consumer has an immediate effect if prices are unfairly raised (leading to reduced profits and loss of market share) or lowered (leading to larger market share but potentially net losses).

With perfect competition, prices are going to be set by consumer demand, and producers cannot influence how those prices are determined. Therefore, actions like dumping are destructive; it distorts how markets are expected to work. Consumers are price makers and the other side (producers, suppliers, wholesalers, and retailers) are price takers. This means that they do not set prices but must accept prices based on consumer preferences and levels of competition.

When perfect competition is the dominant market force, conditions are ideal in several ways and these conditions add to a healthy economy. All of these conditions must be in place at the same time to achieve a *perfect* market:

1. *A series of small producers compete with one another*: a market controlled by one or more large companies cannot be perfectly competitive. A larger producer can control prices through volume,

and that affects smaller firms. In 2016, Walmart's discounting policies and online sales had led to retailers cutting an estimated 44,000 jobs across the United States:

> Walmart's dominance has created an environment where it's difficult for retailers to compete in an overcrowded market. The issue is complicated by recent changes in the retail industry, with more shopping being done online—another factor that is creating more competition for retailers.[2]

In a robust economy, a greater number of small outlets is considered a healthy attribute of perfect competition. In the modern world of online sales and deep discounts, this model is disappearing in many areas.

2. *Substitution is easy*: products and outlets can be replaced without difficulty or sacrifice of price levels. This is also healthy because consumers have choice. If one store is remote and inconvenient, offers poor service, or fails to offer adequate variety and choice, consumers simply go to a different store.
3. *Entry and exit is simple*: competitors can easily enter the market as new participants or exit without significant loss. For example, opening a grocery store, clothing boutique, or computer repair shop normally are simple moves unless local licensing and regulatory restrictions are imposed. However, opening a new railroad is cost-prohibitive and the requirement of land rights, the cost of tracks and cars, and many other aspects of that business are significant barriers.
4. *Perfect information is available*: consumers can make valid comparisons in terms of price and quality among several products. This prevents producers from making untrue claims or promises.
5. *The market is efficient*: producers can offer products to customers at the lowest possible cost, and market prices are reasonable for both sides.

Perfect competition is characterized by these five attributes creating equilibrium or conditions close to equilibrium so that both sides—producers and consumers—are satisfied. Changes to price or quantity would be counterproductive and would destroy the equilibrium. None of

Theory of the second best
A theory explaining that when market distortions cannot be controlled directly in order to remove negative conditions, a second-best condition or outcome is the most desirable.

the participants in this market would be able to improve their situation without harming another participant.[3]

These are concepts only and not conditions that can ever be achieved in an ever-changing market. So why are they important? Markets that are assumed to be *perfect* set a standard or benchmark for measuring conditions. Comparison is the best method for judging conditions and outcomes. Remembering that efficiency is a desirable goal, the *theory of the second best* tells economists and others that when market situations cannot be controlled or remedied, the second-best outcome is the most desirable one.[4]

ASSUMPTIONS IN THE PERFECT MARKET

In perfect competition, a larger number of competing producers is viewed as a healthy condition. When this occurs, the overall market and a set of competitors perform as a sector rather than each producer acting individually. This brings order and predictability to the market.

Perfect competition requires equilibrium for producers as well as consumers—a general agreement about output and price. However, competitive forces constantly challenge this view of perfection and try to achieve an edge. This does not always result in a positive outcome. As previously demonstrated, if one producer raises prices, customers will promptly seek an alternative—either a substitute product or a different provider of the same product. The consequence of raising prices is loss of market share and profits.

Recognizing the value of equilibrium, a producer can compete in many ways beyond changing prices. For example, auto manufacturers and home builders compete within their industries by offering free extended warranties on newly offered products. This is a form of non-price competition. It allows a company to attract customers with a promise of quality and protection for the same price as a competitor who is offering

the product but without the extra protection. It has been proven to be such a good idea that virtually all auto manufacturers and home builders now offer free warranty contracts.

Even so, price dominates the concept of perfect competition. Taken to the extreme, perfect competition results in a zero profit margin. In this condition, competition must consist of a producer who is reducing prices; then all other producers will also lower prices to maintain competitive status. Eventually, all members of the sector will end up with a zero profit.

As a concept, perfect competition is interesting but impractical. As soon as any one competitor expands and increases volume of revenue, perfect competition will no longer be possible. Larger firms compete by offering discounts, and may even sometimes force competitors out of business. The examples of Walmart in suburban areas or of Amazon in the bookselling business make this point. Beyond discounted prices, perfect competition is also distorted when two competitors merge, creating a much larger single entity, perhaps one able to put many smaller competitors out of business completely.

For example, a chain of grocery stores merges with another of similar size and can discount prices on many levels. As a result, locally owned grocery stores and pharmacies lose large portions of market share and eventually are forced out of business.

The concept of perfect competition sets standards in a competitive world. However, other market structures are not subject to competitive forces.

THE MONOPOLY

A *monopoly* is a form of market structure in which one company operates an industry without any competitors. This form has a negative reputation and is viewed widely as an abusive and unhealthy economic system. However, there are instances in which a monopoly makes sense.

Monopoly
A market structure with a single company and no competitors.

A monopoly can reduce its supply of goods or services in order to drive up prices and increase profits. However, in that instance, consumers may purchase less, so that the potential for a

monopoly's profits is not unlimited. In practice, the opposite may occur, since:

> . . . monopolists typically increase prices by using political machinery to limit the output of competing products—usually by blocking low-cost substitutes. By limiting the supply of these competing products, the monopolist drives up demand for its own. Thus, in contrast to conventional theory, the monopolist actually produces *more* of its *own* product than it would in a competitive market, not less. But because production of the substitutes is restricted, *total* output falls.[5]

The size of a company is not a determining factor in whether a monopoly exists. In the 1920s, many industries were beset by monopolies large and small and even small companies often created negative response:

> It is the violation of no confidence to say that building construction has gotten into bad repute in this community. There was a general disposition to keep away from it as a thing diseased. Capital avoided it. The wise dollar preferred almost any other form of activity or no activity.[6]

The pricing power that is assumed to fall to the monopoly is limited by the market. Many monopolies that are granted through government regulation or legislation sell products and services, but if the price moves higher, consumers will buy less, reducing the monopoly's profits. This is the same economic force existing in other forms of the market. Consumers react to prices regardless of whether they are imposed by dozens of competitors or by one company.

The overriding attribute of a monopoly is its status as the sole company and existing barriers to entry. A monopoly holds power through regulation, high costs of operation for a new competitor, or even political power and influence. For example, a utility company may be granted an exclusive right to provide gas and electric services in a defined market. This is a sensible restriction because high capital costs make the monopoly a necessity. This is one form of monopoly.

Another form exists because one company owns the intellectual rights to its products and services. For example, the Microsoft Windows system

has control over most of the market of PC users. This is maintained because the cost of competing is high and development of a new and different system is prohibitive. The only way users can choose another system is to select the Mac system offered by Apple.

THE OLIGOPOLY

Oligopoly
A group of companies in an industry, competing with one another but preventing any new competitors from entry.

Contrasting a monopoly, an *oligopoly* is a group of companies working together to control a market and prices, and to prevent any new companies from entry. In this situation, the primary barrier to entry is the actions of the companies to maintain control. Even though members of an oligopoly compete against each other, they perceive an advantage in limiting the competition to their specific group.

Just as a monopoly cannot drive up prices indefinitely, the oligopoly is restricted by market forces. If prices go up, consumers buy less. Because of this, members of an oligopoly are likely to end up behaving in their own interests, lowering prices to take a larger market share. This violates the often unspoken agreement among the members to collude and keep prices high, but as markets resist, the tendency is for one or more companies to lower prices. This form of competition ultimately may destroy the oligopoly.

For example, auto manufacturing operates as an oligopoly. The process of making vehicles requires considerable investment in plants and machinery, expertise, and skilled labor. Suppliers are limited and often controlled by major manufacturers. Prices for finished products tend to be competitive within narrow bounds. A model of a given size and engine quality is likely to be priced similarly to the competitor's model. All manufacturers may also work with a single or limited numbers of suppliers for many parts. BMW experienced a shortage of steering gears provided by supplier Bosch GmbH in 2017 that created a slowdown in manufacturing. Ironically, the oligopoly of auto manufacturers may depend (for some parts) on a monopoly or oligopoly of suppliers:

> The hiccups in the normally smooth operation show how dependent manufacturers are on a global, smoothly running supply chain. Even small disruptions anywhere along the line can cascade into delays in getting the company's big money-making products off the assembly line and into showrooms.[7]

The potential for supply chain disruption resulting from this situation points out the flaws in a monopoly or oligopoly and the unhealthy consequences for the market. However, these consequences may be unavoidable due to external barriers to entry in many industries such as auto manufacturing and its suppliers.

MONOPOLISTIC COMPETITION

Monopolistic competition
A market structure with many competitors, offering similar products to the market with minor differences.

The fourth market structure is called *monopolistic competition*. This is a market structure with many competitors offering similar products or services; consumers benefit from the slight differences in products offered.

There are many examples of this type of market. For example, beauty supplies, restaurants, and health products function in an industry with many competitors. Each producer attempts to present its range of products in a way that consumers will prefer over a similarly priced competitor. A restaurant advertises specials and provides exceptional customer service; a brand of beauty products promises their facial cream will make you look younger; and an airline promises added leg room and reliable service; however, in all of these industries, differences in price and quality clearly are similar or identical, even though products are not always the same.

Monopolistic competition contains four specific attributes:

1. *Abundant number of competitors*: this market structure contains numerous competing companies.

2. *Price stability*: prices for products and services are also competitive. If any one company attempts to raise its prices, it would lose market share and profits due to the similarities among substitutes offered.
3. *Consumer awareness*: the buyer understands the differences among products, not only in terms of price but also for other features. In this market, brand loyalty often is an essential ingredient in maintaining market share.
4. *Low barriers*: in this market, barriers to entry and exit are low. This ensures a liquid and accessible market for the consumer; there is no shortage of choices.

The role of equilibrium in monopolistic competition relies on the curve of average revenue and average cost. The net difference between these two, multiplied by quantity, equals total profit. This is illustrated in Figure 14.1.

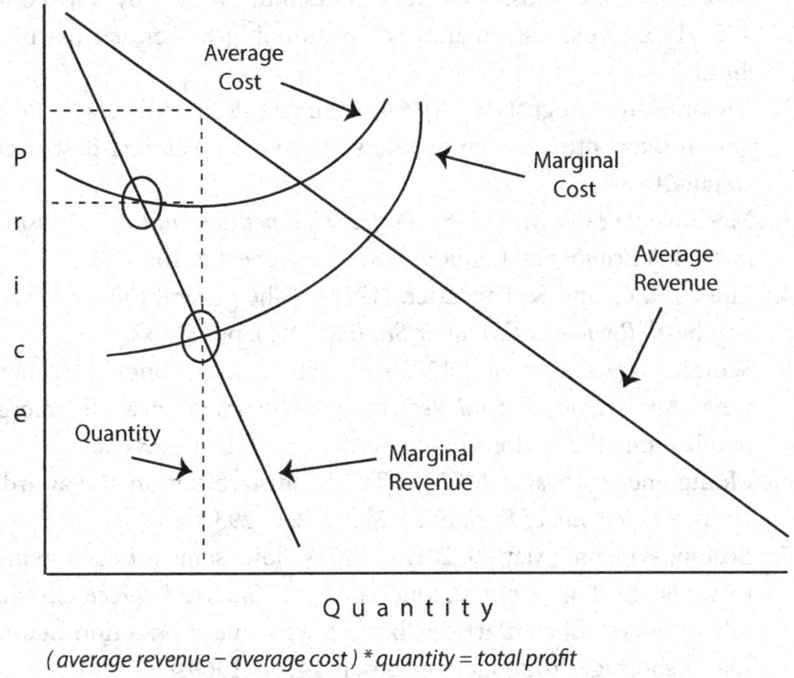

Figure 14.1 Equilibrium in monopolistic competition

This is different than the equilibrium analysis applied to perfect competition. The curves of marginal and average costs reflect the narrow profit margin characteristic of monopolistic competition. For the business owner who is involved in this market, awareness of how these curves evolve as markets grow (or shrink) is essential in order to anticipate future profitability.

Economists refer to this market structure as *imperfect competition* in contrast to stark differences in quantity and price seen in other markets, as well as in contrast to perfect competition. However, even though it may be imperfect, this form of market reflects reality more often than perfect competition.

ENDNOTES

1. Sanger, David E. (November 3, 1987). "Japanese chip dumping has ended, U.S. finds." *New York Times*, https://www.nytimes.com/1987/11/03/business/japanese-chip-dumping-has-ended-us-finds.html.
2. Taylor, Kate. (August 15, 2016). "Walmart destroyed retail." *Business Insider*, https://www.businessinsider.com/walmart-destroyed-retail-2016-8.
3. Machovec, Frank M. (1995). *Perfect Competition and the Transformation of Economics*. London, UK: Routledge. pp. 101–102.
4. Lipsey, R. G. and K. Lancaster. (1956). "The general theory of second best." *Review of Economic Studies*. 24(1). pp. 11–32.
5. Schmitz, James A. Jr. (July 12, 2016). "The cost of monopoly: A new view." *Minneapolis Federal Reserve*, https://www.minneapolisfed.org/publications/the-region/the-costs-of-monopoly-a-new-view.
6. Montgomery, Royal E. (1926). "The Landis arbitration and award." *University Journal of Business*. 4(3). pp. 260–293.
7. Boston, William. (May 29, 2017). "BMW slows some production due to parts shortage from supplier Bosch." *The Wall Street Journal*, https://www/wsj.com/articles/bow-slows-some-production-due-to-parts-shortage-from-supplier-bosch-1496071360.

Part III

Macroeconomics

15

GROSS DOMESTIC PRODUCT

Abstract

Macroeconomics is the study of overall national growth—covering several topics not on the individual level of businesses and consumers, but throughout an entire nation. A key indicator in macroeconomics study is gross domestic product (GDP), the dollar value of growth per year. However, this can be calculated in many ways and, contrary to popular belief, GDP is an estimate and not an exact value.

GDP is a key macroeconomic measure of the overall economy and how it is performing. It is the total value of goods and services produced and sold each year. This measurement can be computed in several different ways, making it confusing and not always comparable to past reports. GDP can be calculated based on production, income, or expenditure; it can also be represented as *nominal GDP*, used to not only calculate a nation's productivity, but also to compare to other countries. This version of GDP is based on current price levels and adjusts for inflation or deflation.

Gross domestic product (GDP)
The measurement of all goods and services produced and sold each year, as a measurement of economic health and improvement.

Complicating the formula for GDP, each segment of the economy is broken down and studied separately; and the sum of industrial GDP is

> Nominal GDP
> The measurement of GDP based on current prices, including adjustments for inflation or deflation.

calculated on a per capita basis to arrive at a mean standard of living. In other words, the complexities of calculation make GDP an estimate, not an exact outcome.[1]

However, even though GDP is the product of estimates, it provides an essential comparative statistic and outcome of a nation's economy. This sole economic value has been described as the *world's most powerful statistical indicator of national development and progress.*[2]

THREE WAYS TO CALCULATE GDP

In theory, calculations of GDP by production output, income, or expenditure should all end up with the same value or something very close. However, this is not always the case.

> Production approach
> GDP that is calculated as the sum of output by producers in all sectors of the economy.

The *production approach* adds all output by producers for all sectors of the economy. The *expenditure approach* counts production only to the extent that goods and services are sold to someone. And the *income approach* assumes that GDP is represented by the total of producers' income.

The production approach is the most direct method even though, given that some goods produced this year will remain in inventory, there are going to be inaccuracies. Offsetting this is the fact that some of last year's inventory would be sold in the current year. Overall, production should be very close to the expenditure version of GDP; and the income approach should also reflect the same dollar values. The three methods should not vary significantly from one another over a series of years.

The *production approach* has three steps:

1. Domestic output is estimated based on sector-specific market activity (including year-to-year changes in inventory levels).
2. The costs of materials, supplies, and other factors are estimated.

3. Cost of materials is subtracted from estimated output to obtain the value added or GDP in the annual economy. This value is also called *GDP* at *factor cost*.

The *income approach* is based on the total income of all producers in the economy. This method is termed gross domestic income (GDI). Although this should be the same number the production method yields, errors may distort the outcomes enough to make them slightly different. It equals all incomes paid for factors hired, including wages, interest, rent, and profits. Income, overall, is calculated in five classifications: wages paid for labor, profits earned by producers, interest and investment income, farm income, and non-farm unincorporated business income.

<u>Income approach</u>
GDP that is calculated as the total of all producers' income.

The *expenditure approach* is calculated as the sum of goods and services sold by producers. When goods are produced but not yet sold, an oddity in accounting rules defines these goods as those producers have bought for themselves. In other words, the expenditure approach counts all goods produced and should be identical to the outcome of the production approach.

<u>Expenditure approach</u>
GDP that is calculated as goods produced and sold.

In summary, the three methods for calculating GDP should all end up with similar values. Small inaccuracies are assumed so the three methods will not end up with the exact same GDP value, but over the years all should publish results that are reliable and close to one another.

GDP, calculated under any of the aforementioned methods, should come out to a reliable estimate based on the formula:

$$C + I + G - X = GDP$$

where: C = consumption
I = business investment
G = government expenditures
X = exports less imports

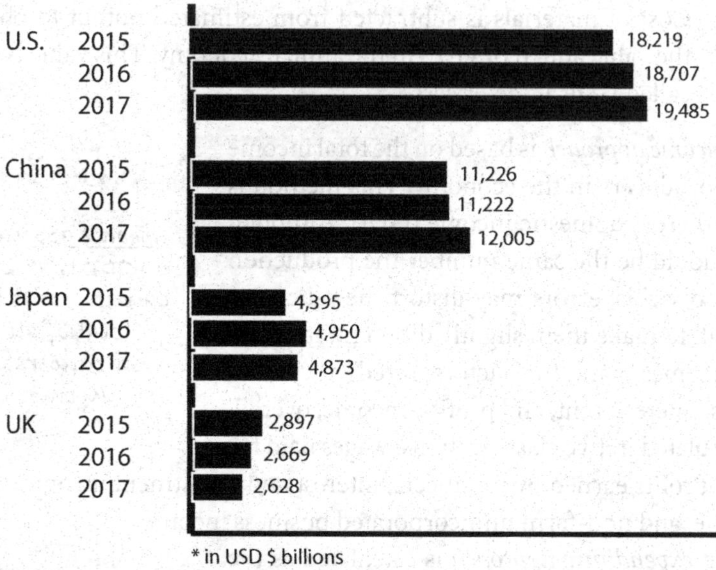

Figure 15.1 GDP by country, three years[3]

A comparison of GDP by country is useful as well because it reveals individual growth as well as comparative growth. Four of the world's largest economies (United States, China, Japan, and the UK) are summarized for three years on this basis in Figure 15.1.

Gross national income (GNI)
The summary of a country's growth based on activity within the country and including owners residing elsewhere.

GROSS NATIONAL INCOME (GNI)

The GDP of a country is widely understood as the growth of a nation's economy, separate from the economic status of other nations. Another indicator is a country's *gross national income (GNI)*, also called gross national product. This is a summary of ownership including those participants in a country located overseas. While GDP limits its analysis domestically; GNI is focused on location.

For example, the GNI for four countries in 2016 (latest reported data, in USD $ billions) was:

United States	18,968,714
China	11,154,194
Japan	5,096,371
UK	2,587,657[4]

The simplified calculation of GNI starts with GDP and adds income paid into a country by people and businesses in other countries; less payments made from the country to others outside of the country. It accounts for income from investments earned by outsiders and paid in, net of money moving out in the opposite direction. This is a crucial distinction from GDP, which is the market value of all goods and services produced domestically, but not adjusting for the movement of money between countries.

GNI is calculated from GDP, as:

$$GDP + FX = GNI$$

where *GDP* = gross domestic product
FX = net of income earned abroad by local citizens, minus income earned domestically by foreigners and shipped abroad

If all enterprises within a country were owned by citizens living in that country, GDP and GNI would be identical. GNI adjusts for citizens operating abroad, and for noncitizens operating locally. These variances can be significant when the levels of commerce between these groups are substantial. The United States used GNI as a primary measurement of production up until 1991 when it switched to GDP.[5]

LIMITATIONS OF GDP

Explanations of GDP are complex. Making the matter even more difficult to quantify, many groups have criticized the calculation because it does not consider the impact on the environment. However, this point of view ignores the facts: GDP is a measurement of results, not of cause

and effect. In some respects, proponents of clean policies often overlook, ignore, or downplay the importance of financial outcomes and trends.[6]

Another limitation of GDP analysis is the observation that higher levels do not translate in every case to improved standards of living. This has been true notably in many large economic sectors such as the healthcare industry. It may be that in many economic systems or in some countries, improvement in the GDP does not reach all economic sectors. However, this social issue is not a flaw in GDP or its calculation. It is a problem not directly related to economics, even though the effect is apparent. Income distribution is not even, and it must be kept in mind that GDP is both an estimate and an average, not a reflection of overall changes in living conditions.

The calculation is flawed and limited without doubt. It does not include unpaid work or black market transactions. These would be difficult or even impossible to accurately estimate, but the point is that reported, legal, and documented results represent only a portion of the entire economy. Estimates of these unreported economic values vary from as low as 15% of reported GDP in Canada, up to as high as 70% in the United Kingdom. In the United States, estimates are that between 20% and 50% of the true overall economy is unreported.[7]

These excluded goods and services are not limited to illegal or black market transactions. The value of unpaid household labor is a substitute for services that would have to be paid for if the person performing these services were not available. Making the accuracy of GDP even more difficult, suspicions are that some countries—such as China—inflate their GDP and overreport annual growth.[8]

ENDNOTES

1. Dawson, Graham. (2006). *Economics and Economic Change.* Upper Saddle River, NJ: FT Press. p. 205.
2. Lepenies, Philipp. (2016). *The Power of a Single Number: A Political History of GDP.* New York, NY: Columbia University Press. p. ix.
3. Chart prepared by the author, based on data from *Knoema*, https://knoema.com/aewtuqe/gnp-and-gdp-by-country.

4. *World Bank*, https://data.worldbank.org/indicator/NY.GNP.MKTP.CD.
5. Grimm, Brice T. (March 2, 2007). "The statistical discrepancy." *Bureau of Economic Analysis*, https://www.bea.gov/system/files/papers/WP2007-2.pdf.
6. Gertner, Jon. (May 13, 2010). "The rise and fall of GDP." *New York Times Magazine.*
7. Holcombe, Randall G. (2004). "National income accounting and public policy." *Review of Austrian Economics.* 17(4). pp. 387–405.
8. Ingraham, Christopher. (May 15, 2018). "Satellite data strongly suggests that China, Russia and other authoritarian countries are fudging their GDP reports." *SFGate*, San Francisco, CA.

16

UNEMPLOYMENT AND LABOR FORCE PARTICIPATION

Abstract

Among the macroeconomic measurements available, one of the most widely cited is the national unemployment rate. This single percentage is cited as evidence of presidential success or failure, policy decisions, and the shape of the future. However, unemployment involves more than the single percentage cited by media sources; the labor participation rate also should be tracked to understand the cyclical forces at work.

The *unemployment rate* is the percentage of people who are out of work but who are available to work and are looking for a job. The *labor force* is the combination of employed and unemployed people. And the *labor participation rate* is the percentage of the labor force who are currently holding a job or seeking a job.

These definitions explain the scope of the employment and unemployment picture. This is all reduced in media reports to the single *unemployment* percentage, but that often is not given in the true or accurate context of what is going on in a national economy.

> **Unemployment rate**
> The percentage of people available for work and currently looking for a job.

Labor force
The total number of employed and unemployed people.

Labor participation rate
The percentage of the labor force currently with jobs or actively seeking work.

Unemployment may also be reported inaccurately. For example, if the past month saw 200,000 new jobs created, how is that defined? Some sources count all jobs, including part-time work—and others report the equivalent of full-time jobs. For example, of those 200,000 new jobs created, if 50,000 were jobs of 20 hours per week (or approximately half-time), an accurate full employment report would list these as 25,000 equivalent full-time jobs. This means that rather than 200,000 new jobs, last month's full-time equivalent was 175,000.

A basic definition of the unemployment rate (*R*) is equal to the number of people currently looking for a job or unemployed (*U*), divided by the number of people in the labor force (*LF*):

$$U \div LF = R$$

However, this rate does not always translate to the opposite employment rate. If many jobs currently held are part-time, the distinction is an important one. The *underemployed* are people with jobs who are not working full-time or to their capacity. Among this group are many people who desire full-time jobs but cannot find them along with those who are working two or more jobs. This occurs when employers are required to provide benefits to anyone working more than a specified number of hours per week; those employers may hire many part-time workers in order to avoid providing health insurance, retirement, and other benefits.

Underemployed
People working part-time and those working beneath their capacity.

If an individual is underemployed, it is not accurate to count that as equivalent to a full-time job. If a person holds two part-time jobs and both are counted in the jobs number, it inflates the true number of currently employed people. Therefore, economists need two statistical tracking devices: the unemployment rate and the labor participation rate. The

former reports the percentage of people in the labor force not working. The latter tracks the percentage of those available to work, but not currently employed. Both should be reported to reflect the equivalent of full-time work; otherwise, the widespread hiring of part-time workers distorts both outcomes.

UNEMPLOYMENT AND ITS ECONOMIC AFFECTS

The unemployment rate—even though it is a simplified version of what is occurring—is used widely as a key metric for the economy. This is a valid form of simplification. Economists acknowledge that high or growing unemployment reduces demand domestically for goods and services. Fewer people are earning money, so demand falls.

Another consequence of high unemployment is reduction in import activity. With fewer people in the labor force who are able to earn money, demand for imports will fall. Due to overall economic weakness, exports also are likely to decline. A growing unemployment rate adversely affects domestic activity as well as international activity. It also decreases tax collections, so the government must reduce spending or operate with a deficit.

Unemployment is also used to make judgments about inflation. When unemployment declines, it translates into a shortage of workers for available jobs. This leads to higher wages offered; when labor is at a shortage, compensation rises, and that creates inflationary pressure. When unemployment is high, conversely, workers will accept lower pay in order to gain employment. Weakness in demand leads to stagnant or declining wages.

The impact of unemployment on the economy depends on the type of unemployment that is currently driving the economic engine. There are three primary types of unemployment in effect at any time:

> Structural unemployment
> A form of unemployment caused by replacement, reduction, or outsourcing of current jobs, or replacement of a labor force with robotics.

1. *Structural unemployment*: is a consequence of jobs being replaced, reduced, or outsourced. A lack of people with required skills also translates into structural

unemployment. A factor adding to structural unemployment is the growing usage of robotics, especially in manufacturing settings: "The rapid adoption of new technologies in the workplace, especially robotics and artificial intelligence, has motivated some researchers to determine what effects such technologies may have."[1]

2. *Frictional unemployment*: results when workers must seek employment based on their skills and experiences by moving elsewhere due to lack of jobs in one area.
3. *Cyclical unemployment*: results from economic changes, notably seasonal. For example, retail employers will hire workers for the holiday season and then lay off those workers when the season is over.

> Frictional unemployment
> A form of unemployment resulting from the need of workers to move in order to find work suitable for their skills when such positions are not available in their area.

> Cyclical unemployment
> A form of unemployment caused by seasonal changes in the business sector, resulting in temporary hiring and laying off employees.

The reported levels of unemployment are published with *seasonal adjustments* due to cyclical unemployment. These adjustments are made by the U.S. Bureau of Labor Statistics (BLS), which explains the nature and rationale for making adjustments:

> Over the course of a year, the size of the labor force, the levels of employment and unemployment, and other measures of labor market activity undergo fluctuations due to seasonal events including changes in weather, harvests, major holidays, and school schedules. Because these seasonal events follow a more or less regular pattern each year, their influence on statistical trends can be eliminated by seasonally adjusting the statistics from month to month. These seasonal adjustments make it easier to observe the cyclical, underlying trend, and other nonseasonal movements in the series.[2]

Additional distinctions in types of unemployment include *hidden* unemployment, the result of not counting people who have given up and are

no longer seeking work. Although still part of the labor force, the hidden unemployment of long-term workers means that in the statistics of the macro-economy, these people are no longer counted as unemployed.

Seasonal adjustments
The modification of reported unemployment to remove the influence of known seasonal changes in the economy.

Additional definitions of unemployment types also are found in economics literature. According to most government analyses, *long-term unemployment* is defined as when people have been looking for jobs for 27 weeks or more. This is a flawed descriptor, however. Some people search for jobs actively and try to find positions every day; others are more casual and less urgent in their efforts. The single 27-week definition does not distinguish between those types of long-term unemployed workers.

Long-term unemployment
Condition describing workers looking for jobs for 27 weeks or more.

The real unemployment rate includes three classifications:

1. Unemployed people who have not looked for jobs during the most recent four weeks but have tried to find work during the last 12 months.
2. All people who have given up looking for a job, defined as discouraged workers.
3. Those with part-time jobs who would prefer full-time jobs (the underemployed).

Real unemployment
A definition of unemployment as described by the U.S. BLS to include three categories of the labor force.

Under this definition, real unemployment is usually higher than the rate using different calculations. Most of those definitions ignore discouraged workers and drop them from calculations of the labor force; and consider part-time jobs as *jobs* for the purpose of calculating the number added in the economy. The real unemployment rate went as high as 16.4 percent on May 2009 during the 2008 to 2009 recession.[3]

High inflation, however it is measured, affects economic health. In addition to the obvious impact of unemployment on consumers and households, the social impacts of a country not using its labor resources effectively is a negative outcome of growing unemployment. Many take jobs beneath their skill level due to a lack of jobs, reducing economic efficiency. When unemployment reaches extreme levels, it can lead to political and social unrest.

IDEAL UNEMPLOYMENT LEVELS

Full employment
The condition in which everyone wanting a job has a job at a level of compensation that is acceptable.

Economists offer some idea about *ideal* employment levels. To many people, *full employment* means an unemployment rate below 5%. This level is accomplished when everyone who wants a job is able to find a job at a wage level that is acceptable. There will always be at least some people who will not accept jobs even when many jobs are available.

Why 5%? In order to be *full*, employment can never reach 100% because some members of the labor force are unemployable or simply do not want to work. The U.S. Full Employment Act (passed in 1946 and amended in 1978) defined full employment at no more than 3% unemployment for those aged 20 or older.[4]

There are two definitions as a result of the law and economic practice. Legislation defined *full employment* based on a percentage of current unemployment. Economists qualify this by specifying that work is available, and that jobs are held by all of those who *want* to work. The 5% rate is somewhat random, however, with many preferring to cite 1 to 2% unemployment—but this may exclude underemployment, the consequence of workers not being able to find suitable full-time work for their skill levels. A refinement of the definition of full employment is the level for which there is no cyclical unemployment.[5]

Economists would agree that some level of unemployment is *ideal*, although the level is not agreed upon by everyone. But is the

full-employment rate the same as an ideal rate? A distinction is made between full employment and another type—full employment without added inflation (the ideal rate). The *ideal rate of unemployment* can exist, at least in theory, when inflation does not rise consequently. This also has been called the non-acceleration inflation rate of unemployment or the inflation threshold. This is illustrated in Figure 16.1.

> **Ideal rate of unemployment**
> The unemployment rate that can be sustained without growth in inflation.

Three possibilities are considered in this analysis. It requires comparison between the long-run curves and short-run curves of unemployment. The long-run curve is assumed to remain unchanged and is represented by the vertical solid line. The initial short-run curve is revised, also

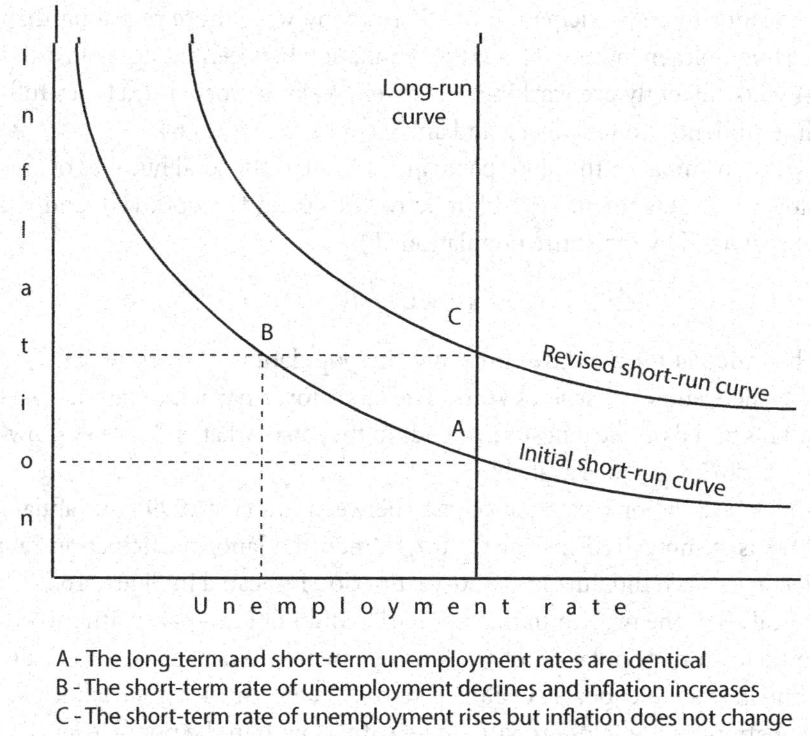

Figure 16.1 Ideal rate of unemployment (Prepared by the author)

changing the relationship between unemployment and inflation—and adjusting the ideal unemployment level to a different position.

Point A shows when the long-run and short-run unemployment rates are the same. If the short-run rate declines (point B), inflation increases. The ideal rate of unemployment is achieved when unemployment rises but inflation does not change—shown as point C.

The unemployment rate is used throughout the economy to judge trends and to determine whether matters are improving or deteriorating. However, in this process, the labor participation rate is often overlooked even though it may be even more revealing than the rate of unemployment.

THE LABOR PARTICIPATION RATE

The labor force participation rate is in many ways more revealing than the unemployment rate. This is the population between the ages of 16 and 64 who currently are working or actively seeking work. It excludes full-time students, homemakers, and anyone over the age of 64.

The formula for the labor participation rate is the total number of employed (*E*) plus unemployed but actively looking for work (*U*); and the sum divided by the entire population (*P*):

$$(E + U) \div P$$

This calculation measures not only the population of working age, but also the trend over several years. The labor force participation rate rises or falls based on the long-term trends in the job market and reveals growing or shrinking jobs available.

The U.S. labor participation rate between January 1999 and January 2018 is summarized in Figure 16.2.[6] When the labor participation rate declines—as it did during the 20-year period indicated in Figure 16.2—it reveals that the growth in the job market did not keep pace with growth in the overall population of working age people. Another factor is a decline in available jobs. A healthy economy is one in which the labor participation rate reflects growth in line with growth in the population. The unemployment rate only reports current conditions, whereas the labor

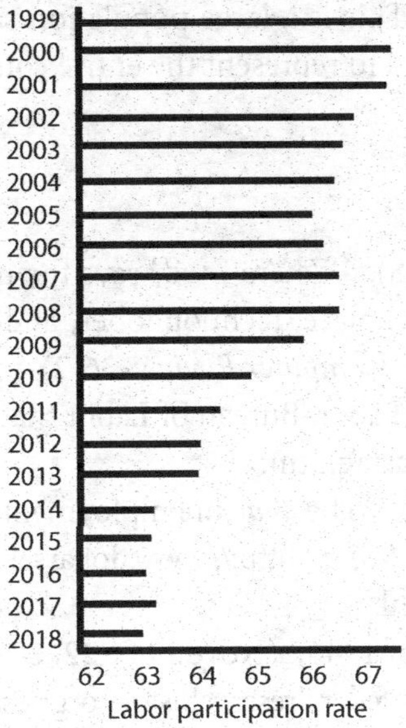

Figure 16.2 Labor participation rate (*Source*: U.S. BLS. www.bls.gov)

participation rate—when reviewed over many years—summarizes the trend in the job market.

The decline in labor participation further reflects a recessionary economy. The approximately 6% decline in labor participation from 1999 to 2018 appears as a broad recessionary job market. It is not a summary of the number of jobs available or created each quarter, as the unemployment rate reports, but rather the *rate* of increasing or decreasing job rates for a changing population. Although the labor participation rate fell by 6% in 20 years, the U.S. population grew to 329 million, a 17% increase over the 1999 population. If the labor participation rate had remained unchanged, it would reflect that jobs increased to keep pace with the working-age population.[7]

The government-published outcome for unemployment, labor participation, and other statistics are not exact numbers but estimates based on detailed statistical analysis. Unemployment is calculated as the result of a monthly survey. This Current Population Survey is conducted by the Census Bureau and evaluates approximately 60,000 households and a

total of 110,000 people. This is a large population sample and is drawn from every state, intended to represent the entire country.[8]

ENDNOTES

1. McClure, P. K. (2018). "'You're fired,' says the robot: the rise of automation in the workplace, technophobes, and fears of unemployment." *Social Science Computer Review*. 36(2). pp. 139–156.
2. U.S. Department of Labor, Bureau of Labor Statistics (BLS), https://www.bls.gov/cps/seasfaq.htm.
3. Miller, John. (2009). "The *real* unemployment rate hits a 68-year high." *Dollars and Sense*, http://www.dollarsandsense.org/archives/2009/0709miller.html.
4. "Employment Act of 1946," (November 22, 2013). *Federal Reserve History*, https://www.federalreservehistory.org/essays/employment_act_of_1946.
5. O'Sullivan, Arthur and Steven M. Sheffrin. (2003). *Economics: Principles in Action*. Upper Saddle River, NJ: Pearson Prentice Hall. p. 335.
6. U.S. Bureau of Labor Statistics, www.bls.gov.
7. U.S. Census Bureau, www.census.gov.
8. U.S. Census Bureau, Current Population Survey (CPS), www.census.gov/programs-surveys/cps.html.

17

INFLATION AND RECESSION

Abstract

Two forces control the macroeconomy in many respects and set up benefits or consequences for the microeconomy. These forces—inflation and recession—are constant forces in every economic system. *Inflation* is the increase in prices of goods and services caused by changes in supply and demand and in the producer's changes in the factor market. Recession is a change in the economy often described as the negative side of a business cycle in which economic activity declines.

Of all the forces affecting the economic health of a nation, inflation is often the most severe. In some extreme cases, inflation has gotten out of control and ruined an entire economy. Inflation is the rise in prices of goods and services; as prices move higher, consumers are forced to make choices. They may buy fewer goods at higher prices or seek cheaper alternatives. For producers, inflation has an equally devastating effect. Because consumers buy fewer goods, producers must decide whether they can afford to lower prices or settle for a lower volume of sales. As this occurs, the marginal cost declines, meaning that producers might not be able to cover their expenses.

Producers are also consumers. They buy materials and pay for labor. As the cost of these factors of production rise, producers must either pass costs along to consumers or seek alternative efficiencies to keep costs under control.

MYTHS ABOUT INFLATION

Many consumers and business owners believe they understand inflation—but they might not have it right. Several myths surround this topic.

For example, some people think that *inflation is not an especially important topic* and does not affect them. Even among new business owners, the idea persists that if costs rise, you simply pass on the higher costs to consumers. Although this is true to some extent, the economic reality remains: as prices rise, consumers buy less, and the consequence is less profit, not more. Underlying this reality is inflation. Although it is strictly defined as higher prices for goods and services, inflation also erodes the purchasing power of money.

For example, $100.00 in December 1998 had the same purchasing power as $153.28 in December 2018. Going all the way back to 1978, $100.00 at that time was equal to $371.10 at the end of 2018. This means that to buy the same goods in 2018 that you paid $100 for in 1978, you would need $371.10. Your dollar does not go as far due to inflation. (A free inflation calculator can be found at https://data.bls.gov/cgi-bin/cpicalc.pl?cost1=100.00&year1=197812&year2=201812.[1])

Inflation, in other words, has a very profound impact on producers and consumers. The related myth that rising costs can be passed on in higher prices ignores the economics of the situation. Consumers ultimately control prices based on how much they decide to buy, their ability to sacrifice or find substitutes, and in many cases the choice to do without.

Another popular myth is that *purchasing power does not have a direct impact* on how consumers or business owners behave; it is merely a statistic. In extreme cases, severe inflation not only impacts the ability to function within an economy, but it also adversely affects gross domestic product (GDP). For example, in 2015, Venezuela experienced a 160% increase in inflation; and in 2016, it went to 302%. In these same years and as a direct consequence, GDP declined by 6.2% and the following year by 6.5%. Due to the resulting decline in the value of Venezuela's currency (the Bolivar), the country's imports fell 23% in

2015 and 40% in 2016. By the first quarter of 2018, inflation had risen to a rate of 454%.[2]

For those who are used to 2 and 3% inflation and are unaware of the devastation that is possible, direct impact is easily minimalized. But it can be severe. For example, another myth is that *interest rates are raised or lowered as a result of inflation.* In fact, baseline rates are set by the Federal Reserve. Rates are changed due in part to inflation, but even more so by the Fed's desire to control inflation and keep it in check. To curtail growing inflation, the Fed (operating as the central bank of the United States) may increase rates, hoping this will cool down the rate of economic growth and inflation. Likewise, the Fed may lower the baseline rate when inflation is low, attempting to generate more economic activity. To a business owner, the Fed's attempt to control inflation may be disturbing because a pure economist would prefer that the basic forces of supply and demand would be allowed to operate freely and without government or central bank influence.

Yet another myth is that a *breakeven return on investments* is equivalent to the current rate of inflation. In other words, if inflation is 2.5% and an investment earns 3%, it beats inflation by 0.5%. This is not true. Because earnings are also taxed, the true breakeven rate must combine inflation and taxes. To compute the true after-inflation, after-tax breakeven rate, the current rate of inflation must be divided by the net after-tax income:

$$i \div (100 - E) = b$$

where i = rate of inflation
e = effective tax rate
b = breakeven yield

For example, assume that inflation is 2.5% and an individual pays a combined federal and state income tax of 35% (of taxable income). This is the effective tax rate. Breakeven yield is:

$$2.5 \div (100 - 35) = 3.85\%$$

If this individual earns 3%, they are losing 0.85% after calculating inflation and taxes.

Consumer Price Index (CPI)
A measurement of inflation, comparing current prices of a selected group of goods and services to their prices in the past.

Fixed basket
Any index that is used to represent a larger market, such as CPI.

Deflation
The opposite of inflation; annual reduction in prices of goods and services.

Disinflation
An alternate name for deflation.

CALCULATING INFLATION

The U.S. rate of inflation is based on the *Consumer Price Index* (CPI), published by the Bureau of Labor Statistics (BLS). CPI was computed from a base value of 100 at the beginning of 1982. Each year's calculated differences in price are calculated from this base.[3]

CPI is referred to as a *fixed basket* tracking index. This is because CPI is based on a fixed set of goods and services intended to represent the overall economy. This fixed basket includes goods such as milk, airline tickets, furniture, and gasoline, for example. Because a selected group of products is used to represent the entire economy, CPI is like the Dow Jones Industrial Average, which is made up of 30 stocks that are intended to represent the entire stock market of nearly 4,000 companies.

The following example shows how CPI calculates inflation. The index for 2016 was 240.0 and for 2017 it was 245.1. To find the annual inflation from these values, we must calculate the difference and then divide by the earlier index value:

$$(245.1 - 240.0) \div 240.0 = 2.1\%$$

Based on this, the 2017 inflation rate was 2.1%. The annual rates between 1982 and 2018 are summarized in Figure 17.1.

Besides inflation, a few other terms should be remembered. *Deflation* (also called *disinflation*), is a decrease in prices in any period. For example, in 2009, a year of deflation occurred at 0.4% below the previous year. In periods of deflation,

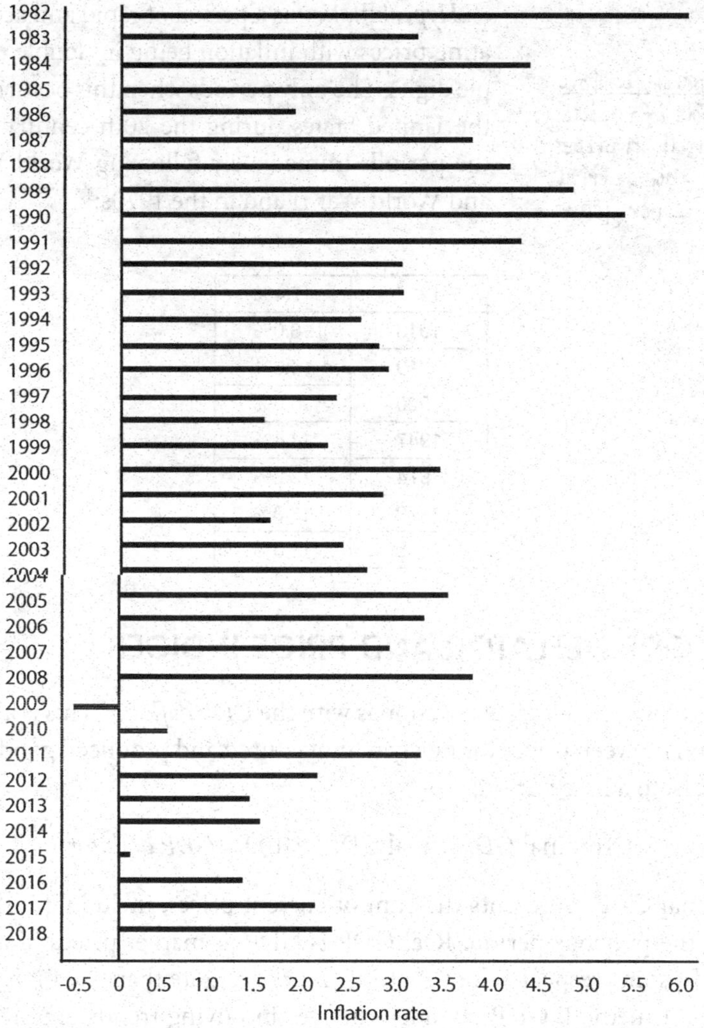

Figure 17.1 Annual rate of inflation in the United States (*Source:* Bureau of Labor Statistics, www.bls.gov)

consumers might spend less, expecting prices to move even lower. This leads to smaller GDP for the year of deflation and possibly for the following year as well. The United States experienced deflation during the Great Depression at a rate of 10.3% in 1932.

Hyperinflation
Periods of rapidly expanding prices in double or triple digits per year.

Hyperinflation is a period of rapid and accelerating prices with inflation being in double or triple digits. The only periods when this occurred in the United States during the 20th century were the periods immediately following World War I and World War II and in the 1970s:[4]

1917	17.4%
1918	18.0%
1919	14.6%
1920	15.6%
1947	14.4%
1974	12.3%
1979	13.3%
1980	12.5%

THE GDP DEFLATOR AND PRICE INDICES

Another way to calculate inflation is with the *GDP deflator*. This is a comparison between prices for newly manufactured and produced goods and services, to a base period:

$$(\text{Nominal } GDP \div \text{real } GDP) \times 100 = GDP\ deflator$$

Nominal GDP represents the sum of current prices, including inflation from the previous period. Real GDP is GDP at market prices of a base year. In some respects, the deflator is more accurate than the more popular CPI method. GDP includes changes in buying trends among consumers, whereas CPI is rigidly fixed to include only specified goods and services. Therefore, CPI might miss some price changes that significantly affect the health of the current economy. A counterargument to this is that CPI, due to its conformity to a preestablished basket of goods and services, is consistent and represents comparisons of the same inflationary trend over many years.

An alternative to CPI is a selective grouping of goods or services. Setting up a *price index* allows economists to judge limited sectors of the

economy. For example, a transportation company might be interested in tracking a price index of gas and oil companies to predict inflationary trends in its industry.

A *quantity index* calculates price changes between periods and includes prices based on different volumes of production. This can measure the effects of rising or falling production based on changes in demand as a symptom of business cycles and gradual economic trends.

Both price and quantity index calculations also contain limitations. Central banks and governments may rely on these to gauge the overall health of a national economy, which may lead to changes in taxation and interest rates, either of which may be used in an attempt to influence economic growth and momentum. Taxes or interest rates may be raised to slow down inflation by reducing GDP; alternately, taxes or interest rates may be lowered to encourage GDP growth. This type of government intervention in the markets, referred to broadly as *Keynesian economics*, is based on ideas promoted by British economist John Maynard Keynes in the 1930s. Keynes believed that stimulus spending by governments would influence activity, notably increasing demand among consumers and lead to a healthy economy.

Opposing this view, American economist Milton Friedman disagreed with Keynes. He promoted the idea of a free market economy. This was called the theory of *consumption function*.

These different economic points of view demonstrate the complexity of how matters like

Price index
An index of a limited grouping of goods and services to track inflation within one industry or sector versus the more generalized inflation represented by CPI.

Quantity index, also called a volume index
The quantity of goods produced during a period, reflecting price changes based on volume.

Consumption function
An economic theory developed by Milton Friedman that the free market works best without government influence.

GDP and inflation actually work on a national level. Of course, these vary based on methods of calculation, but the underlying concern is whether central banks and government can influence how consumers behave—and whether they should attempt to exert influence at all.

THE COST OF INFLATION

Even among those who understand inflation, the overall costs might not be entirely appreciated. There are many costs associated with rising prices. These include:

1. *Loss of purchasing power*: as prices rise, money does not buy as much. Reduced purchasing power is an attribute of higher prices that is often overlooked when studying inflation. Over many years, this can become significant. Both consumers and business owners suffer the long-term effects of inflation.
2. *Reduced GDP*: as inflation rises, goods and services become more expensive. Consumers spend less and real wages (after-inflation income) decline. This translates to reduced GDP.
3. *Loss in real value of savings*: consumers decide between spending and savings. But savings, often tucked away in a *safe* account, lose value even before calculating taxes when inflation is taken into account. For example, if inflation is 2.5% and a savings account pays 1.5%, the loss in real value is 1% per year.
4. *Increased unemployment*: inflation slows GDP, and this means employers hire fewer people and sometimes lay off current employees. With lower GDP, demand declines, thus employers need fewer employees.
5. *Greater chances of recession*: the business cycle will improve as long as inflation does not rise and when GDP climbs. However, when inflation does rise, GDP flattens out and the result may be a turn in the business cycle and the beginning of a new recession.
6. *Higher interest rates*: inflation has an often unrecognized impact on lenders. As purchasing power declines, it translates to lower profits for lenders, therefore interest rates are raised. This affects variable rate borrowers as well as business owners who are seeking

debt capital to expand their businesses. Higher interest rates have a dampening effect on business growth. Some are helped by inflation. Homeowners with fixed rate mortgages can repay the debt with cheaper, devalued money. Governments also benefit from inflation for the same reason—they can repay federal debt with cheaper money.

7. *Lower competition overseas*: because the prices of goods and services increase and cause inflation, exporting activity becomes less competitive. For many business owners who are working only domestically, this is not always acknowledged as an impact of inflation. However, it does have an impact; lower exports mean an overall decline in business activity.
8. *Uncertainty*: among the most serious consequences of inflation is the uncertainty about future prices and economic health. This directly affects profit margins expected in the near and far future. Consequently, businesses are not likely to invest in expanded inventories, additional outlets, capital assets, or hiring more people. The expectation of a downturn directly affects behavior among both consumers and business owners.

Deflation also has immediate and direct impacts on businesses and consumers. If prices move lower, consumers may delay purchasing decisions in a belief that future prices will be even lower. This means demand falls, leading to higher unemployment and a reduction in the amount of wages that employers are willing to pay their labor force.

INFLATION AND EXPECTATIONS

Inflation is not universal. It refers to a general or average increase in prices for goods and services. However, some prices rise and others fall, but inflation measures only the average. For example, air travel may be more popular than automobile travel due to rising costs of gasoline as well as the need to buy meals and stay in hotels. As a result, air fares are driven upward. That is inflationary to the extent that people will pay more for airline tickets. However, due to less auto trips, lower-cost hotel

Adaptive expectations Types of expectations about future inflation based on past rates and a belief about their effect on the future.

rates may decline. That deflation is likely to be absorbed in the overall inflation rate and is not counted separately.

People develop a set of expectations about inflation. As they notice prices rising for food, gasoline, utilities, and other goods, they are likely to expect continued growing prices into the future. These *adaptive expectations* track a prior set of prices that consumers thought would happen in the future against the actual rate that occurred. In comparison, *rational expectations* reflect estimates of future inflation without bias, and are based on the ideas proposed by American economist John F. Muth:

> Muth's notion was that the professors, even if correct in their model of man, could do no better in predicting than could the hog farmer or steelmaker or insurance company. The notion is one of intellectual modesty. The common sense is *rationality*: therefore, Muth called the argument *rational expectations*.[5]

These distinctions are important because they determine how consumers and business owners behave. If a business owner subscribes to the adaptive model, it would be assumed that if last year inflation grew by 5%, the coming year should also expand by the same rate. However, if that business owner applied rational expectations, an estimate would be based on observation of current price trends without regard to past inflation.

Rational expectations Types of expectations about future inflation assuming experts were no better at estimating the future than anyone else capable of rational thought.

Expectations are reflected in how central banks adjust interest rates. When the expectation is that inflation is growing, higher interest rates *should* slow down inflation as the argument goes. That is a Keynesian approach to the issue of business cycles—that expectations can be controlled or altered by intervention. The opposite belief states that business cycles occur naturally

and should be left alone without attempts to intervene. Under this theory, inflation and deflation are likely to occur as part of the business cycle and not as the result of government or central bank controls.

CHALLENGES IN MEASURING INFLATION

The objective measurement of inflation demands that we make distinctions between changes in price (in the case of CPI, price refers to a set basket of goods and services) and in the price shifts that are a result of changes in value.

The changes in value are likely to result from adjustments in the volume of production, the levels of quality or performance, and improved production processes resulting from inventions in technology. The resulting price shifts—whether rising or falling—are not products of inflation, but the results of noninflationary changes.

In price index accounting for inflation (as in the case of CPI, for example), the starting and ending price levels are determined by application of a weighted average. This is the result of multiplying the unit price for each component by the average number of products being purchased by consumers. Because the results are generated through surveys of households thought to be typical of the overall market, index-based versions of CPI are statistical estimates and not exact values. The calculation also varies by the base year employed.

> **Base effect**
> The effect on current inflation calculation when the base year in the comparison is exceptionally high or low. The effect may overstate or understate current inflation.

The outcome of measuring inflation with weighted averages is affected by the *base effect*, the influence of inflation during the selected base period. For example, if the base year's inflation was unusually low, the current rate may be overstated; or if the base year's rate had spiked above the average, the current year may be understated.

The problem of measurement often leads to modifying inflation as reported due to perceived base effects on outcomes. The rationale for adjustment is that the measurement must be changed from time to time to keep pace with changing

market preferences. However, the fact that CPI and other measures are not precise, but are based on statistical estimates, reveals the difficulty in measuring this important economic indicator. It is *not* the last word in how inflation affects consumers or business owners, and it is never an exact factor in the economy.

> <u>Seasonal noise</u>
> The periodic distortion of inflation caused by a change in buying activity identified as seasonal.

Adjustments may be made to what is considered a *typical* consumer, to the basket of goods and services, or to the method of weighting specific components. In other words, the calculation of inflation contains many variables. This means not only that it lacks precision, but also that the outcome itself can be changed and rationalized at any time. Another form of adjustment is the seasonal adjustment to inflation known as *seasonal noise*. The intention of seasonal adjustment is to remove the seasonal impact of higher or lower activity among consumer buying. The same type of adjustments called *statistical noise* are made in the reporting of unemployment rates and other cyclical changes.

THEORIES OF INFLATION

> <u>Triangle model</u>
> A Keynesian explanation of inflation, consisting of three distinct causes.

The previously mentioned Keynesian theory of economics claims that inflation results from economic pressures, either from the demand side or the supply side. Under this theory, three types of inflation are identified, collectively referred to as the *triangle model*.[6] The demand-pull version is inflation that is caused by government and business spending, which creates economic growth through excess demand. The cost-push form of inflation results from reduction in supply, which in turn creates higher prices resulting from increased scarcity. And *built-in inflation* is created when wage earners seek income to keep up with inflation that is perceived to occur from outside influences, but instead creates inflation

on its own, setting up a circular effect (fear of inflation creates more inflation, which in turn sets up more fear).

Contrasting Keynesian economic theory is *monetarism*. Economists who subscribe to this view believe that a growing or shrinking money supply is the primary cause of inflation or deflation, and that a free market economy is the path to a strong economy. Milton Friedman makes a case for this theory in observing the economic contraction of the Great Depression and blaming it on the abandonment of strong monetary policy:

> **Built-in inflation** A form of inflation created when wage earners fear inflation and seek higher income, creating a circular effect of ever-higher inflation.

> The contraction shattered the long-held belief, which had been strengthened during the 1920s, that monetary forces were important elements in the cyclical process and that monetary policy was a potent instrument for promoting economic stability. Opinion shifted to the opposite extreme—that money does not matter, that it is a passive factor that chiefly reflects the effects of other forces, and that monetary policy is of extremely limited value in promoting stability.[7]

Another concept is called the *Austrian School*. This theory blames inflation on differences among markets when newly created money and credit are introduced to the market. This theory was developed by Austrian-American economist Ludwig von Mises. He stated that inflation should be measured as an increase (or decrease) in quantities of money not offset by the need for money. Price inflation results from this disparity. Mises explained inflation in terms of increases in the money supply:

> **Austrian School** An economic theory stating that inflation results from the introduction of money and credit when the quantity of money is not offset by a demand for money (resulting in inflation).

> "In theoretical investigation there is only one meaning that can rationally be attached to the expression Inflation: an increase in the quantity

of money (in the broader sense of the term, so as to include fiduciary media as well), that is not offset by a corresponding increase in the need for money (again in the broader sense of the term), so that a fall in the objective exchange value of money must occur."[8]

The many different points of view about the causes of inflation demonstrate the complexity of this topic. Not only is its calculation elusive and the result of estimates (meaning there is no definitive or exact rate of inflation), but its causes are debated among Keynesian, monetarist, and Austrian theories.

For the business owner, this means that inflation must be viewed with the knowledge of how inexact it is. The effects clearly are felt by every business, and the struggle between prices and profitability in a competitive market are unavoidable.

RECESSION

Recession
A period of negative GDP in the economy.

Closely related to inflation is the cyclical trend known as *recession.* This is the condition when an economy suffers from negative GDP. It is a natural part of the business cycle, and it may be brief (lasting only a few months) or extended (several years).

The free market economist has faith in the business cycle and believes that if left alone, the economy will return to growth. Keynesian economists believe that government intervention is necessary to control recession and the related effects of inflation on the behavior of GDP. Definitions vary; one popular description of recession is negative GDP for two or more fiscal quarters.[9]

Governments often believe they can control the economy and prevent or reduce recession. Actions include lowering taxes, enacting stimulus spending, and encouraging demand through changes in regulation. Central banks try to end recessions by making changes in interest rates and the money supply. Efforts by governments and central banks often fail to achieve the desired outcomes and may make matters worse.

Attributes of recession include outcomes beyond reduction in GDP. Consumption is also likely to fall during recessions, as well as investment activity and net exports. If a recession exceeds a 10% decline in GDP or lasts longer than four years, it is defined as a *depression* in the economy.

Depression
A severe extension of recession of 10% or more negative GDP or lasting more than four years.

Recessions create fear and apprehension among business owners and consumers. Despite attempts by the government to stimulate the economy during a recession, this generalized dread about the economy is difficult to end. Business cycles tend to move through their upward and downward movements in their own time and cannot be rushed. A business owner responds to a recession (or anticipation of a recession) by reducing the employee force and saving available profits rather than investing in higher inventory levels. These defensive moves are natural responses to a downturn but may also create longer recessions.[10]

In a similar vein, consumer confidence falls in a recession, so that people buy fewer goods and may elect to save rather than to spend, anticipating the need for cash in the future. The consumer's apprehension about investing or spending is often reflected in the stock market. Many past recessions have been preceded by weakness in the markets by a few months up to a year before the recession is recognized officially; but the record is not conclusive. Since 1948, ten recessions were forecast by stock market declines, but 10 other declines did not lead to recessions.[11]

Some recessions also are anticipated by a weakening real estate market. However, the correlation between weak real estate trends and economic recessions is not precise since real estate weakness can last longer than a recessionary cycle.[12]

Recession, like inflation, cannot be simplified by pointing to any one cause. It is part of the business cycle described in the upcoming chapter; however, governments and central banks, believing in their own power and influence, defy the business cycle and continue to believe that their actions and decisions can control all aspects of the economy.

This assumption—held not only by governments and central banks, but also by many economists—contains three parts: (1) governments are

well-equipped to evaluate business failure and to judge efficiency; (2) governments are more qualified than the private sector to establish market efficiency through adjustments; and (3) the motive by government to fix economic problems is altruistic and not based on self-interest or a desire for more power. This belief was explained by South Korean economist Ha-Joon Chang, as an idea that it is "assumed the state knows everything and can do everything."[13]

Most economists, like most business owners, reject this theory, especially if they have had dealings with the government and have seen how inept agencies can be at addressing the most basic of business problems.

ENDNOTES

1. Bureau of Labor Statistics (BLS), https://data.bls.gov/cgi-bin/cpicalc.pl?cost1=100.00&year1=197812&year2=201812.
2. Gupta, Girish. (April 11, 2018). "Venezuela inflation 454 percent in first quarter: National Assembly." *Reuters*, https://www.reuters.com/article/us-venezuela-economy/venezuela-inflation-454-percent-in-first-quarter-national-assembly-idUSKBN1HI2MO.
3. Bureau of Labor Statistics (BLS), https://www.bls.gov/cpi.
4. Ibid.
5. McCloskey, Deirdre N. (1998). *The Rhetoric of Economics*. 2nd ed. Madison, WI: University of Wisconsin Press. p. 53.
6. Gordon, Robert J. (1988). *Macroeconomics: Theory and Policy*, 2nd ed. New York, NY: McGraw-Hill. Chapter 22.4.
7. Friedman, Milton and Anna Jacobson Schwartz. (1963). *A Monetary History of the United States, 1867–1960*. Princeton, NJ: Princeton University Press. p. 300.
8. Mises, Ludwig von. (1963). *The Theory of Money and Credit*. New Haven, CT: Yale University Press. p. 240.
9. Shiskin, Julius. (December 1, 1974). "The changing business cycle." *The New York Times*.
10. Samuelson, Robert J. (June 14, 2010). "Our economy's crisis of confidence." *The Washington Post*.

11. Siegel, Jeremy J. (2002). *Stocks for the Long Run: The Definitive Guide to Financial Market Returns and Long-Term Investment Strategies.* 3rd ed. New York, NY: McGraw-Hill. p. 388.
12. Shiller, Robert J. (June 7, 2009). "Why home prices keep falling." *The New York Times.*
13. Chang, Ha-Joon. (1994). *The Political Economy of Industry Policy.* London, UK: Macmillan. p. 25.

18

THE MACROECONOMICS BUSINESS CYCLE

Abstract

The interaction of economic activity, from growth (boom) to stagnation (recession), defines the range of changes and the overall business cycle. This cycle is characterized by fluctuations in the gross domestic product (GDP), establishing trends in either direction. Although the phases of the business cycle are predictable, the timing and duration of each phase are not. Some business cycles may occur within a matter of months, whereas other cycles last for many years.

The *business cycle* is the trend of expansion and contraction in the economy as GDP moves over time, either increasing during times of growth or declining during weaker times. This cycle is a naturally occurring series of changes in economic growth.

> **Business cycle**
> The constantly evolving status of the economy and its expansion or contraction as the GDP moves over time.

The role of business and government within the business cycle is debated endlessly. The government and central bank attempt to control the business cycle through regulation, taxing policy, and interest rates. Some economists believe this is the proper role of government. Others believe business should be largely left alone and

allowed to function within the business cycle with little or no governmental interference.

PHASES OF THE BUSINESS CYCLE

Peak
The top level of the business cycle, when economic activity has expanded to a high level.

Trough
The bottom level of the business cycle, when economic activity has declined to a low level.

The business cycle moves through distinct phases. In a normal series between *peak* and *trough*, the cycle moves from expansion to recession. In an extreme version of a recession, in which the economy declines severely, a depression may result, ending only when a recovery (new expansion) occurs. These phases are illustrated in Figure 18.1.

The expansion is characterized by increasing employment, producer income and volume of output, increasing wages, and robust demand for goods and services. On the consumer side, demand grows, and so does investment as higher wages provide more flexibility in both spending and savings.

At the peak of the business cycle, expansion has been exhausted and the maximum degree of growth has been reached. The momentum of expansion slows, and the healthy indicators slow down and then stop.

In a recession, demand slows down and then declines with increasing acceleration. Producers tend to continue increasing output at first, not realizing that the economy has peaked and turned. This creates excess supply in the market. Consequently, prices begin to fall as consumer demand is reduced. Revenue falls and wages follow. Employers may lay off employees, creating growing unemployment. In a severe recession, these trends continue in severity as well as time, creating a period of depression.

A trough is the bottom level of the cycle, when the negative attributes of recession slow down and then end. Both demand and supply reach a low point and the decline is reflected in slow or negative growth in GDP.

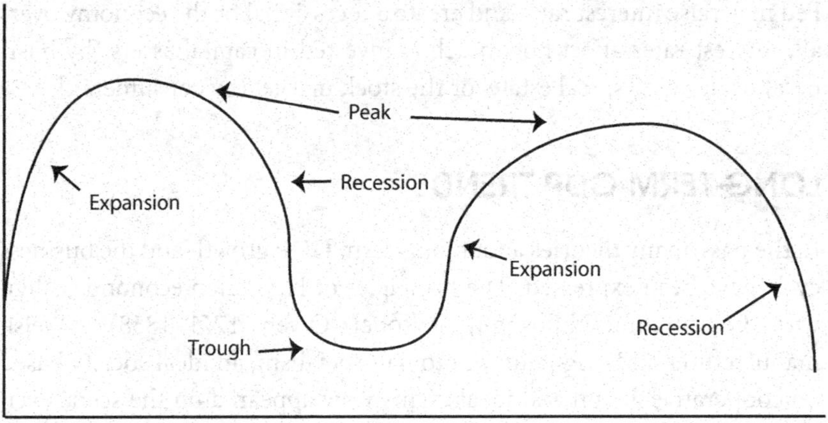

Figure 18.1 Business cycle and its phases

After the trough, a new period of expansion begins, and the business cycle is repeated.

UNDERLYING CAUSES OF THE BUSINESS CYCLE

In an ideal world, cycles would not occur at all. Full employment and equilibrium would be established and then could remain without change. However, cycles do occur for several reasons, all of which are predictable.

These cycles are created by many factors, including increased spending by consumers (creating higher demand), which also affects prices. Expansion is also caused by government spending on social programs, national defense, and other budget items. If this spending is not matched with savings elsewhere or changes in tax levels, it creates inflation. On the opposite side, when consumers and governments reduce levels of spending, the economy slows down and moves into a recession. Just as expansion is optimistic, a recession is characterized by pessimism among consumers and producers.

The cycle is also influenced by policies of the central bank. If the Fed attempts to control the cycle by raising or lowering interest rates, money supply changes and so does the cycle—often with unintended consequences within the economy. For example, to slow down inflation, the

Fed may raise interest rates and create a recession. For the economy overall, interest rates affect how much is invested in capital assets (by business) or in savings, real estate, or the stock market (by consumers).[1]

LONG-TERM GDP TRENDS

In the past, many theories about long-term GDP growth and the business cycle have been expressed. The principles of Keynesian economics align with the economic philosophy of Robert Owen (1771–1858), a Welsh manufacturer and originator of utopian socialism, an ideal society based on cooperative action and ideals. This view appeared on the scene even before Karl Marx and his socialist movement.[2]

The importance of Owen's socialist view is its evolution to Keynesian thinking. Owen was criticized during his lifetime by those arguing that the utopia Owens envisioned would result in greater poverty and that the cooperative requirement would turn the economic world into a singular workshop in which people were forced to work for the common good and not to pursue their individual interests.

During Owen's lifetime, economic cycles were believed to be caused solely by a combination of overproduction and under-consumption (in other words, disequilibrium). Owens, like Keynes, later favored socialism as the solution and promoted government intervention to control business cycles. These ideas became the core of Keynesian economics in the 1930s and to the modern era—many economists subscribe to this idea.

Contradicting socialism and government intervention to control the cycles, the major influence on economic growth has been improvements in technology. Today, business cycles are recognized by most economists as caused by a complex set of variables, but it is free enterprise and not government control that determines economic growth and GDP advancement.

However, in some economic theories, economic fluctuation is studied rather than the more rigid business cycles. This point of view sees the concept of a *cycle* as less descriptive than the fluctuations occurring increasingly as cause and effect of economic conditions, but not cyclical in any sense.[3]

Keynesian economists state that government regulation and oversight is essential in order to avoid a series of business cycles and resulting crises. Free market advocates state that interference by the government in the business cycle tends not to control negative outcomes, but to make them worse, or even to cause them. Keynesian economics became the *norm* after the Great Depression of the 1930s but tends to fall out of favor as economic conditions improve. The Keynesian theory was rekindled after the recessionary period that began in 2007. It appears that the view favoring government intervention is most likely during periods of recession, whereas free market economics is favored during times of expansion.

BUSINESS CYCLES AND THE PURPOSE OF MACROECONOMICS

The primary opposition to Keynesian economics is the Austrian School theory. Under this economic theory, business cycles are created by excessive credit issued by banks and by central banks moving interest rates too low. The consequential expansion of the money supply creates misallocation of resources in the economy, and the artificially created economic boom is inevitably followed by a bust. This is characterized by investments being sold at a loss and contraction of the money supply.

Both Keynesian and Austrian views are at the extreme, and most economists view the business cycle in between the two. Governments do intervene and often harm the economy, and this is not a way to control the business cycle. At the same time, some regulatory oversight is necessary to prevent uncontrolled inflation or recession, but the business cycle tends to operate best when markets are free to compete.

Observing that most economists think in between the extremes, the argument comes back to the purpose of macroeconomics in the business cycle. By testing whether economic health is improving or declining, economists can see how the behavior of businesses and governments cause the trends and react to them. With this information in hand, economists may work with business owners to foresee economic change and

to take actions designed to identify effective decisions in the segments of the business cycle.[4]

THE PRODUCT-BASED BUSINESS CYCLE

One theory, the *product-based business cycle*, sees cyclical movement in the economy as the direct result of the life cycle of products in the market. As products are introduced and gain popularity, the economy expands; and as products move out of favor, the economy loses steam and contracts.

This idea cannot be applied within an economy because many products circulate at any given time and will not tend to find or lose favor at the same time. It can be applied to nations on a macroeconomic basis, however. Developed nations have the capital to invest in development of new products and technology; less developed nations cannot match this investment level and tend to focus on the marketing of existing products. Businesses must keep pace with newly developed technology and products or they lose their ability to compete.

The product-based cycle is only partially valid. It identifies how businesses compete or fail to compete; however, products are marketed continuously and not cyclically. Therefore, this theory may explain why some businesses compete and thrive, while others fail to compete and fall behind. However, this concept does not explain how the business cycle behaves on a macroeconomic basis.[5]

This theory is appealing because it simplifies the causes of the business cycle and is easily understood. However, the impact of products and technology does not occur in a cyclical manner. The true causes and effects of the business cycle are more complex. These causes include government and central bank policies; changes in regulation, interest rates, and taxes; hiring trends among businesses; international trends in inflation and export/import activity; and political influence, to name a few. The larger picture of business cycles is more complex and may further represent the mood of a population. An optimistic consumer is confident enough to increase spending, creating higher demand and profits for producers. A pessimistic consumer is apprehensive and reduces spending in favor of a more defensive position. This decline in demand lowers producer profits.

The causes of consumer moods may take many forms, often political or geopolitical in nature.

The overall causes and consequences of business cycles (or fluctuations) cannot be comprehended as a singular set of events or conditions; and although the cyclical movements are observed in hindsight, they cannot be simplified or explained as belonging to any one reason for movement. The course of a cycle is predictable, but its duration and combination of causes cannot be known accurately.

ENDNOTES

1. Romer, Christina D. (September 1994). "Remeasuring business cycles." *Journal of Economic History*. 54. pp. 573–609.
2. Draper, Hal. (1990). *Karl Marx's Theory of Revolution, Volume IV: Critique of Other Socialisms*. New York, NY: Monthly Review Press. pp. 1–21.
3. Mankiw, Gregory. (Summer 1989). "Real business cycles: A new Keynesian perspective." *The Journal of Economic Perspectives*. 3(3). pp. 79–90.
4. O'Sullivan, Arthur and Steven Sheffrin. (2003). *Economics: Principles in Action*. Upper Saddle River, NJ: Pearson Prentice Hall. p. 57.
5. Vernon, Raymond. (May 1966). "International investment and international trade in the product cycle." *Quarterly Journal of Economics. 5*. 80(2). pp. 22–26.

19

CONSUMPTION VERSUS SAVINGS

Abstract

The natural conflict between consumption and savings describes an aspect of economic behavior that evolves as disposable income increases or decreases. The propensity to consume or to save further influences the overall economy and the multiplier effect, which is the tendency for one form of behavior to create and promote secondary activity. These economic behavior propensities are analyzed on a macroeconomic basis although the components of each attribute occur individually among consumers, business owners, and producers.

Consumer behavior is a topic of continuous study among economists. The reason for this focus is clear: consumers tend to apply available income in one of two primary ways—consumption and savings. The decision to favor one or the other defines how the overall economy behaves.

MARGINAL PROPENSITY TO CONSUME

The *marginal propensity to consume* (MPC) is an economic principle observing that as *disposable income* grows, consumers tend to also increase spending. The degree to which this occurs is the propensity to consume; and the level of additional income spent is the marginal

Marginal propensity to consume (MPC) The level of additional spending that occurs per each added dollar of disposable income.

Disposable income The level of net income available after needed expenses that may be spent or saved.

propensity to consume. For example, in one family, an additional dollar of disposable income generates added spending of 85 cents. The MPC in this example is 0.85.

This is an analysis of behavior. What does the average consumer do with added dollars of disposable income? When someone receives a raise in monthly pay, the propensity to increase consumption is a clear attribute among consumers; but it may not be at 100%—meaning some portion of disposable income will be saved or invested. In some cases, consumers may consume more than 100% of newly acquired disposable income. This requires reduction of savings and investments or taking on added debt. The *consumption function* is shown in Figure 19.1.

The MPC is a ratio between changes in consumption and changes in disposable income.

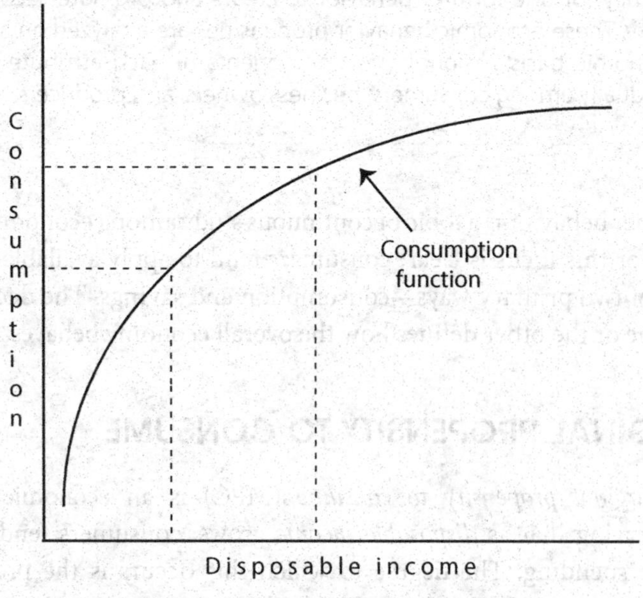

Figure 19.1 Consumption function

It is not specifically limited to a ratio between zero and 100. If the consumer spends more than the disposable income, it represents a decrease in previously accumulated savings; and if a consumer reduces the level of consumption below zero, that reduced level creates a minus, or negative MPC. Consumption above available disposable income, also called *autonomous consumption*, tends to occur despite limitations of income. It is accommodated by eroding savings or increasing debt.[1]

Autonomous consumption
Levels of consumption above disposable income, thus creating a negative savings or increase in debt.

Breaking the disposable income level into two parts (consumption and savings) is a simplification of what is done with disposable income, but it is an effective formula that is used to understand how consumers behave when their disposable income rises. But what happens if disposable income falls? Economists (especially Keynesian economists) believe that as a generalization, when disposable income falls, consumption does not also fall. Consumers tend to reduce savings levels to compensate for less disposable income, rather than spending less. There is a two-part analysis at work. If disposable income rises, spending also rises. If disposable income falls, spending does not change.

Changes in interest rates would initially be thought to affect the MPC; but it does not. If interest rates are lowered, consumers have less incentive to save, so consumption may consequently rise. If interest rates rise, consumers can save less and still reach a future goal for savings levels (higher interest compounded over many years equals larger savings balances).

MPC VARIANCES BY STANDARD OF LIVING

MPC does not follow a predictable course. Tendencies for the use of disposable income vary based on wealth—not only for individuals but for entire nations as well.

MPC tends to be higher among poorer countries, and lower among richer countries. The cost of basic needs (versus wants) will be a lower overall percentage of total income when income levels are higher, so with

more disposable income available, the decision to save is easier. Consumption wants can be satisfied at a lower overall ratio of disposable income. For poorer nations, this margin is much smaller, so MPC is greater.

From the business owner's point of view, focusing on one socioeconomic class over another depends on the product or service; however, some realities cannot be ignored. In order to increase the volume of revenue, it may be desirable to emphasize poorer classes, where the propensity to consume is greater, and to seek higher price points of products that are made available to richer classes. A moral aspect to this comes into play, but as a reality of business, these propensities cannot be ignored. Therefore, different ranges of products are found in poorer neighborhoods than in richer ones. In grocery stores, for example, a poor economic area is likely to sell a higher volume of cheap but unhealthy food. In a rich economic area, similar stores may favor marketing expensive luxury foods.

Local and regional taxation can also be used by governments. For example, in poor neighborhoods, the propensity to consume will be reduced by increasing taxes; even when the same taxes are imposed on rich neighborhoods, the effect will not be as severe. Not only can consumers afford higher taxes, but with a lower propensity to consume, the impact is not as great. These localized examples apply equally to entire nations considering the propensity to consume, responding to taxes, and favoring imported goods (in some cases) over domestically manufactured or grown products. The propensity to consume cannot be studied as an analysis of dollars spent but is more accurately understood as a percentage of disposable income given to consumption.

MARGINAL PROPENSITY TO SAVE

Marginal propensity to save (MPS)
The application of a portion of disposable income to save as opposed to consume.

Disposable income is either consumed or saved. When a consumer decides to make a purchase above the level of disposable income, savings are reduced, or personal debt is increased. Working within a current budget, disposable income not consumed is saved. The *marginal propensity to save* (MPS) is the percentage of disposable income not used to consume.

This *savings function* is the remainder of disposable income after consumption. If a consumer spends above disposable income levels, the savings function will be negative, representing either a reduction in dollars saved or an increase in debt. The analysis of the savings function is a comparison between disposable income saved versus total disposable income.[2]

Savings function
The degree of savings of disposable income.

The MPS is also distinguished by whether savings are changed within the current budget or are a response to changes in income. For example, if a family's income remains the same but certain recurring payments stop because a debt has been repaid, the decision could be made to increase monthly savings by the amount of payment. However, if a family receives an increase in monthly pay of $200 and decides to save $150 per month, it is called *induced savings*.

Induced savings
The increase in a savings function due to increases in disposable income resulting from higher overall income.

THE MULTIPLIER EFFECT

The analysis of MPC or MPS must be studied beyond the immediate effect on a family's budget and on immediate levels of how disposable income is applied. The *multiplier effect* describes how an economic decision (consuming or saving, for example) by a consumer creates a secondary impact in the economy, or new demand. By the same argument, decisions by producers also create a multiplier effect or *new supply*. This changes what is called the *circular flow of income*.

Multiplier effect
The tendency for economic decisions to have impacts on the economy beyond the initial transaction.

The circular flow of income represents the way that added income moves through the economy, and the way that new production generates more income. Injections of spending into the economy carry through to other sectors of the economy. This idea is illustrated in Figure 19.2.

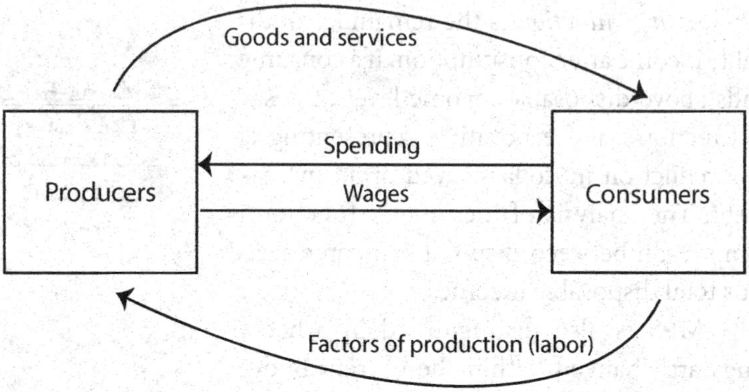

Figure 19.2 Circular flow of income

Circular flow of income
A model of economic activity in which money as well as goods and services are exchanged between producers and consumers, thereby creating secondary benefits to other participants.

In this basic circular flow relationship, producers hire and pay workers, and those workers represent factors of production (labor). Consumers use their earnings in spending, which returns revenue to the producers.[3]

In practice, the circular flow of income is more far-reaching. This is the multiplier effect, demonstrating that new economic activity is not limited to the immediate transaction. For example, as the population in one city grows, a manufacturer opens a new factory and hires employees to start up two shifts. The new factory requires the purchase of land as well as materials and machinery. The newly hired workers create a large increase in the number of people traveling to the neighborhood each day and in response, several new restaurants and other retail establishments are opened. Workers can now spend part of their income locally by having meals at these new restaurants or buying other products close to where they work. This increased demand leads to yet more outlets being opened. The circle is completed when the original producer, seeing higher demand, hires workers for a third shift. The circle continues to expand as demand leads to supply, and supply creates new demand.

The volume and dollar level of the circular flow of income depends on population, disposable income, and the types of products and services demanded (and supplied). As commerce grows, so does income for consumers, and this generates more disposable income. The measurement of the multiplier effect includes tracking the propensity to consume and the propensity to save over time.

A *reverse multiplier effect* is also possible. If income is taken out of the circular flow, it also carries through to other parts of the economy. This may be caused by the closing of a facility that employs large numbers of people, which decreases the propensity to consume out of concern about a recession in the business cycle or tax increases.

> <u>Reverse multiplier effect</u>
> A reduction in the circular flow of income, resulting from a decline in an MPC.

For example, let's assume that a manufacturing facility employs over 300 people in three shifts and has been in operation for five years. A decline in demand leads to closure of the factory and 300 employees become unemployed. Local retail outlets suffer as a result and close their doors, leading to more unemployment. The effect is further experienced among suppliers as overall orders for raw materials decline due to local recessionary changes.

Just as the multiplier effect is created by investment, exports, and even government expenditures, the reverse multiplier effect is experienced when investments fall, when exports decline, and when taxes are increased.

ENDNOTES

1. Colander, David C. (2004). *Microeconomics*, 5th ed. Boston, MA: McGraw-Hill/Irwin. p. G-1.
2. Blanchard, O. (2006). *Macroeconomics*, 4th ed. Upper Saddle River, NJ: Pearson Education. p. 59.
3. Daraban, Bogdan. (May 2010). "Introducing the circular flow diagram to business students." *Journal of Education for Business*. 85.5. pp. 274–279.

20

THE ROLE OF GOVERNMENT

Abstract

Many in government believe their proper role is to manage and even control the economy. History has demonstrated that this is impossible; and that government interference in the business cycle often has unintended consequences both for individual business owners and for the overall economy. The combination of fiscal and monetary policies is believed to be the path to controlling inflation, unemployment, and more. Taxing power and control over interest rates further creates this impression. However, the role of government and central banks in the economy should be limited to appropriate fiscal and monetary policies and should not be used in the pursuit of political aims. The result of government involvement in the economy creates a *political economy* that may be harmful to the business community.

What role should the government play in the economy, and what role does it play? To many, the government itself is the essential and indispensable economic force in a nation. To others, the government should leave businesses alone and allow the business cycle to follow its natural course.

In either case, governmental policies can help an economy to remain stable and avoid excessive versions of the business cycle. Government and central bank actions can reduce the momentum of inflation, lower unemployment, and make it easier for businesses and consumers to be approved for loans. But this is a controversial topic.

Many people would argue that the power of class envy and a desire for redistribution of wealth is a driving force in the economy. Once politics enter the picture, the message may be tailored to appeal to a segment of the voting public, but this often means offering ideas that defy rational thought. These ideas include universal free health care, guaranteed college education, guaranteed minimum income, and taxation of the wealthiest citizens as a punitive measure for accumulating money. The appeal of such programs ignores many economic realities, and the problem is not that the world is unfair but that many people do not understand the basics of the economic system.

GOVERNMENT INTERVENTION

What happens when the government tries to exert complete control over the economy? The rationale is rarely to improve economic results like gross domestic product (GDP), profitable businesses, or employment numbers. The usual reason for a government to attempt taking control is in the interest of *social justice*. This usually means that some people earn too much money and others don't earn enough, so government policies aim at redistributing wealth away from some people and giving it to others.

Other governments have believed that the business cycle should follow free market principles without government intervention. This translates to lowering taxes, removing regulations, and eliminating tariffs on exports and imports.

Most countries end up with economic systems and policies that incorporate some aspects of both philosophical viewpoints and combine some governmental policies with the free market. Most economic systems that are in effect today are free markets and follow the capitalistic ideal. This allows producers and consumers to (1) own and invest in property, (2) compete for profits, and (3) enjoy a wide breadth of product and service choices and prices. Competition may be fierce in a capitalist system, but it also is recognized as a healthy attribute of the economy.

In this free market system, every participant—producers as well as consumers—is free to make choices regarding what is bought and sold,

how prices are set, and how much of a product is produced and provided to the market. These decisions, for the most part, are not determined or controlled by any authority. The system works because even as producers set prices with profits in mind, consumers ultimately control the prices of goods and services. If a price moves too high, consumers buy less or move to another competitor. If price moves too low, the producer will not be able to earn a profit. This middle ground—equilibrium—is the core principle of a healthy free market economy. In this interaction between producer and consumer, government involvement is usually a negative factor.

unfair competition
Practices that set up competitive advantages for one company at the expense of all others and in which that advantage is gained through misrepresentation or illegal practices.

There are exceptions. When a company breaks the law or achieves an unfair advantage to control its market, regulators will step in and act to correct the unfairness of a situation. The nature of *unfair competition* is that one or more companies takes advantage of competitors to control the market.

Unfair competition takes several forms, including:

1. *False advertising*: promises or misleading statements inducing consumers to purchase products when the claims are not true. Examples include weight loss or hair growth products that do not work and get-rich-quick schemes. A related form, offering warranties but not honoring them, is false representation.
2. *Bait and switch*: marketing in which a company promises one product but ends up trying to sell a *knockoff* or lower-quality substitution. For example, a car dealership offers a new car at a low price but has none available when the consumer visits the showroom and offers them a more expensive model. This also is referred to in the law as unauthorized substitution.
3. *Intellectual property theft or infringement*: If a company or individual owns a trademark or other intellectual property (patent or copyright), it provides exclusive rights. However, a competitor might use a product or duplicate it without permission. Examples

> include misuse of a company's well-known logo to promote a competing product. A patented process, strategy, or formula might be stolen, which is misappropriation of a trade secret. If someone publishes a book, article, or other artistic work that was created and copyrighted by the original author, it represents copyright infringement.

In these situations, the law sets up remedies and can be used to prevent unfair competition, and even to file lawsuits and recover damages. However, these are extreme cases; in the normal operation of the economy, government involvement is viewed by most business operators in a free economy as interference and not as a necessary force.

HOW GOVERNMENTS ACT IN THE ECONOMY

Beyond setting up laws and regulations to prevent unfair competition, governments have influence over economic activity and results. Government involvement in the economy takes one of two general roles. It may try to promote economic growth, and it may try to regulate economic activity.

The government uses tools at its disposal to exert influence and control. These tools include taxation, spending programs (stimulus), regulation, and (through the central banking system) control over interest rates or changes in the amount of money in circulation.

In addition, new regulations or laws are enacted to either promote or curtail private business activity. These come in many forms: enterprise zones promote activity and the openings of new businesses, and regulation prevents industry from continuing to operate or from increasing their activity. A government's *fiscal policies* are directly influential on economic growth. These policies include changes in tax rates or legislation to provide benefits to a specific industry. Another fiscal policy impacting the economy is government spending. An increase in spending

> Fiscal policies
> Government programs designed to affect the economy, including taxing policies and laws and government stimulus programs.

is referred to as stimulus—in the belief that government spending is the best way to end recessions and increase employment.

Fiscal policies are promoted as economically motivated. However, they often are a form of politically motivated ideas. Spending in a sector or area may be intended to gain and keep votes for the party in power, for example. Increased taxes move money from the private sector to the government. However, if the government uses the added revenue to grant favors to some voters or businesses, it represents a redistribution of wealth. This is not a positive factor in the economy. Businesses will be less productive and the GDP and employment will both suffer as the result of increased taxes. When taxes are reduced, businesses have greater incentive to create profits and consumers have added incentives to spend more.

Economic influence also comes from the central bank in the form of *monetary policies*. In the United States, the Federal Reserve is the central bank and it influences the economy through these policies.

The central bank regulates the money supply and, independent from the political power structure, can increase or decrease the amount of money in circulation. The central bank can also increase or decrease interest rates. With more money circulating, the economy is likely to grow; with less money in circulation, inflation declines as the economy slows down. Through a central bank policy of *quantitative easing*, the economy is influenced directly. This involves purchasing government securities and increasing the money supply.

The combination of fiscal policies and monetary policies influence the economy and may be used to encourage growth or to slow down growth when inflation begins rising. The question remains, however, whether the government has the right to influence the economy (versus trusting the

> Monetary policies
> Economic policies enacted by the central bank, including changes in interest rates or to money in circulation.

> Quantitative easing
> A monetary policy in which the central bank lowers interest rates by purchasing government securities and increasing the money supply.

natural course of the business cycle), and whether it should be involved in this way.

GOVERNMENT RIGHTS AND DUTIES

To many, a government's function is to control economic trends and to influence the business cycle. This broad power is accepted on the assumption that the government knows what is good or bad for economic growth better than the private sector. The same people who believe this also believe that it is a proper function of government to control markets through regulation and taxing policies. However, separating monetary or fiscal policy from politics is not an easy matter, and political economics may hold greater sway than *real world* economics.

Politically speaking, some observers also believe it is a duty of the government to use its powers to adjust the economy for the purpose of correcting inequality. This gets translated into proposed policies like *making the rich pay their fair share* or *providing subsidies to poorer areas.* These may be viewed as compassionate programs, but they often are also used to attract voters and to exploit one sector to benefit another.

Economists who favor government intervention cite the desire for equality as justification for many policies. However, history has shown that programs to redistribute wealth are not effective. For example, in 1964 President Johnson announced his war on poverty. The total spent by 2016 was over $15 trillion. However, the absolute poverty line (the percentage of people unable to meet their basic needs) was 10.5 percent in 1966 and has risen since then and remained between 12 and 15 percent ever since. Attempts by the government to end poverty have not succeeded but have cost a profound amount of money.[1]

Arguments against government intervention are convincing. The strongest is the fact that governments are likely to make bad decisions, even more so than private companies. Governments are influenced by political interests and they tend to spend money inefficiently. A government that tries to influence the economy is also likely to decrease or remove personal freedom for consumers and businesses by forcing them to comply with economic regulations. The most often cited purpose in

government programs is to create equality of opportunity; and this belief further claims that governments are impartial. Because governments are political, this is not a likely factor in determining how governments act to exert economic influence. Added to this are the well-known inefficiency and excessive costs of government programs, which all points to the low likelihood of successful intervention by government.

ENDNOTES

1. Rector, Robert and Rachel Sheffield. (September 15, 2014). "The war on poverty after 50 years." *The Heritage Foundation.*

BIBLIOGRAPHY

Adams, Henry Brooks. (1907). *The Education of Henry Adams* (1999 ed). New York, NY: Modern Library.

Arthur, Charles. (March 6, 2013). "Google Glass: Is it a threat to our privacy?" *The Guardian*, https://www.theguardian.com/technology/2013/mar/06/google-glass-threat-to-our-privacy.

Artuc, E., S. Chaudhuri, and J. McLaren. (2010). "Trade shocks and labor adjustment: A structural empirical approach." *The American Economic Review*. 100.

Barrett, Rick. (November 10, 2010). "Companies find outsourcing can backfire as quality, customer service suffer." *Journal Sentinel*.

Blanchard, O. (2006). *Macroeconomics*, 4th ed. Upper Saddle River, NJ: Pearson Education.

Blough, Roger. (August 1, 1967). *Forbes*.

Bomey, Nathan. (November 26, 2018). "GM poised to close plants in Michigan, Ohio, Maryland, will cut 15% of salaried workers." *USA Today*, https://www.usatoday.com/story/money/cars/2018/11/26/gm-general-motors-plant-closures-job-cuts/2113275002/.

Boston, William. (May 29, 2017). "BMW slows some production due to parts shortage from supplier Bosch." *The Wall Street Journal*, at https://www/wsj.com/articles/bow-slows-some-production-due-to-parts-shortage-from-supplier-bosch-1496071360.

Boudette, Neal E. and Jeff Bennett. (March 26, 2011). "Pigment shortage hits auto makers." *Wall Street Journal*.

Boyes, William and Michael Melvin. (2015). *Microeconomics*, 10th ed. Boston, MA: Cengage Learning.

Branigan, Tania. (March 13, 2011). "Tsunami, earthquake, nuclear crisis—now Japan faces power cuts." *The Guardian.*

Bunkley, Nick. (January 2, 2017). "GM's journey from Volt to Bolt. A troubled vehicle paved the way for more audacious bets." *Automotive News*, https://www.autonews.com/article/20170102/OEM05/301029932/gm-s-journey-from-volt-to-bolt.

Bureau of Labor Statistics (BLS), https://www.bls.gov/cpi.

Canal, Emily. (October 16, 2018). "Why Amazon is making it easier to buy 'Shark Tank' products." *Inc.*, https://www.inc.com/emily-canal/shark-tank-amazon-retail-site-online-store.html.

Carlson, Peter. (September 4, 2007). "The flop heard round the world." *The Washington Post*, http://www.washingtonpost.com/wp-dyn/content/article/2007/09/03/AR2007090301419.html.

Census Bureau, www.census.gov.

Chang, Ha-Joon. (1994). *The Political Economy of Industry Policy*. London, UK: Macmillan.

Clark, Don and Juro Osawa. (December 10, 2010). "Power blip jolts supply of gadget chips." *The Wall Street Journal*, https://www.wsj.com/articles/SB10001424052748703766704576009071694055878.

Colander, David C. (2004). *Microeconomics*, 5th ed. Boston, MA: McGraw-Hill/Irwin.

Companies History, http://www.companieshistory.com/mattel/.

Daraban, Bogdan. (May 2010). "Introducing the circular flow diagram to business students." *Journal of Education for Business*. 85.5.

Dawson, Graham. (2006). *Economics and Economic Change*. Upper Saddle River, NJ: FT Press.

Debreu, Gerard. (1972). *Theory of Value: An Axiomatic Analysis of Economic Equilibrium*. New Haven, CT: Yale University Press.

De La Merced, Michael J. (January 19, 2012). "Eastman Kodak files for bankruptcy." *The New York Times*, https://dealbook.nytimes.com/2012/01/19/eastman-kodak-files-for-bankruptcy/.

De Lea, Brittany. (June 4, 2018). "Next recession not far off, economists predict." *Fox Business*, https://www.foxbusiness.com/markets/next-recession-not-far-off-economists-predict.

Dicke, Tom. (2010). "The Edsel: Forty years as a symbol of failure." *Journal of Popular Culture*. 43(3).

DiGangi, Christine. (November 25, 2015). 7 horrifying moments of Black Friday insanity. *WHIOtv7*, https://www.whio.com/lifestyles/holiday/horrifying-moments-black-friday-insanity/ridWk1JxpJeN4b0yOcuo0N/.

Dollery, Brian and Joe Wallis. (2001). *The Political Economy of Local Government*. Cheltenham, UK: Edward Elgar.

Draper, Hal. (1990). *Karl Marx's Theory of Revolution, Volume IV: Critique of Other Socialisms*. New York, NY: Monthly Review Press.

Edwards, Phil. (February 3, 2016). "All 512 animals Teddy Roosevelt and his son killed on safari." *Vox.com*, https://www.vox.com/2015/7/29/9067587/theodore-roosevelt-safari.

Ellin, Abby and Jeanette Torres. (November 19, 2012). "Hostess, Twinkies: 5 game-changing strikes. *ABC News*, https://abcnews.go.com/Business/strikes-shut-companies/story?id=17743234.

Estrin, James. (August 12, 2015). "Kodak's First Digital Moment." *The New York Times*, https://lens.blogs.nytimes.com/2015/08/12/kodaks-first-digital-moment/?smid=pl-share.

Federal Aviation Administration (FAA), https://www.faa.gov/about/office_org/headquarters_offices/ato/service_units/systemops/slot_administration/.

Federal Reserve History. "Employment Act of 1946," https://www.federalreservehistory.org/essays/employment_act_of_1946.

Fitzpatrick, Sheila. (2000). *Everyday Stalinism: Ordinary Life in Extraordinary Times: Soviet Russia in the 1930s*. Oxford, UK: Oxford University Press.

Fox, Justin. (June 11, 2001). "When bubbles burst tulips: Dot-coms. Hey, manias happen. But most don't lead to economic disaster." *Fortune*, http://archive.fortune.com.

French, Doug. (2006). "The Dutch monetary environment during tulipomania." *The Quarterly Journal of Austrian Economics*, 9(1).

Friedman, Milton. (2017 ed.). *Price Theory*. New York, NY: Routledge.

Friedman, Milton and Anna Jacobson Schwartz. (1963). *A Monetary History of the United States, 1867–1960*. Princeton, NJ: Princeton University Press.

General Motors Corp., Securities and Exchange Commission Form 10-K for the Year Ending December 31, 2006, http://www.sec.gov/Archives/edgar/data/40730/.

Gertner, Jon. (May 13, 2010). "The rise and fall of GDP." *New York Times Magazine*.

Gordon, Robert J. (1988). *Macroeconomics: Theory and Policy*, 2nd ed. New York, NY: McGraw-Hill.

Greenwald, B. and J. E. Stiglitz. (1986). "Externalities in economies with imperfect information and incomplete markets." *Quarterly Journal of Economics*, 101(2).

Grimm, Brice T. (March 2, 2007). "The statistical discrepancy." *Bureau of Economic Analysis*, https://www.bea.gov/system/files/papers/WP2007-2.pdf.

Gupta, Girish. (April 11, 2018). "Venezuela inflation 454 percent in first quarter: National Assembly." *Reuters*, https://www.reuters.com/article/us-venezuela-economy/venezuela-inflation-454-percent-in-first-quarter-national-assembly-idUSKBN1HI2MO.

Hardin, Garrett. (1968). "The tragedy of the commons." *Science*, 162 (3859).

Harsanyi, John C. (1982). "A simplified bargaining model for the n-person cooperative game." *Papers in Game Theory*. Theory and Decision Library. Dordrecht, Netherlands: Springer.

Hauschild, Marc. (May 30, 2017). "Supply shortage sees BMW production plummet." *The Manufacturer*, https://www.themanufacturer.com/articles/supply-shortage-sees-bmw-production-plummet/.

Herper, Matthew. (February 10, 2017). "Why did that drug price increase 6,000%? It's the law. *Forbes*, https://www.forbes.com/sites/matthewherper/2017/02/10/a-6000-price-hike-should-give-drug-companies-a-disgusting-sense-of-deja-vu/#117084e071f5.

Holcombe, Randall G. (2004). "National income accounting and public policy." *Review of Austrian Economics*, 17(4).

Home Depot, https://www.homedepot.com/b/Kitchen-Water-Filters/N-5yc1vZarmz; Amazon, https://www.amazon.com/s/ref=nb_sb_noss

_2?url=search-alias%3Dgarden&field-keywords=water+purification +&rh=n%3A1055398%2Ck%3Awater+purification.

https://www.bcbusiness.ca/9-dumbest-fads-ever-to-make-money.

https://www.intelligenteconomist.com/laffer-curve/.

https://www.investors.com/politics/editorials/income-tax-revenues -trump-tax-cuts-economic-growth.

https://www.statista.com/statistics/286526/coca-cola-advertising-spending -worldwide/ andhttps://www.cheshnotes.com/pepsico-advertising-and -marketing-budget/.

https://www.usatoday.com/story/money/cars/2018/11/26/gm-general -motors-plant-closures-job-cuts/2113275002/.

Ingraham, Christopher. (May 15, 2018). "Satellite data strongly suggests that China, Russia, and other authoritarian countries are fudging their GDP reports. *SFGate*, San Francisco, CA.

Keyes, Daniel. (August 18, 2017). "Walmart's online sales continue upward trend." Business Insider, https://www.businessinsider.com/walmarts-online-sales-continue-upward-trend-2017-8.

Knoema, https://knoema.com/aewtuqe/gnp-and-gdp-by-country.

Kreps, David, Robert Wilson, Paul Milgrom, and John Roberts. (August 1982). "Rational cooperation in the finitely repeated prisoners' dilemma." *Journal of Economic Theory*. 27(2).

Kuhn, David Paul. (September 3, 2010). "None of your business: On Obama's public sector cabinet." *Real Clear Politics*, https://www.realclearpolitics.com/articles/2010/09/03/none_of_your_business_on_obamas_public_sector_cabinet_107001.html.

Lambert, Fred. (December 7, 2018). "Tesla would consider buying shuttered GM factories [again], says Elon Musk." *Electrek*, https://electrek.co/2018/12/07/tesla-consider-buying-shuttered-gm -factories-elon-musk/.

Lepenies, Philipp. (2016). *The Power of a Single Number: A Political History of GDP*. New York, NY: Columbia University Press.

Lipsey, R. G. and K. Lancaster. (1956). "The general theory of second best." *Review of Economic Studies*, 24(1).

Loveday, Steven. (August 27, 2018). "2019 Chevrolet Volt slight price increase." *InsideEVs*, https://insideevs.com/2019-chevrolet-volt-price-increase/.

Machovec, Frank. (1995). *Perfect Competition and the Transformation of Economics*. New York, NY: Routledge.

Mackay, Charles. (1841). *Extraordinary Popular Delusions and the Madness of Crowds*. London, UK: Richard Bentley.

Mankiw, Gregory. (Summer 1989). "Real business cycles: A new Keynesian perspective." *The Journal of Economic Perspectives*, 3(3).

Mankiw, N. Gregory. (2017). *Principles of Economics*, 8th ed. Boston, MA: Cengage.

McCloskey, Deirdre N. (1998). *The Rhetoric of Economics*, 2nd ed. Madison, WI: University of Wisconsin Press.

McClure, P. K. (2018). "'You're fired,' says the robot: The rise of automation in the workplace, technophobes, and fears of unemployment." *Social Science Computer Review*, 36(2).

Melvin, Michael and William Boyes. (2002). *Microeconomics*, 5th ed. New York, NY: Houghton Mifflin.

Miller, John. (2009). "The *real* unemployment rate hits a 68-year high." *Dollars and Sense*, http://www.dollarsandsense.org/archives/2009/0709miller.html.

Mises, Ludwig von. (1963). *The Theory of Money and Credit*. New Haven, CT: Yale University Press.

Money, Nathan. (November 26, 2018). "GM poised to close plants in Michigan, Ohio, Maryland, will cut 15% of salaried workers." *USA Today*, https://www.usatoday.com/story/money/cars/2018/11/26/gm-general-motors-plant-closures-job-cuts/2113275002/.

Montgomery, Royal E. (1926). "The Landis arbitration and award." *University Journal of Business*, 4(3).

Navarro, Peter. (August 14, 2017). "China must stop forcing U.S. firms to share intellectual property: Trump trade official." *USA Today*, https://www.usatoday.com/story/opinion/2017/08/14/china-must-stop-forcing-us-firms-share-intellectual-property-peter-navarro-column/563151001/.

Newman, Jared. (April 4, 2012). "Google's 'Project Glass' teases augmented reality glasses." *PC World*, https://www.pcworld.com/article/253200/googles_project_glass_teases_augmented_reality_glasses.html.

Nicholson, Walter and Christopher M. Snyder. (2014). *Intermediate Microeconomics and Its Application*, 12th ed. Boston, MA: Cengage Learning.

Office Wonderland, https://officewonderland.com/listings/lg-55eg5sd-c-55-dual-side-in-glass-digital-signage/?gclid=Cj0KCQiA1NbhBRCBARIsAKOTmUsF851vYcry8eb-Rbq5et2beg3fmmCIpU8TN1Nkx3-LkDAAGiYJihUaAgXvEALw_wcB.

Osborne, Martin J. and Ariel Rubinstein. (1994). *A Course in Game Theory*. Cambridge, MA: MIT Press.

O'Sullivan, Arthur and Steven M. Sheffrin. (2003). *Economics: Principles in Action*, Upper Saddle River, NJ: Pearson Prentice Hall.

Parkin, Michael. (2010). *Economics*. 9th ed. New York, NY: Pearson.

Real Simple, https://www.realsimple.com/work-life/entertainment/shark-tank-products.

Rector, Robert and Rachel Sheffield. (September 15, 2014). "The war on poverty after 50 years." *The Heritage Foundation*.

Rees, Jasper. (January 20, 2012). "The end of our Kodak moment." London, UK: *The Telegraph*.

Robinson, Joan. (1965). *The economics of imperfect competition*. London, UK: Macmillan.

Romer, Christina D. (September 1994). "Remeasuring business cycles." *Journal of Economic History*. 54.

Samuelson, Paul A. and William D. Nordhaus. (2009). *Microeconomics*, 19th ed. New York, NY: McGraw-Hill.

Samuelson, Robert J. (June 14, 2010). "Our economy's crisis of confidence." *The Washington Post*.

Sanger, David E. (November 3, 1987). "Japanese chip dumping has ended, U.S. finds." *New York Times*, https://www.nytimes.com/1987/11/03/business/japanese-chip-dumping-has-ended-us-finds.html.

Sauter, M., E. Comen, T. Frohlich, and S. Stebbins. (July 11, 2018). "When product launches go awry: 50 worst product flops of all time." *USA Today*, https://www.usatoday.com/story/money/2018/07/11/50-worst-product-flops-of-all-time/36734837/.

Schmitz, James A. Jr. (July 12, 2016). "The cost of monopoly: A new view." *Minneapolis Federal Reserve*, https://www.minneapolisfed.org/publications/the-region/the-costs-of-monopoly-a-new-view.

Sciacca, Annie. (November 17, 2015). "Here's one cost to opening a restaurant that might surprise you." *bizjournal*, https://www.bizjournals.com/sanfrancisco/blog/2015/11/cost-liquor-license-restaurant-open-san-francisco.html.

Seidman, Bianca. (September 22, 2015). "Drug price increases 5,000 percent overnight." *CBS News*, https://www.cbsnews.com/news/generic-drug-price-increases-5000-percent-overnight/.

Sendy, Andrew. (November 6, 2018). "Are Tesla solar roof tiles worth it?" *Solar-Estimate*, https://www.solar-estimate.org/news/2018-11-06-are-the-tesla-solar-roof-tiles-worth-it.

Shaw, Adam. (September 2, 2017). "Why economic forecasting has always been a flawed science." *The Guardian*, https://www.theguardian.com/money/2017/sep/02/economic-forecasting-flawed-science-data.

Shaw, George Bernard (attributed). (May 1933). *The Saturday Review of Literature*.

Sheffield, Rachel and Robert Rector. (September 15, 2014). "The war on poverty after 50 years." https://www.heritage.org/poverty-and-inequality/report/the-war-poverty-after-50-years.

Shiller, Robert J. (June 7, 2009). "Why home prices keep falling." *The New York Times*.

Shiskin, Julius. (December 1, 1974). "The changing business cycle." *The New York Times*.

Siegel, Jeremy J. (2002). *Stocks for the Long Run: The Definitive Guide to Financial Market Returns and Long-Term Investment Strategies*, 3rd ed. New York, NY: McGraw-Hill.

Sleter, Greg. (May 9, 2017). "Office Depot Q1 sales down, net income rises." *HomeWorld Business*, https://www.homeworldbusiness.com/office-depot-q1-sales-net-income-rises/.

Small Business Administration (SBA), https://www.sba.gov.

Smith, Adam. (1827). *The Wealth of Nations*. Edinburgh, Scotland: University Press.

Tanzi, Alexandre. (October 16, 2018). "Top 3% of U.S. taxpayers paid majority of income tax in 2016." *Bloomberg*, https://www.bloomberg.com/news/articles/2018-10-14/top-3-of-u-s-taxpayers-paid-majority-of-income-taxes-in-2016.

Taylor, Kate. (August 15, 2016). "Walmart destroyed retail." *Business Insider*, https://www.businessinsider.com/walmart-destroyed-retail-2016-8.

Tucker, Jeffrey A. and Stephan Kinsella. (August 25, 2010). "Goods, scarce and nonscarce." *Mises Institute*, https://mises.org/library/goods-scarce-and-nonscarce.

Van Sickle, John V. and Benjamin A. Rogge. (1954). *Introduction to Economics*. New York, NY: D. Van Nostrand.

Vernon, Raymond. (May 1966). "International investment and international trade in the product cycle." *Quarterly Journal of Economics* 5, Vol. 80, Issue 2.

Weeks, Carly. (July 14, 2011). "Campbell's adding salt back to its soups." *Toronto Globe and Mail*.

Welch, Patrick J. and Gerry F. Welch. (2016). *Economics Theory and Practice*, 11th ed. Hoboken, NJ: John Wiley & Sons.

Woo, Elaine. (April 1, 2015). "Gary Ross Dahl, originator of 70s Pet Rock sensation, dies at 78." *Los Angeles Times*.

Woodhill, Louis. (March 19, 2014). "The war on poverty wasn't a failure—it was a catastrophe." *Forbes*, https://www.forbes.com/sites/louiswoodhill/2014/03/19/the-war-on-poverty-wasnt-a-failure-it-was-a-catastrophe/#52b8eef16f49.

World Bank, https://data.worldbank.org/indicator/NY.GNP.MKTP.CD.

www.oxygenbars.com.

Wynne-Jones, Jonathan. (June 6, 2009). "Computer game Tetris celebrates 25 years." *The Daily Telegraph*, https://www.telegraph.co.uk/technology/news/5460283/Computer-game-Tetris-celebrates-25-years.html.

GLOSSARY

adaptive expectations: types of expectations about future inflation based on past rates and a belief about their effect on the future.

artificial demand: any form of demand created by generating interest in a product or service when no true economic value exists.

Austrian School: *an economic theory stating that inflation results from* the introduction of money and credit when the quantity of money is not offset by a demand for money (resulting in inflation).

autonomous consumption: levels of consumption above disposable income, creating a negative savings or increase in debt.

barriers to entry: conditions preventing or limiting the ability of a business to enter and participate in a market.

barriers to exit: conditions preventing or limiting the ability of a business to exit from a market.

base effect: the effect on current inflation calculation when the base year in the comparison is exceptionally high or low. The effect may be to overstate or understate current inflation.

best response dynamics: the tendency for producers to react to conditions to maximize profits and for consumers to select price and quality to find the best bargain.

built-in inflation: a form of inflation created when wage earners fear inflation and seek higher income, creating a circular effect of ever-higher inflation.

business cycle: the constantly evolving status of the economy and its expansion or contraction as the gross domestic product (GDP) moves over time.

choice theory: the belief that consumers are rational in the way they choose when comparing prices, quality, and reputation of scarce goods.

circular flow of income: a model of economic activity in which money as well as goods and services are exchanged between producers and consumers, creating secondary benefits to other participants.

competitive equilibrium: alternative description of Walrasian equilibrium.

consumer price index (CPI): a measurement of inflation, comparing current prices of a selected group of goods and services to their prices in the past.

consumption function: an economic theory developed by Milton Friedman, arguing that the free market works best without government influence.

cooperative games: forms of interaction based on two competing sides or teams with external rule enforcement.

core values: the well-defined purposes and goals held by a business or person; the expansion of financial considerations to include non-financial ideals about future outcomes of present decisions.

cost of goods sold: (also termed *direct costs*) the expenditures of a business associated directly with the production of revenue as opposed to expenses that cannot be assigned to the revenue produced by one or more products.

cost of production theory: an economic theory observing that the price of goods is determined by the combined application of labor, materials, and capital.

cost-push inflation: a form of inflation caused by decreased supply.

cross-price elasticity of demand: the lower demand of a product with price increases versus higher demand for a substitute available at a lower price.

cyclical unemployment: a form of unemployment caused by seasonal changes in the business sector, resulting in temporary hiring and laying off of employees.

deflation: the opposite of inflation; annual reduction in prices of goods and services.

demand function: the combined motives for consumers of goods and services; a combination of price, availability, convenience, and service.

demand-induced scarcity: a form of scarcity generated when the consumer population grows or when the demand for a product or service is expanded.

demand-pull inflation: a form of inflation caused by increased demand.

depression: a severe extension of recession of 10% or more negative GDP lasting more than four years.

derived demand: reference to the producer's need to purchase materials and labor, facilities, and capital assets in order to produce goods demanded by consumers; the scope of a producer's role as a consumer.

diminishing returns: the tendency for increased factors to yield less per-unit returns in the long run, notably when a single factor is increased but others remain unchanged.

diseconomies of scale: the loss of profitability because of increased production volume, caused by the inability of lowered costs per unit.

disinflation: alternate name for deflation.

disposable income: the level of net income available after needed expenses that may be spent or saved.

dynamic equilibrium: condition when one or more changes or shifts takes place, disrupting the agreement between producer and consumer or shifting equilibrium.

economics: the interaction of scarcity with the wants and needs of consumers and how decisions are made.

economies of scale: the improvement by producers in marginal costs, which may include a small reduction in quality; or the incentives offered to consumers to purchase more of a product for a small discount.

efficiency: the application of scarce resources in the best possible manner and for the lowest possible cost.

elasticity: changes in price or quantity even without corresponding changes in cost that occur within the economy, often due to perception of overall economic trends.

equilibrium: the point where goods and services provided at a given price and quantity perfectly match demand among consumers.

equilibrium shift: a move of equilibrium to a new level, caused by increases or decreases in levels of either demand or supply.

equity: fairness; in the economy, provision of a needed product or service at a lower cost to those who cannot afford a higher price.

expenditure approach: GDP calculated as goods produced and sold.

factor markets: the elements that every business needs in order to create and market its products and services, including raw materials and labor in a manufacturing environment, facilities and capital assets, and technical or intellectual skills in production of specialized products or services.

factors of production: the four attributes required to generate a profit within the constraints of the market.

fiscal policies: government programs designed to affect the economy, including taxing policies and laws and government stimulus programs.

fixed basket: any index used to represent a larger market, such as the consumer price index.

free goods: the ultimate description of non-scarce goods, available to anyone and everyone, and without cost.

frictional unemployment: a form of unemployment resulting from the need of workers to move in order to find work suitable for their skills when such positions are not available in their area.

full employment: condition in which everyone wanting a job has a job at a level of compensation that is acceptable.

game theory: a set of analyses by consumers and producers, both individually and with one another, to better understand how rational people make strategic decisions.

greater fool theory: in speculation, the belief that paying too much for a product or service is rationalized by the belief that someone else (a *greater fool*) will be willing to pay more.

gross domestic product (GDP): the measurement of all goods and services produced and sold each year as a measurement of economic health and improvement.

gross national income (GNI): the summary of a country's growth based on activity within the country and including owners residing elsewhere.

hyperinflation: periods of rapidly expanding prices in double or triple digits per year.

ideal rate of unemployment: the unemployment rate than can be sustained without growth in inflation.

income approach: GDP calculated as the total of all producers' income.

income elasticity: a measurement of demand based on rising income; divide increases in demand by increases in customers' income.

induced savings: the increase in a savings function due to increases in disposable income resulting from higher overall income.

inferior goods: products likely to experience a decrease in demand even when customers' income elasticity is positive.

inflation: an increase in prices leading to a decline in the purchasing power of money.

invisible hand: a force within the economy moving supply and demand toward equilibrium even when participants act only in their own *self-interest.*

Keynesian economics: a set of theories promoted by John Maynard Keynes that government spending can be undertaken to stabilize and improve the economy; also called *demand-side* economics.

labor force: the total number of employed and unemployed people.

labor participation rate: the percentage of the labor force currently with jobs or actively seeking work.

Laffer curve: a belief offered by Art Laffer in the 1980s stating that when federal taxes are raised, revenues fall, and that when tax rates are lowered, revenue grows.

law of demand: the observation that the higher a product's price, the lower its demand will be.

law of diminishing returns: the point where the cost of gaining higher profit is greater than the profit itself.

law of supply: the observation that a higher volume of goods is offered at higher prices, and a lower quantity of products is offered at lower prices.

long-term objectives: the set of actions and outcomes developed with the mission statement in mind, expressing the desires and underlying values of the organization.

long-term unemployment: condition describing workers looking for jobs for 27 weeks or more.

marginal analysis: adjustments in price by producers to achieve the best possible profits or in behavior among consumers to get the best possible price and quality.

marginal benefit: the willingness of each participant in the economy to pay a price for the products or services offered; or for the producer, for the elements in the factor markets needed to produce products.

marginal cost: the added cost of producing the latest added unit.

marginal net benefit: the perceived value of a decision to buy; when the benefit is perceived to be greater than the cost, a decision to buy is more likely to be made.

marginal propensity to consume (MPC): the level of additional spending that occurs per each added dollar of disposable income.

marginal propensity to save (MPS): the application of a portion of disposable income to save as opposed to consume.

marginal revenue: the additional revenue earned when the current level of sales are increased by a single unit; or the revenue earned with the last unit sold.

marginal utility: the utility gained from the last item purchased, which is lower than the utility for buying the original unit.

mission statement: a formalized and brief description of goals, aims, and values for a company, expressed and shared with all stakeholders.

monetary policies: economic policies enacted by the central bank, including changes in interest rates or to money in circulation.

monopolistic competition: a market structure with many competitors offering similar products to the market with minor differences.

monopoly: a market structure with a single company and no competitors.

multiplier effect: the tendency for economic decisions to have impacts on the economy beyond the initial transaction.

Nash equilibrium: a theory where everyone is fully aware of everyone else's strategies and no gain will be achieved by changing a strategy.

negative return: the reduction in gross profits caused by increasing factors of production.

nominal GDP: the measurement of GDP based on current prices, including adjustments for inflation or deflation.

non-cooperative games: forms of interaction with no external enforcement of rules and based on credible threats by one side to the other.

nonscarce goods: any products or materials that are abundant, usually having no economic value.

non-zero-sum game: any interaction in which a net gain is realized by one side.

normal goods: those products with demand likely to increase as consumers' income elasticity is positive.

normal profits: a level of revenue equal to its total costs; the breakeven point required for a business to compete in the market and avoid losses.

oligopoly: a group of companies in an industry, competing with one another but preventing any new competitors from entry.

opportunity cost: the evaluation of costs and benefits undertaken to arrive at a decision, including knowledge of what must be given up as a result.

Pareto optimal: condition when resources are applied with maximum efficiency and when any reallocation would harm one side or the other.

peak: the top level of the business cycle when economic activity has expanded to a high level.

perfect competition: a theoretical condition of equilibrium between producers and consumers (or between producers and suppliers) in which optimal profits are created by the best possible use of factors of production.

perfect complement: the combination of two products that both must be acquired for the intended purpose to be achieved.

perfect information: the belief that consumers make choices based on complete knowledge of all aspects going into those choices.

perfect market: a theoretical condition in which equilibrium between supply and demand are achieved and in which producers operate at peak efficiency and generate the exact level of supply and price demanded by consumers.

perfect substitutes: products that compete within the same market and are priced the same, for which the selection of either represents the same quality but experience different preferences among consumers.

price index: an index of a limited grouping of goods and services to track inflation within one industry or sector versus the more generalized inflation represented by the CPI.

prisoner's dilemma: an idea in game theory that two suspects should both keep quiet when questioned; but each one is unsure whether the other is blaming him so the tendency is to blame a crime on the other suspect even without evidence.

production approach: GDP calculated as the sum of output by producers in all sectors of the economy.

production function: the cost of production and level of competition based on efficiency and application of unique properties, such as utility patents.

profit maximization: the process of determining the level of output, given fixed and variable costs of production, required to generate maximum profits.

quantitative easing: a monetary policy in which the central bank lowers interest rates by purchasing government securities and increasing the money supply.

quantity index: also called a *volume index*, the quantity of goods produced during a period, reflecting price changes based on volume.

rational expectations: type of expectations about future inflation assuming experts were no better at estimating the future than anyone else capable of rational thought.

real unemployment: a definition of unemployment as described by the U.S. Bureau of Labor Statistics (BLS) to include three categories of the labor force.

recession: a period of negative GDP in the economy.

relative price: the price of two or more products, defining how consumers choose between one or the other.

resource demand: the form of demand presented by producers for its factor markets and the goods and services it requires to generate finished products or services.

resource supply: the cost and quantity of factors of production charged to a business based on past and current costs.

reverse multiplier effect: a reduction in the circular flow of income, resulting from a decline in a marginal propensity to consume.

savings function: the degree of savings of disposable income.

scarce goods: any products or materials for which demand is greater than supply.

scarcity: the limitation of all goods and services and of their affordability; the essential element required to set value on anything.

seasonal adjustments: modification of reported unemployment to remove the influence of known seasonal changes in the economy.

seasonal noise: the periodic distortion of inflation caused by changed buying activity identified as seasonal.

static equilibrium: the state of complete agreement between producers or consumers, when no changes in price or quantity occur, and when no demand or supply shifts are underway.

structural scarcity: a form of scarcity resulting from consumers being unable to access goods and services due to geographic, demographic, or income-based restrictions.

structural unemployment: a form of unemployment caused by replacement, reduction, or outsourcing of current jobs, or replacement of a labor force with robotics.

substitute: a product bought by a consumer as an alternative to another product due to obsolescence, quality, convenience, or price.

supply function: the willingness and ability of a producer to offer goods and services based on the cost of goods and pricing considerations.

supply-induced scarcity: a form of scarcity resulting from shortages or unavailability of raw materials, labor, and other requirements of production.

supply-side economics: the belief that lowering taxes and reducing regulation work together to generate greater business activity, leading to greater tax revenues.

theory of production: the process of determining how many goods to produce and at what cost, given the constraints of raw materials and labor, as well as other production investments.

theory of the second best: a theory explaining that when market distortions cannot be controlled directly to remove negative conditions, a second-best condition or outcome is the most desirable.

tragedy of the commons: an economic theory based on a tendency to destroy common areas through overuse rather than preserving the resource through cooperation.

triangle model: a Keynesian explanation of inflation consisting of three distinct causes.

trough: the bottom level of the business cycle when economic activity has declined to a low level.

underemployed: people working part-time and working beneath their capacity.

unemployment rate: the percentage of people available for work and currently looking for a job.

unfair competition: practices setting up competitive advantages for one company at the expense of all others when that advantage is gained through misrepresentation or illegal practices.

utility maximization: the tendency among consumers to seek products they need and want, given the limitations of income and conflicts between spending decisions.

value proposition: a set of defining attributes about why products or services address customer or client needs; the special or exceptional talents of owners and staff; and the qualities in the product and service that set it apart from others.

Walrasian equilibrium: a theory that equilibrium can exist for the entire competitive market, rather than observed in some markets but not in others.

zero-sum game: any interaction in which gains on one side of a transaction are offset by equal losses on the other side.

INDEX

Note: Page numbers followed by "f" indicate figures.